Translated, with Introduction and Notes,

By JAMES A. MASSEY

THOUGHTS on DEATH
and IMMORTALITY

from the Papers of a Thinker,
along with an Appendix of
Theological-Satirical Epigrams,
Edited by One of His Friends

Ludwig Feuerbach

UNIVERSITY OF CALIFORNIA PRESS

BERKELEY, LOS ANGELES, LONDON

University of California Press
Berkeley and Los Angeles, California

University of California Press, Ltd.
London, England

Library of Congress Cataloging in Publication Data

Feuerbach, Ludwig Andreas, 1804-1872.
Thoughts on death and immortality.

Translation of Gedanken über Tod und Unsterblichkeit.
1. Death.   2. Immortality (Philosophy)
I. Title.
B2971.G392E5   1980   218   80-25259

Printed in the United States of America

1 2 3 4 5 6 7 8 9

Contents

Acknowledgments   vii

Introduction   ix

    Feuerbach's Response to the Challenges of His Day   xi

    Biographical Notes   xviii

    The Purpose and Style of *Thoughts on Death*   xxi

    The Argument: Negating Traditional

       Christian Concepts   xxvi

    Reflections   xxxii

    A Note on the Translation   xli

Thoughts on Death and Immortality   1

    Editor's Foreword   3

    I   17

    God   19

    II   Time, Space, Life   48

    III   Spirit, Consciousness   107

Epigrams   175

Notes to the Introduction   253

Notes to *Thoughts on Death and Immortality*   256

Notes to the *Epigrams*   258

90856

Acknowledgments

I completed this book as a Visiting Senior Fellow at Duke University; for the library privileges that this entailed, I am grateful to the Department of Religion. I am also indebted to Professor James Rolleston of the university's Department of Germanic Languages and Literature for helping me relate the genres of Feuerbach's versification to the traditions of nineteenth-century German poetry and to Professor Ruel Tyson of the Department of Religion at the University of North Carolina at Chapel Hill for helping me clarify the different moods of Feuerbach's rhetoric. Mostly, I wish to express my gratitude, admiration, and love for the help given to me by my wife, Dr. Marilyn Chapin Massey, who is one of the foremost scholars in the field.

Introduction

Thoughts on Death and Immortality is a straightforward denial of the Christian belief in personal immortality, a plea for recognition of the inexhaustible quality of the only life we have, and a derisive assault on the posturings and hypocrisies of the professional theologians of nineteenth-century Germany. Its editor claimed that he had had a difficult time convincing the author to allow it to be published; the author's reticence was well founded, for because of the outrage it caused, this book became a major obstacle to Ludwig Feuerbach's attempts to gain a professorship at a German university. All the same, he did not find this exclusion to be particularly tragic. Having taught as a lecturer for two years at the University of Erlangen by the time the book appeared, his scorn was directed at the world of the professional scholar as much as at that of the theologian: "Three things I would not like to be: an old hag, a hack / In the academy, and finally a pietist" (p. 205).[1]

This book, however, is much more than the denial of a particular Christian belief, a belief that the French Enlightenment had already attacked during the previous century. Published in 1830, it was the first public result of an interior dialogue that Feuerbach was to carry on throughout much of his career with major representatives of the tradition of Western philosophy. The concern that pressed this dialogue forward would remain constant: to retrieve the power of philosophical thought for use in the concrete world of directly experienced reality. Feuerbach was convinced that the major obstacle to human happiness was the divided consciousness, the propensity that humans have to compartmentalize their interior lives so that they remain blind to their true relationships to their environment and thus to their full potential. He came to see the dogmatic propositions of Christian theology and the abstract systems of metaphysical idealism from Descartes to Hegel as the primary examples of this division; these propositions and systems of thought remained divorced from empirical reality, while empirical reality remained "thoughtless."[2] Despite his sensitivity to the oppression of his people and the frequent temptation to enter the political arena, he would always choose the instruments of reflection to heal the disease of divided consciousness; his political action would be to transform the German people's awareness of themselves and their needs. The problem was finding the appropriate philosophical tools for this transformation. Feuerbach's developing critique of the philosophies available to him and the resulting growth in awareness of the implications of his own ideas often forced him to revise his position; it may well be that the rich sophistication of his interior conversation and the insights he gained as he articulated his conclusions are more significant than the conclusions themselves.[3]

In fact, the mode of expression that Feuerbach chose for many of these conclusions has been a major obstacle to our understanding and appreciation of his importance. To call for a kind of reflection that opposed systems of thought which overemphasized the criterion of internal logical consistency, he used loosely connected aphorisms, such as "Humanity is the God of humanity" and "Humanity is what it eats." Later interpreters have tied him to these aphorisms and then have either understood them only superficially, condemned them as too abstract, or trivialized them as ideological slogans. Meanwhile, the fertility of the insights that developed these aphorisms has inspired such thinkers as Karl Marx, Sigmund Freud, Friedrich Nietzsche, Karl Barth, Martin Buber, and Ernst Bloch to draw conclusions that have become part and parcel of our contemporary intellectual world. I think, however, that the effort to understand Feuerbach on his own terms will be rewarded by the discovery that he has much to say to us in his own voice as well as through the voices of the great thinkers who took him up. Although he approached it from a direction opposite to ours, he consistently attacked an urgent problem facing contemporary society: rejecting theology and metaphysics for failing to keep their feet in the real world, he attempted to articulate an empiricism that remained open to reflection, an empiricism that could direct scientific data toward their human possibilities. Our problem is less that of rejecting abstract thinking than that of giving science a human direction.

Thoughts on Death is an excellent introduction to Feuerbach, not only because it was one of his first attempts to apply philosophy to concrete reality but also because it is his opening attack on the cultural force that would remain for him the principal example of the divided consciousness and therefore the principal testing ground of his concepts of human reintegration. He intended the refutation of immortality to be a means of pointing out that the emphasis of modern Christianity on the individual self betrays the essential continuity between humans and their terrestrial environment and therefore blinds Christians to the value of life. *Thoughts on Death* is therefore essential for understanding the full-blown critiques of Christianity of *The Essence of Christianity* (1841), the work that contributed the most to his reputation—and to his misappropriation.[4] But perhaps *Thoughts on Death* says more than this. Can Feuerbach contribute to our contemporary attempts to face the reality of being-toward-death? After a brief sketch of his life and thought within the context of the problems of his day, this Introduction will point out important features of the argument of *Thoughts on Death* and will present some reflections on the possible significance of Feuerbach's stand on personal mortality.

Feuerbach's Response to the Challenges of His Day

Most of Feuerbach's writings were published between the expulsion of Napoleon from German lands in 1813 and the March Revolution of 1848.[5] During this period, not only were expectations rising for the reform of a loosely united three dozen states and many more smaller domains still dominated by medieval political and social structures, but also liberals and conservatives alike, from the intelligentsia to the ruling nobility, were fairly certain that, sooner or later, something like the upheavals

of France would come to pass. Napoleon himself had contributed to the conviction that it was impossible to turn back the
clock: his rule had collapsed many of the small Rhineland principalities into a few much larger bodies and had imported
administrative reforms that the weight of their past had kept the
Germans themselves from achieving. In southern Germany,
including Feuerbach's homeland, Bavaria, the decade after
Napoleon's defeat produced constitutions that in some respects
curbed the injustices of absolutist paternalism. During the very
war to get rid of him had arisen for the first time the effective
use of the ideology of modern Germany unity, for at least some
of the patriots believed that only a single nation under arms
could repulse the national army of France. However, it was not
just the new opportunities in Napoleon's reformed administrations and the leveling effect of the war that had somewhat loosened the rigid class structure and given new hope of advancement to the weak middle classes. Since the 1780s, the Germans
had experienced one of the greatest literary and cultural outbursts that Western civilization had yet seen. The modern
humanistic ideals of personal fulfillment espoused by the classicists, the romantics, and some of the idealist philosophers had
given impetus to educational reforms and a certain prestige to
anyone who had benefited from the results of these reforms in
the improved gymnasiums and universities. Perhaps just as
important, these intellectuals and writers had gained the freedom for their accomplishments with few of the advantages of
riches or princely heritage; among others, Lessing, Herder,
Schiller, and Goethe were minor officials in small German
states. (For that matter, it escaped no one that the French
emperor himself had been of common origin.) Perhaps culture
as well as blood, money, or military accomplishment held a key
to advancement and fulfillment.

Ultimately, however, the need for economic reform much
more than modern humanistic ideals or liberation sentiments
would move the Germans into the world of the modern nation-
states. Because of a sudden spurt in the European population
which had begun just before the turn of the century, there were

more mouths to feed than German production could bear. Already drained by the war, the almost exclusively agrarian states awoke to the peacetime commercial supremacy of England, which was at least two decades ahead of central Europe in industrialization. The lack of political and therefore economic unity to gear up to compete with England was a serious obstacle to the needed overhaul. Furthermore, although the German economy achieved a generally steady and occasionally strong rate of growth up to the end of the nineteenth century, the more industrialized the country became, the more the lowest classes grew vulnerable to the fluctuations of the new international capitalism, having gradually been forced to abandon the land to compete for subsistence in the spreading blight of the newly industrialized cities.

Who was going to be able to deal with these problems? Where was the leadership that would provide the focal point of power and foresight necessary to overcome centuries of political stagnation and divisiveness? Should this power be used to give Germans legal rights and participation in the affairs of government, or should it be used to strengthen the largely intact old orders? Much of the Catholic population of southern Germany felt somewhat akin to Austria, but few could dream that Austria would ever be an agent of reform. Prussia was clearly the other most powerful state and the one most serious about reform, but after the war, the attempts of Ministers Heinrich Friedrich Karl vom und zum Stein (1757-1831) and Karl August von Hardenberg (1750-1822) to modernize governmental processes along French and English lines were being rolled back by the most conservative and militaristic group competing for power, the great feudal landowners of Prussia's eastern provinces. And it did not help the morale of the groups hoping for modernizing change when between 1825 and 1835 the last representatives of the cultural movement, the one great source of German pride and self-identity other than military might, passed away—the critic Jean Paul in 1825; the composer Carl Maria von Weber in 1826; the leading romanticist Friedrich Schlegel in 1829; Hegel, Stein, and the historian Barthold Georg Niebuhr in 1831;

Goethe in 1832; the theologian Friedrich Schleiermacher in 1834; the naturalist Wilhelm von Humboldt in 1835. In years to come, the primary question would be how much one was willing to sacrifice for the sake of a strong leader.

With the advantage of the hindsight gained from the perspective of the 1860s, in which the rule of Otto von Bismarck (1815-1898) was accepted at the cost of most of the goals of liberalism, it is difficult to see how democratic forces could have reversed the tide of conservative reaction. The nobility had the best statesmen; it could use the military organizations, still intact after the war, to suppress dissent; it was able, for the most part, to keep the loyalty of the peasant majority of the population; and it had on its side the appeal to images of the peace and tranquillity of the German past in a period following great upheavals. Still, perhaps none of this power would have been sufficient to clamp the lid back on were it not for the deep and abiding religiosity of the people. The postwar years saw a strong, emotional religious outburst throughout the German states; its conservative tone strengthened the authority of the established religious leaders, and most of these, both Protestant and Catholic, worked strenuously to restore the old faiths alongside the "legitimate" German thrones. Thus the people who had called for more individual rights, for constitutional government, and for German unity were forced to watch in frustration as Metternich, with Prussia obediently concurring, established the German Confederation, which brought little more unity than had existed under the old German Empire and which was immediately seen as a diplomatic debating club for the preservation of the status quo. The most visible expression of this frustration were the societies formed by the university students, many of whom had risked their lives in the war for the ideal of a united Germany. Although these organizations were not uniformly reformist—some of them shared militaristic and anti-Semitic tendencies—Metternich saw them as a threat, and a few relatively harmless demonstrations were enough to enable him, in 1819, to convince the German states to censor public political discussion and to form boards of inquiry to prosecute anyone suspected of associating with the "seditious demagoguery" of the students.

Even when the forces for reform began, with the help of France's July Revolution of 1830 (the year that *Thoughts on Death* was published), to gain momentum and to defy the reinstated commissions of inquiry, nothing like the forum for public discussion which had preceded the outbreak of the first French Revolution existed in Germany, with the sole exceptions of the journalistic writings of Heinrich Heine (1799-1856) and Ludwig Börne (1786-1837). These two men avoided harassment by emigrating to Paris, and their satirical writings escaped censorship as long as they kept their critiques indirect, either by writing about the events in France and letting their readers draw their own conclusions from the contrast with German affairs or by using the language of aesthetics. This lack of political discussion and the political naïveté that it fostered contributed to the failure of the March Revolution of 1848, for the participants in the Frankfurt National Assembly had to spend an enormous amount of energy in choosing and making explicit the options open to them on almost every question, and by the time they finally completed a constitution, the threatened governments had taken back their power.

Perhaps it is possible to exaggerate the fear of its vulnerable central position in the continent as a contributing factor to the militaristic emphasis in Germany's eventual unification; and it is impossible to gauge the effect on later German history of the dangerous sense of inferiority and isolation that grew out of the contrast between the outcome of the German reform attempts and the corresponding political successes in western Europe and America. The paralysis of fear, however, seems to have been one of the most powerful forces of this period. The revolution never would have gotten as far as it did had not the nobility sensed beforehand that an upheaval was imminent; many of them stood aside in guilt and in mortal fear of what the peasants, whom they had used so successfully, might do to them. On the other hand, the economic reformers who led the breakthrough were so afraid of the social upheaval that could be trig-

gered if the poor classes rose that they quickly threw in their lot
with the upper classes, thereby isolating themselves from what
might have become their strongest base of support. Meanwhile,
fear of political oppression had moved some of the leaders of
student societies to emigrate in the 1820s, even to America—
Feuerbach himself seriously considered this after the failure of
the March Revolution of 1848—and cells of liberal émigrés
grew in Switzerland and France.

Personal experience made Feuerbach aware of the dangers
attending the liberal call for reform. His father, Paul Johann
Anselm Feuerbach (1775-1833), a prominent reformer of the
penal law code, was forced to move the household twice because of his political candor, the second time from Munich to
Bamberg when Feuerbach was ten. At the age of sixteen Feuerbach wrote his mother, Wilhemine Feuerbach née Tröster, that
while on a tour through Bavaria he had stopped at Mannheim
to visit the grave of Karl Ludwig Sand, the student leader who
had been executed for murdering J. A. Kotzebue, the dramatist
suspected by the students of spying for Russia. The Feuerbach
family, like many others of the middle class, must have been
sympathetic to the student societies, for in the letter Ludwig
enclosed some blades of grass from Sand's grave, explaining
that he knew how much she had loved the student leader.[6] In
1824, he had just arrived to begin studies at the University of
Berlin when he became the object of daily surveillance by the
police assigned to the commission to investigate the student
societies; on the basis of a "tip" that he and his four brothers
were conspirators, the commission interrogated him twice
before allowing him to matriculate. He soon found out the reason for this harassment: one of his brothers, Karl, a professor
of mathematics at a gymnasium in Erlangen, had been among a
group of people jailed for their public criticism of German conditions. Although the police could not make charges stick, Karl
was detained for fourteen months, during which he attempted
to commit suicide twice; he never fully recovered from the
experience. And six years later, Feuerbach learned that attempts
at religious reform were not exempt from repression, for the

censorship authorities confiscated *Thoughts on Death* soon after it appeared in the bookstores.

Later, at the height of his fame, Feuerbach had to answer the charge of remaining aloof from the revolutionary movement to which his writings had contributed because, as a delegate to the Frankfurt Parliament, he had maintained almost total silence during its deliberations. Something like this accusation was leveled at the theoretical conclusions of his writings. During the early 1840s he had declined to participate in the radical journals of Karl Marx, Friedrich Engels, and Arnold Ruge (1802-1880), the leading political editor of his day; in turn, Marx and Engels had criticized his writings as being too abstract to be useful for the analysis of the concrete conditions of oppression.

To what extent were these attacks justified? It seems to me that his contemporaries acquired the impression that Feuerbach would be a political leader because of the passionate directness of much of his writing and because some of his conclusions—for example, that religious belief is actually an expression of human social needs—had practical political implications. Feuerbach, however, knew that there was a difference between expressing an idea and putting it into effect, and he remained skeptical of the political capacities of his people—he once said that the Germans were nothing but living books—and therefore of the success of any German political revolution during his lifetime. Certainly the fear of harassment played a large part in his hesitation to enter public affairs; although he was sensitive about his exclusion from the professional ranks and deeply hoped to make a name for himself, he published *Thoughts on Death* anonymously and considered doing this with some of his later works. In actuality, though, this cultivation of seclusion stemmed just as much from his desire to be left alone, to remain independent of religious, political, and academic alliances in order to gain objectivity in his thinking, as it did from caution. Moreover, he was aware that Goethe and other distinguished authors had published anonymously in order not to distract readers from the content of their books. It was this content, the "objective idea," the intellectual truth of a problem, with which

Feuerbach would remain primarily concerned. The resignation of the individual to the search for the truth, the excitement of discovery in this search, and the struggle for a mode of expression that would directly communicate the truth to the widest possible audience explain the passion of his writings. However his ideas are assessed, he designed his writings to change opinion rather than to provoke action.

Biographical Notes

Feuerbach was born in Landshut, Bavaria, on July 28, 1804, of parents who were determined to protect him from the strong, traditional Catholicism of southern Germany by giving him a solid Lutheran upbringing. During his years of study at the gymnasium in Ansbach, he had a deep, Scripture-oriented piety, taking private tutoring in ancient Hebrew to supplement his studies of the Bible. By the time he had chosen to enter the University of Heidelberg to prepare for the ministry, however, something had shaken his faith from its anchor in scholarly study of the Scriptures. It may have been the influence of his religion instructor, Theodor Lehmus (1777-1837), at that time a disciple of the Heidelberg theologian Karl Daub (1765-1836), whose explanation of Christian doctrine used the philosophical categories of Hegel in opposition to both the prevailing biblicism and rationalism of the day. In addition, while spending a few months in preparatory study, Feuerbach read and outlined Herder's *Letters Regarding the Study of Theology* (1780-1781), which may have inculcated a distrust both of the orthodox doctrine of verbal inspiration and of critical-scholarly exegesis, for in Herder's opinion the Bible was the result of direct poetic outbursts of the simple religion of the people and could be understood only by imaginative assumption of this simplicity. At any rate, soon after the start of classes at Heidelberg, Feuerbach developed an extreme distaste for the "spider's web of sophisms"[7] of Professor H. E. G. Paulus (1761-1851), one of the leading nineteenth-century proponents of rationalistic, critical exegesis, while finding Daub the only professor of theology worth hearing. Since what Feuerbach liked in Daub were his Hegelian categories, it was not long before the idea of learning these firsthand dawned on him.

Although he convinced his father to support the continuation of his study for the ministry at Berlin because of the great theologians in residence there, when he arrived, in the spring of 1824, Feuerbach was no longer sure that he wanted to become a minister. He had originally been drawn to philosophy as a way of expressing religious belief, but he no longer saw philosophy and theology as compatible, apparently in contradiction to Hegel's assumption that the content of dogma, rightly understood, could be articulated philosophically without being destroyed. His final decision was not long in coming: during the winter semester of 1824-25, Feuerbach found himself unable to complete the courses of two of the leading Christian academics of his day, the church historian Johann August Wilhelm Neander (1789-1850) and the theologian Schleiermacher, because "to my soul, which demanded truth, i.e., *unity, decisiveness, the absence of qualifications,* the theological mishmash of freedom and dependence, reason and faith was odious to the point of death,"[8] while the philosophy of Hegel was the "Bethlehem of a new world."[9] From that point on philosophy would be both his tool for articulating the relationship between humanity and its world and a weapon for criticizing the "mishmash" of theology.

Prevented by finances from finishing at Berlin, Feuerbach returned to Bavaria to complete his doctorate in philosphy at the University of Erlangen and to begin his short-lived career—from 1829 to 1835—as a lecturer on the history of modern philosophy. His dissertation, *Reason: Its Unity, Universality, and Infinity* (1828), and *Thoughts on Death* are the creations of a brilliant follower of Hegel who is beginning to work out the implications of some of the master's ideas. In the meantime, however, his lectures on philosophy triggered a further confrontation with representatives of modern thought, especially Bacon, Descartes, Leibniz, and Pierre Bayle, from which he

would emerge with two conclusions that demanded a new beginning in philosophy: Christian theology masked the true human
origin and the nature of religious belief, and Hegel's philosophy, the culmination of the idealist tradition, was the deifica-
tion of thought at the expense of humanity.[10] In different ways,
both traditions were bound to a manner of thought that be-
trayed the concrete humanity they should have served. *The
Essence of Christianity,* the result of his first conclusion, argued
that the traditional theological doctrines, rather than having a
divine referent, were hypostatizations of humanity's most basic
needs, of which religious faith, if rightly understood, was an
authentic expression. The two works that embody his call for
the reform of philosophy, *Preliminary Theses for the Reform in
Philosophy* (1843) and *Foundations of the Philosophy of the
Future* (1843), were his first attempts to forge the criteria of a
way of thinking that penetrated and remained close to the concrete, empirical world.

   Although Feuerbach's thought continued to develop, it remained near to the two constructive emphases of these three
works—the elucidation of the origin of religion in humanity
and its relation to the natural environment, and the attempts to
articulate a humanistic empiricism. His publications after 1848
were largely ignored, however, perhaps because the critiques of
Marx and Engels were accepted by the radicals, or perhaps
because his own mode of thinking remained close to the literary
and philosophical tradition from which he parted, while many
of the other German leaders had begun to struggle with pressing
economic, political, and social concerns.[11] Meanwhile, financial
problems increased his isolation. In 1837 he had married Berta
Löw and moved with her to Bruckberg, near Ansbach, where
the porcelain factory of which she was a part owner had been
their main source of support. In 1860 the factory went bank-
rupt, and the family settled into a very modest home near Nuremberg with almost no income. Although prohibited from serious literary work because of declining health, Feuerbach continued to keep abreast of political affairs, enthusiastically

applauding the movement for women's emancipation and the
publication of Marx's *Capital* (1867). In 1870, he joined the
German Social Democratic party, which paid tribute to his
humanism with a huge procession attending his burial in the
Johannesfriedhof in Nuremberg two days after he died on Sep-
tember 13, 1872.

The Purpose and Style of *Thoughts on Death*

In 1828 Feuerbach sent his dissertation to Hegel as a testimonial
to his discipleship. Rather than describing and defending the
contents of the dissertation, however, his accompanying letter
proposed that it was necessary for the philosophy of his mentor
to take a new direction in the future! Feuerbach clearly considered himself capable of working in this new direction, for
Thoughts on Death embodies the proposal of the letter. By the
same token, the ideas in the letter will serve to explain the major
themes of this work.

Feuerbach is certain that Hegel's philosophy contains nothing less than the seeds of a new epoch in world history because
for the first time a conceptual system has adequately explained
the connection between universal ideas and concrete realities,
between God, humanity, and the world. Until now, however,
this new world epoch has been established merely theoretically,
merely within the arena of professional philosophical debate,
while the culture does not base its life on reason; the modes of
perception with which humanity presently approaches reality
assume a split between the thing and its concept and between
God and the world, and these modes of perception are now part
of the flesh and blood of the culture, having been assimilated
for over a thousand years. Therefore the new epoch can be
established only by a direct attack; in order to be effective
enough to uproot the old assumptions and to become humanity's new mode of perception, Hegel's ideas must be lifted out
of their interior connections within his system and must be

brought to bear on the "thoughtlessness" of the culture; they must become "incarnated," must be given a concrete shape that everyone can understand.

But what is the mode of viewing reality that must be dethroned? To Feuerbach, the culprit is theoretical selfishness. Practically since the beginning of Western history, people have understood the individual person, the self, even the personhood of God to be the single absolute source and criterion of all reality. It is as if the concern for the self has sucked all the meaning out of the nonhuman world of which the human is also a part. People do not understand that God is also a "nature," is the source of the impersonal reality with which our creaturely destinies are also bound. Moreover, people do not understand the unity of personhood with the natural world through the "natural world" of their bodies. Thus people understand death as nothing but the mode of transportation of the detached, limitless self into a higher world, not realizing that death is the ultimate expression of their unity with *this* world.

Now it is Christianity, which Feuerbach calls the religion of the pure self and of the pure self as God, that has led the way in maintaining the strength of this theoretical selfishness. The refutation of the belief in the soul-without-end in *Thoughts on Death* will be effective only if it exposes the entrenched misconception behind this belief: Christianity misunderstands human finitude and expresses its error by imagining a world higher than the real one. Thus the denial of immortality will also be a means for "negating the previous world-historical modes of viewing time, death, life here, the hereafter, I, individual, person, and the person viewed as beyond finitude and as absolute, namely God, etc., in which are contained the basis of history heretofore and the source of the system of both orthodox and rationalist Christian representations."[12]

Again, however, as the letter to Hegel states, it is not enough merely to elaborate philosophical arguments in order to make the ordinary human recognize the folly of his or her ingrained presuppositions and then be willing to change them. The ideas must be embodied in a striking way, and the many voices that

Feuerbach assumes throughout *Thoughts on Death* show his struggle for a manner of expression that will make his assertions immediately clear to any person with a mind. Most of the prose combines logical, even scholastic argumentation with appeals to a "you," the familiar form of the German second person singular pronoun. Then, just before the conclusion to the prose, Feuerbach inserts poetry that recapitulates the themes of the argumentation. This conclusion begins with a prayer to the divine Spirit, also addressed as a "you," which recalls the Psalms or Augustine's meditations in the *Confessions.* The work ends with a long series of epigrams that make a joke out of every contemporary German school of academic theology, not only because they maintained the belief in immortality, but because of the overwhelming stupidity of their attitudes and ideas. I suggest that underlying these forms of expression are both Feuerbach's reading of the mood of his culture and his theory of how to engage this culture with the written word.

The tone of Feuerbach's argumentation throughout is one of utter conviction, the logical steps being wielded like a hammer with which to pulverize the opposition; indeed, his favorite method of arguing is to point out the utter absurdity of the implications of the position to be refuted. Apart from Feuerbach's own conviction as to the truth of what he was saying, *Thoughts on Death* is supposed to proclaim the onset of a new age, and a revolutionary statement should be expressed, not in the cold categories of philosophy, but with religious passion and conviction. Only passion makes history; that is, only if absolute certainty is brought to bear against already entrenched religious certainties can it hope to dislodge them.[13] The appeal to "you, dear reader" may seem at first to contradict this exalted religious tone; yet it, too, is intended as an incarnation of the argument, to effect a connection between the intellectual conclusions and the audience, a connection of which the language of the profession was incapable. Actually, it also contains a note of humor intended to distance the author from, as well as to put him in contact with, his readers: the personal address apes the personalism he is attacking, and the address to God in prayer gives witness of one who is capable of singing a hymn of praise to a God who creates us for this earth—and nowhere else. Feuerbach would remark later that ironic humor is the method par excellence of uniting the abstract with the concrete, for it demonstrates the freedom and clarity of the thinker who is able to maintain control of intellectual truth while allowing no one to mistake its concrete import.[14]

To the young Feuerbach, though, the language of prose was still not sufficiently direct. He inherited the theory of Herder and the romantics that poetry is the most "immediate" language; it expresses with simple naïveté the deepest wishes not only of the individual but of an entire culture. Since poetry is the language of the heart, it, and not theology, expresses the religious convictions for which the mind must find reasons.[15] He also had to admit, however, that he had reversed the way in which poetry is engendered: to "embody" the philosophical ideas, he concretized them in imaginative language—a method that hardly guarantees artistic success. The problems of this poetry are compounded by the contrast between the form of verse he used and the tone he attempted to achieve. He wrote in highly rhythmic rhyming couplets—we would call it doggerel verse—which in English sound like nursery rhymes; these cannot carry the weight of the solemnity of such lines as, "Oh harsh life, bitter being! / Oh being full of pure struggle and pain!" (p. 155). The overall effect is more that of a college student filling up spare time than of the celebration of death depicted in the great romantic poetry that Feuerbach may have had in mind (such as Novalis's *Hymns to the Night*). Still, Goethe had given respectability to this popular verse form. Furthermore, the fact that Feuerbach used poetry is more important than the poetry's actual artistic merits; the idea was to counter the deeply felt hope for immortality with a language that would evoke the experience of death-in-life.[16]

The problem of explaining the linguistic function of the *Epigrams* is different from that of explaining the verse because the elegiac couplet was well suited to Feuerbach's display of caustic wit. The German humanists had already developed a tradition of epigrammatic satire; by Feuerbach's time, it had become an accepted method for declaring a literary war on one's opponents. Almost every figure of the classical and romantic schools had written epigrams; in 1796, Goethe and Schiller had published their "ironical-satirical" couplets, which had left unscathed few members of contemporary German literary and philosophical circles. Again, in 1827, Goethe published epigrams, which he had written during the previous decade, under the title *Tame Xenien* (Feuerbach used the latter word—which is Greek—as his own title); although these attacked both the literature and the social mores of the German Restoration, it may well be that Feuerbach had Goethe in mind when, in his introductory "Prefatory Admonitions and Rejoinders" (pp. 172-173), he criticized a fellow German satirist for being too mild.

The question is, How does such an expression of ridicule and disdain "embody the idea" and change minds? Although the mature Feuerbach was somewhat embarrassed by the *Epigrams* —partly because an enthusiastic editor had added about a dozen of his own—in 1830 he must have wanted to see them published, despite a fairly realistic assessment of the danger of criticizing the forces in power. He must have known that he was committing an unforgivable sin against the professorial caste, an unveiled attack that showed a total lack of respect for exalted academic reputations. On the other hand, though, anger lowers inhibitions. Utterly capable of writing these attacks was the young man who could also write to his father, a highly authoritarian figure in his life, that "when I want to learn Paulus's insights"—Paulus was the professor whom his father especially wanted Feuerbach to hear in Heidelberg—"I do not need to attend his lectures, but only to go to the best tavern in the neighborhood."[17] Yet even Feuerbach's dangerous all-out attack on the academics was intended to strengthen his argument. When one is convinced of a truth, and when this conviction places one against all the odds of the status quo, then the expression of that truth must include as strong a statement of opposition as possible (p. 232). It seemed to Feuerbach that the powerful "negation" of language could actually silence one's opponents.

Perhaps the best way of clarifying the strange literary character of this work is to explain that, despite its passion and despite the intrusion of the self-conscious literary stylist—or, rather, by means of his passion and style—its author was attempting to demonstrate a certain kind of objectivity. By objectivity the idealist Feuerbach did not mean the detached faithfulness to external data of the contemporary scientist, although he certainly wanted to proclaim his detachment from any and every theological school. His truths, his "objects" were ideas, and his concept of objectivity was to be faithful to the truth of a matter despite what others might wish that truth to be. He presupposed that his audience wished to be immortal, and he sympathized with that hope, acknowledging that its source was real, "living pain" (p. 213); but to act from this presupposition meant to assert the objective truth of human mortality as strenuously as possible, to demonstrate "passion for the object" in order to overcome the ancient controlling force of this wish.

The Argument: Negating Traditional Christian Concepts

The historical introduction to *Thoughts on Death* (pp. 1-14) qualifies an assertion of the letter to Hegel; the Christianity of the pure self is not Christianity as manifested throughout history but is Christianity in its modern form, in the pietism, rationalism, and moralism that are themselves the logical outcome of the Reformation. These movements are the objects of most of the attacks of the *Epigrams*. In contrast to the genuine ancient faith of Catholicism and of the medieval mystics, the new pietism, the emotional religiosity that was characteristic of the religious "awakening" of the post-Napoleonic period, is accused of degrading human nature by its "sin consciousness" and emphasis on the necessity of divine aid and of leading the retreat of religion into the dark recesses of vague feeling, while rationalism is singled out mainly for its nitpicking scriptural exegesis and its lack of historical awareness. The philosophical argument of the prose, however, concentrates on the error that the modern movements share: viewing the individual self as the only model for perfection, as the sole source of meaning and fulfillment. This concentration on the self is the result of modernity's break with the sense of community, with the belief that the identity of humans and therefore the value of life is given by the commonality within which one lives. Even dualistic, otherworldly, medieval Catholicism relied on the sense of community because it believed that the church incarnated on earth the supernatural union of its members. Only with the Protestant reliance on the belief of the individual could the doctrine of personal immortality gain supreme importance, for the now isolated self is restricted to its own reality in its search for ideals of perfection. However, the ideal of the perfect self must remain merely ideal, merely an interior intention; it must always be frustrated on earth because of the restrictions of the crude laws of the material reality that it no longer understands or appreciates. Out of this frustration, religious individualism invents a more perfect world, one that exists after this "meaningless" life, as the only appropriate complement to its ideals.

In order to conteract this error, the entire argument attempts to return the self to the real limits that it has violated by its imaginative invention of the afterlife. It proceeds step by step to detail the attributes that demonstrate the finitude and therefore the mortality of the individual human being. To exist is to exist concretely, with concrete qualities; each set of qualities, in concretizing existence, limits it; if I am a human, I am not a dog, and therefore my subjectivity is not all of reality. Thus individual existence is limited by the infinity of the Creator (pp. 14-49), by its subjection to the laws of time and space (pp. 49-77), by its intrinsic connection to an organic, mortal body (pp. 77-117), and by its merely finite capacity to exercise the infinite powers that characterize it as human, such as self-consciousness, reason, and will (pp. 117-152). While this logic of limitation enjoins resignation to the inevitability and finality of death, the conclusion argues that the inexhaustible quality of the limited time that we have is far superior to a life that would be defined primarily by its eternal duration (pp. 232-247).

The process of returning the self to its limits involves Feuerbach in criticizing the accepted usages of philosophical categories that are central to Christian belief. Most important of these is his rejection of a divine-human analogy that rests its case exclusively on the attributes of person-to-person love. God conceived as merely an infinite person is nothing but an expression of selfishness, because unlimited subjectivity is the infinite mirror and therefore the infinite affirmation and guarantor of the eternal perdurability of the individual's subjectivity. The analogy is wrong because it leaves out the intimate connection between God and extrapersonal being and therefore isolates the human subject from its extrapersonal environment. Feuerbach understands personhood, or the self, as the uniqueness of a reality, that by which it is not anything or anybody else, that by which a reality excludes connection. If God is *merely* a person, then he is not nature; if he is not nature, he is not everything and therefore not infinite. Rather, God must be conceived as the source of nature as well as of personhood, as the source of extrapersonal being. He must be understood as the source of those realities of the universe which limit our being, which frustrate our desire to be infinite. For example, as eternal, he is the source of the consuming power of time, which, as the expression of his eternal presence, is also the expression of the transitoriness of all reality in the face of infinity. In Feuerbach's terms, there is an opaque or a dark side of God which consumes individual reality as well as affirming it (p. 89). To worship *this* God is to surrender one's personhood as much as to experience its affirmation, and the fact of the ultimate surrender of death protects against the selfishness of the hope for an eternal reward.

Feuerbach confirms this assertion of the impersonal side of God, of God's love as a fire that consumes individuality, by working out the implications of the self-surrender of human love. The experience of love expresses the community of being; thus the need to love expresses the need of distinct beings for unity. Love, however, would be impossible if we were merely persons, for personhood is the principle of exclusion. In more

contemporary terms, the basis of love is not the attraction of
one uniqueness for another uniqueness, but the attractiveness
of what we share, of what unites us. Our love for one another
expresses our desire for unity with the infinite human reality of
which we both partake. The condition of the possibility of
human love is therefore the ability to surrender selfhood to this
higher reality. (The argument of the last two paragraphs is on
pp. 14-49.)

At this point we need to digress in order to explain the philosophical position behind such a statement. The young Feuerbach affirmed the philosophical tradition that was committed
to the vision of the ultimate unity of reality and that expressed
this commitment by explaining how external, sensible, individual reality is the manifestation of invisible, spiritual, universal
reality. The philosophy of Hegel had explained the unity of God
with the world to Feuerbach's satisfaction because, by evolving
a set of dynamic categories that had included the universe in the
process of God's self-articulation, it had overcome static spirit-
matter dualism. The model for the dynamism of these categories was organistic: individual realities are seen as the visible tips
of the icebergs of spiritual systems of vital growth. This position explains, for example, Feuerbach's stress on the inner connection between the individual human body and the "universal
organic system" of terrestrial nature. Still, the universal reality
at the source of human individuality is "more real" than the
human individual, for humans are limited expressions of
"humanity itself," the perfect ideal of humanity which is realized but never exhausted in individuals. (So, too, the individual
human body is an imperfect expression of the "organic body
itself"; the death of an individual, rather than being caused by a
mortal wound, is ultimately due to the fact that the finite body
is consumed before the infinite body in which it participates
[pp. 102-105]!)

This, then, is the philosophical vision informing Feuerbach's
stress on the community of being at the expense of individualism. Love expresses the summit of humanity because its object
is the universal unity that makes us what we are—finite embodi-

ments of universal powers. As Feuerbach explains the human
powers of self-consciousness, reason, and will, the argument
for mortality follows this same path: we are not self-consciousness (or reason, or will) itself, but merely single finite manifestations of the universal self-consciousness.

This description of love as expressing the commonality of
being is an attempt to make humans unlock the boundaries of
subjective consciousness, to see humanity as intrinsically
involved even with a world that contains the proofs of human
limitation. That interrelatedness is the structure of reality, especially of human reality, is argued by means of a description of
the fact that even our inner subjective identity is always shared.
Our life arises from unconsciousness, and not just from the
darkness of the womb or the total blackness before conception.
Before we gain the maturity to assert ourselves as independent
beings, the only consciousness we have is that imparted to us by
our nurturers. Even after we have made our independent
stands, we are never completely autonomous; our life story pro-
gresses by becoming entwined with the consciousness that
others have of us. In fact, if the major theme of the life story is
growth in the capacity to love, then our lives are much more a
story of sharing our consciousness than of gaining our own, for
as we approach the twilight of life, the shared consciousness, in
our memory and the memory of others, gains ground against
the consciousness of our selves that remains. The physical event
of death, then, is the expression of the ultimate act of sharing,
of self-donation, for the boundary between our selves and
others is totally obliterated, totally surrendered to others' consciousness of us (pp. 124-133). Here Feuerbach gives an ancient
theme a modern twist: the love that is the very incarnation and
fulfillment of human life is ultimately expressed in death.

Feuerbach reaches a crucial point for overcoming spirit-mat-
ter dualism in his attempt to describe the intrinsic unity between
the individual human soul and its body without destroying the
distinction between universal, spiritual reality and its external
manifestation. (This argument is preceded by a long teleological
discussion to show that the stars could not support life because

the purpose and fulfillment of the cosmos is earth, which is therefore the only heavenly body containing the conditions for life [pp. 59-89]. The quaintness of this philosophy of nature should not distract from the point of the argument: life depends on the presence of certain conditions; these conditions limit as well as promote life; accordingly, the system that engenders individual human life also snuffs it out.) He takes his stand for soul-body unity from two principles: (1) the human body is a living, dynamic unity and thus is not primarily defined by the "dead" attributes of materiality, weight, and divisibility, which best describe a stone; it is "immaterial matter'; and (2) there is a distinction between the soul as a particular life principle of a particular body, which passes away with the body for which it is destined, and the soul that exists "in itself," which is the spiritual, universal soul and therefore beyond the conditions of individuality (pp. 94-117).

Whatever the merits of this argument, the supposition behind it is that the Christian explanations for the perdurability of the soul after the death of the body are made possible because of the devaluation of the human body; traditional Christianity treats the body as lifeless matter, as the shuckable skin of the soul rather than as the one place in nature where bodily existence is "resurrected," is raised into self-conscious bodily existence. Thus the logic of the argumentation moves from the assertion of the dynamic unity of the human individual to the denial of the existence after death of any human individuality. To Feuerbach, though, the resolution of the split between the soul and the body is more important than is this resolution's usefulness for one more argument against immortality. His letter to Hegel asserted that Christianity misunderstands finitude, human limitation, and expresses this misunderstanding in the image of a world that is supposedly higher than this world. Further, the most powerful image that Christianity has used to describe immortality is not that of an ethereal soul, but the picture of individual existence in heaven, the picture of the heavenly body. Thus it is at this point that Feuerbach breaks off his argument in an attempt to show exactly how the devaluation of the real human body leads to the image of the eternal heavenly body (pp. 105-108, 116-117).

The stress on the primacy of the self leads the Christian to see individuality as being distinct even from one's own incarnate self, one's body. Because the now-isolated self no longer recognizes the body's limits as its own, it is free to imagine a fulfillment that is not bounded by these limitations. Feuerbach states that the self in this condition exists as if in a dream, in which the controls of thinking according to law are released from their rule over the imaginative powers. Given free rein in the imagination, the desire to be immortal incarnates the object of its desire, gives it concrete, apparently objective existence—and behold the glorified heavenly body! In other words, the image of the heavenly body is like the hallucination that is produced out of intense desire once that desire is no longer bound by the limits of reality. While the real heavenly body is the earthly body, the Christian's underestimation of its value leads to a gap, a hole, in the real world; Christianity, however, is sufficiently aware of this gap to feel the need to fill it, so it replaces the body that it has misunderstood with the image of a body in a higher world. This description of the process by which something deeply wished for takes on an independent reality is Feuerbach's tentative first step into the psychology of religion. Instead of an argument to prove the limits of human individuality from the laws of this world, it is an attempt to uncover the origin of an image to show that heaven isn't there.

Reflections

We have a longer life expectancy than that of any other human era, and yet we also seem to have a greater "death expectancy" —that is, it appears that our Western culture, like no other before or beside it, is obsessed with the meaning of death, dying, and the life we have allotted to us. Maybe this is not a paradox, however; maybe our preoccupation is actually a result of our hopes for long lives; the chances of being cut off before our time are increased the longer we expect to live, and thus our worry increases proportionally. On the other hand, this cannot be the sole source of our preoccupation; the people of Feuerbach's time did not have our life expectancy, and yet, according to him, they were obsessed with escaping death. Perhaps Feuerbach stood just far enough into our modern age to be capable of reflecting on the trend that we have felt growing in us. Perhaps, despite his strange language, he has something to say about our concern with death. I will reflect on three phases in his argument: his theory as to the source of modernity's focus on personal immortality, his arguments to return the self to its "natural" place, and his attempt to replace the doctrine of immortality with ideals that are bounded by our mortality.

Feuerbach connects the modern emphasis on the immortality of the soul with our culture's change in perspective on the most important source for human meaning: it is now the individual, and no longer the community, that is absolute. He thinks that this change has involved a loss, the loss of the sense that each of us is given our identity, and therefore our significance, by a human group more real than the sum of its members and that therefore the ultimate criteria of the worth of our lives are the values of this community. This loss is destructive because it means the surrender of realistic ideals; the Roman, who gained personal identity from serving the empire, the Greek, who was dedicated to the common ideal of the embodiment of beauty, even the medieval Christian, who believed that the church was the terrestrial manifestation of the supernatural world—all these worked for goals that humans are capable of attaining. Once this sense of communal identity was rejected, the individual was cut off from seeing value in any reality other than the isolated self, and therefore the new culture focused on an unreal goal, the immortal individual of the hereafter, to replace the goals proportionate to human capacity, those of the trans-individual human communities of this earth.

This is a statement of historical origins. Presupposing that humans are mortal, it answers the question, How did the ideal of personal immortality, this attempt to escape death, take over our culture? In order to understand what Feuerbach was driving at, though, we have to ask the meaning of another presupposition behind this historical sketch: In what way does the sense of community prevent humans from trying to escape death?

It is easy to imagine a possible answer. Perhaps the human cannot bear to stand alone before death. Perhaps it is impossible for the self to be totally sensitive to life at every instant— for this is also to shoulder the entire burden of one's approaching death—and so it must deaden some of its awareness in order to continue to live. Perhaps the human must forget part of itself in order to receive the security of the larger identity that the community affords. After all, to be part of a community is to be immortalized in some sense. The group into which I was born was here before me; if I submit to its rules it will sustain me, comfort me as I approach death, and remember me when I am gone. The sense of community has long been a way of lessening the terror of death; at the cost of releasing oneself from one's autonomy, one can be supported by a larger structure along the way. The strong hold of community coherence until the modern age may be due in great part to this kind of response to the experience of approaching death.

I think that Feuerbach's description of life as a process of self-imparting not only takes up this logic but presses it further: it is not that I *choose* to give up part of myself in favor of a larger whole, but, rather, that my human structure demands it. This description begins by applying to the relationship between the individual and the community the classical Christian argument for creatureliness: the consciousness of human autonomy is false because the human is totally dependent for its very self-assertion on what it receives from nurturing consciousnesses. Thus the image of the self-sustaining individual is an illusion from the start. Also, though, the process of maturing human life includes the process of self-surrender, of the self-as-conscious diminishing as the self-as-object grows. As time goes on, I become more and more an object; you and I can observe the self that I was. The fullness of humanity gained when the human reaches its peak is really the fullness of the self as remembered object. And the point of death is the completion of this process of objectification; it is the submergence and impartation of the self without remainder into the community, for at this point I exist only in its consciousness of what I was. Feuerbach's description of the morality of self-donation thus advises humans to accept what the human structure dictates anyway.

The full content of Feuerbach's historical assertion, then, is that, although all cultures have had to face the problem of death, the sense for self-donation to the community has prevented them from entering on the modern Western illusion of the eternal perdurability of the self. However, apart from questioning the accuracy of this statement, it may be very difficult for us to accept this stress on the primacy of community. Isn't Feuerbach concealing the fact that each of us is unique precisely when we have to face the reality of our own death, that we become irreplaceable precisely when we undergo death all on our own? And therefore isn't the ideal of self-submergence for a community just another dream of transcendence, an over-idealization of the communal instead of an overidealization of the self? Doesn't it hide the fact of the ultimate lie of any project, either of the community or of the individual, all of which must end at the same negative point?

While there may never be a completely satisfying answer to the realism of these questions, they miss the logic of Feuerbach's argumentation, which is that the process of individual life, because of the necessity of its relation to other beings, consumes the self until, at death, there is little enough left of that reality, the loss of which would be painful. The philosophical principle behind this is that being is communal, that God is everything in its unity as well as in its distinction, and that therefore the singly existing reality strives to overcome its isolation. In humans, the sources for the drive to overcome isolation are all those aspects that speak relatedness, whether they are the body or the conscious powers of thinking and willing. Feuerbach calls these aspects the *not-self,* and for him, the process of growth, of gaining human maturity, involves consenting to the growth of the not-self. Although he speaks of the necessity of affirming the dark side of God, who out of his love created the laws of the consumption of the self, Feuerbach is not advocating a masochistic self-subjection that contradicts the logic of his philosophy. The dark side in us is that part of our humanity in which the laws of our death are written, just as the drive for unlimited life is written in the self. The consent to being human involves the consent to allowing ourselves to be engulfed and used up only because it is consent to the laws of death working in us. From this perspective, the consent to subjection to the community is not an escape from the aloneness of our death, but the consent to let our aloneness die a little each day.

Still, it can seem to be inaccurate and unfair of Feuerbach to accuse Christianity of splitting the individual from community; the Christian message has often carried to the pinnacle of heroism the ideal of self-donation. Moreover, this very ideal has been the source of Christianity's compelling power to create community: if all of us are equally creatures of God, then our life in service to him must include service to others. Far from attacking this ideal, however, Feuerbach's argument attacks a particular form of self-understanding that Christianity has appropriated, because he thinks that it excludes the possibility of donation of the self not only to other humans but even to God. The modern, individualistic Christian knows and tries to express the distance between the creature and God. However, since the only models left for explaining the reality of God are the attributes of personhood raised to the infinite power, Feuerbach's Christian sees in God only those qualities that affirm the supreme importance of oneself. Surely the object of such infinite personal concern could not be allowed to pass out of existence! This young rebel from theology, soon to profess atheism openly, is attacking modern Christianity for taking the mysterious, negating power of the love of God out of the religious relationship! In addition to this, though, the modern focus on the self has made it of supreme importance that each individual gain an everlasting reward for experiencing the frustrations to unlimited expansion here on earth. The individualistic Christian can proclaim his or her unworthiness to the skies, but the fact

remains that subjection to God is a form of egotism insofar as
its goal is self-perpetuation.

Feuerbach's picture of the Christian individualist, then, is
one of an isolated self that is unable, and perhaps unwilling, to
be released from its own interior. It is therefore locked into a
continual oscillation toward one or the other of the only two
extremes left to it, the extremes of total abnegation and self-
humiliation—in Feuerbach's terms, a reverse form of self-
centeredness—and of infinitely expanding consciousness to the
point at which no limit to the self can be envisioned. Perhaps we
can further understand this picture by returning to the previous
description of the experience of the self in reaction to the reality
of its approaching death. The self can accept or try to run away
from the vision of its end. The condition of acceptance, however, is the admission of the porousness of the self, of its interior relation and therefore vulnerability to all the forces that
endanger and even consume it. Since individualism is a vision of
reality that does not allow for this porousness, it cannot accept
death, and Feuerbach's criticism is an attempt to block the
strategies that the locked-in self devises to control its fate and
thereby escape reality. In his view, the irony of the attempt to
free the self from its oncoming death is that it involves it in
missing the values of life. For the self living inside its magical,
all-inclusive world, heaven has already begun, and it is able to
float above the eternal conflict of reality, unhindered by anything but the limits of its imagination. More recent thinkers
interpret this phenomenon as the expression of the desire to be
God, which prevents the human from becoming human.[18]

The human body is the crucial obstacle to the self's project to
escape limitation; as we have seen, Feuerbach argues that the
traditional Christian soul-body dualism is yet one more attempt
by individualism to deny any connection with this all-too-evi-
dent drag on one's autonomy. The doctrine of the immortality
of the soul "splits humans into an otherworldly, inconceivable,
shapeless soul, which is hostile to both form and nature, and
into a crude, spiritless body, which is hostile to the soul" (p. 2).
Certainly I can mentally distinguish myself from my body; the

very freedom I have to imagine something beyond my finitude
is based on the capacity that distinguishes the human from all
other living beings, the capacity to make an interior division
between my self and my immediate environment. But can I
really step outside of my environment? Is the I that I am in
opposing myself to my body totally independent of my body?
Or rather, even if the relation of the self to the body were nothing but the relation of opposition—which it clearly is not—
doesn't my I depend on my body for its act of division? If this is
true, then when its opposite is consumed, so is the self. It is
death, rather than escape from death, that comes into the world
with self-consciousness, for the human individual is the only
being that must reflect on the fact of death before it arrives. My
body, rather than being the opposition that I must overcome in
order to escape the world, is the external expression of my
anchor in it.

This argument has a certain weakness; Feuerbach's idealist
presuppositions at this stage of his career made him understand
individuality to mean mortality because the individual is the
material manifestation of an ideal, spiritual species. Only with
his later rejection of these presuppositions would he be able to
see the expression of sexual love as the powerful proof of the
subsumption of individuality to the laws of the biological species.[19] The structure of his argumentation here, though, already
moves in this direction and perhaps justifies me in adapting
more contemporary discussions of this theme.[20] As no other
experience, the sexual expression of love overcomes human isolation and thus is an essential mode of communication for the
self. The onset of sexual awareness, however, can be extremely
threatening to the project of escaping death, for it is the experience of an impersonal force in an individual which, in its apparent independence of one's wishes, denies one's control over
one's fate. Moreover, the ultimate expression of sexual love can
be another human, who, in his or her youth, is the embodiment
of the laws of the replaceability of the individual within the species. Once again we return to the dilemma of the modern individualist: the fear of submitting to vulnerability can prevent living human communication.

Thus Feuerbach's criticism of individualism comes down to saying that the self, once detached from the laws of nature and the support of the human community, suffers the destructive consequences of being able to look nowhere but to itself for the justification of its existence. In addition, his historical judgment is that modern Christianity's individualistic interpretation of the religious relationship has contributed to this problem. I think that both of these judgments deserve serious consideration. Our culture has experienced the gradual restriction of religion to the private realm, the rejection of its communal structure in favor of reliance on personal experience alone, and we are beginning to see the consequences of this. Even if one at some time feels totally liberated by an inward self-surrender to God, still, without being able to release something of one's responsibility to the visible support of a human community, its rituals, and its mores, one is encouraged to try to live out of a dangerous introspective concentration. To stand totally alone before one's God or totally alone before one's death may well result in the same kind of paralysis, that of living exclusively out of one's private fantasy. Meanwhile, in a contemporary ethos in which individualism is not relieved even by the religious sense of self-surrender, we watch people who cannot commit themselves to any community, person, or project for fear of hampering their freedom simultaneously suffer the guilt and sense of meaninglessness that comes from lacking the experience of their affirmation by a protective structure.

Feuerbach's final attempt to put the individual self back into its real limits is to oppose to the hope of a life after death an affirmation of the quality of the life that we lead before death (pp. 232-247). He describes the peak experiences of human life as the experiences of infinity within the conditions of finitude. For example, the experience of the self-donation of love unites the personal and nonpersonal aspects of the human because, in the experience, the finite individual realizes its unity with "humanity itself," with the infinite ideal of the species. Here I already experience my death, the annihilation of my individual personhood before infinite reality, but I also experience the realization of my capacity to stretch to infinity. Thus finitude is conquered from within finitude. To the protest that even these experiences are transitory, Feuerbach replies that death itself can be a transitory experience. Only humans experience death before it takes place; the completion of my death and its outcome are experienced by other living people. Thus the major crisis in a human life is not the point of death itself but the realization by the living human that one will really die. The choice of what to do about death, then, is the choice about what life to live. One can make death the constant theme of one's life by hoping for life only after this life—Feuerbach calls this living as if one were dead—or one can decide to live now, to live with the intensity that allows the self to be consumed. For Feuerbach, the second choice is to conquer death within life.

Once again, however, the young Feuerbach's idealist philosophy gets in the way of the direction of his assertions. For the picture of heavenly bliss he substitutes human participation in infinite, universal powers, "humanity itself, consciousness itself, thought itself," the ideals of philosophical activity, which, as they stand, are too abstract to claim a life of total dedication. However, the intent of his assertion of these ideals is clear; he is exhorting humans to give up trying to be everything in order to become something, to temper the desire to become infinite by accepting the limited experiences of infinity which he thinks are available to us. As we have seen, this compromise is possible only with the restraint of the self, only with the surrender of personhood to some kind of ideal that the human perceives as being greater than itself.

Perhaps, though, just at this final point, the unalloyed realism of our contemporary world once again calls out in protest. We know all too well that the desire to exist without limitation need not be destroyed by being translated into identification with a group. We have seen that in fact the destructive possibilities are much greater when individual egotism explodes into the collective egotism of a group whose desire for self-aggrandizement is totally out of the control of the individuals who compose it. It is precisely this contemporary realism that seems to shatter our capacity to trust any longer the collective ideologies of our world, be these either religious or secular. And here neither Feuerbach nor the Freudian psychology that he inspired can help us, for their project was restricted to dispelling illusions, and we have come to the point where we have to entertain the possibility that, while there appear to be no communal ideals worth the risk, human life cannot function without some intimations of immortality, without some dream that we are involved in a destiny that is greater than our own. We must have someone or something to trust in, in order to be released from our narcissism. We must be willing to act out a commitment, not blindly, but in the face of the fear that this group or this person might betray us. And the only effective motivating forces seem to be those dreams like the religious dreams that expand our lives to superhuman dimensions. The project of our day seems to be no longer that of destroying illusions but that of being able to find and accept those illusions that promise to enhance our human creativity. I will leave it to the reader to decide whether the doctrine of personal immortality is a destructive or a creative illusion.[21]

A Note on the Translation

Because of the way *Thoughts on Death* was originally received,[22] the young Feuerbach never planned a second edition in a form close to the first; when he included it in his collected works, he substantially revised the prose from the perspective of his new philosophical position and left out the vast majority of the epigrams.[23] The many typographical errors are evidence of the great haste with which the version of 1830 went into print—Feuerbach did not see the final proofs (pp. v, vii, viii). Johann Adam Stein, the original editor-publisher, who is mentioned in the title as "one of his [Feuerbach's] friends," somewhat mitigated this problem by adding a list of the most serious errors at the end of the book.[24] The spaces between paragraphs in the translation correspond to Feuerbach's paragraphing, but the vast majority of the paragraphing within these sections is my own.

The translation presented two major editorial problems: how

to carry over into English the flavor of the different modes of discourse and how to furnish the necessary background information without distracting the reader or betraying the distinctly antiacademic intention of the author. For example, it was Feuerbach's habit to sprinkle his writing with Latin, Greek, and French, and even with Spanish and English. In *Thoughts on Death* these words and phrases have varying importance according to whether they are located in the prose or in one of the two types of poetry. In the prose, Feuerbach used some non-German words for their technical meaning, some to display the range of his erudition; I left all but a few of these in the translation, confining my explanations to those not familiar to English readers or not found in English dictionaries. There are very few non-German words in the rhyming verse, and these were probably used merely to fit the meter; therefore I translated all of them. The *Epigrams,* however, presented a different problem, for here the different languages were a function of Feuerbach's attempt to be humorous. Thus it was necessary to include all the non-German words, along with the necessary explanatory notes. The notes of Feuerbach and of his editor-publisher are indicated by an asterisk and located at the foot of the corresponding page, as in the original, while my notes are consecutively numbered and follow the translated text.

I was not able to reproduce the heavy beat or the rhymes of the doggerel verse; my partial excuse for this is that the verse is hardly poetry but a didactic attempt to clothe philosophical ideas in aesthetic form. Moreover, many of the rhymes are forced, and the meter is often violated. The *Epigrams* sound much closer to the German, with a pungent snap in the second line of the couplet when they work. They show much of the earthy humor of Feuerbach's Bavarian homeland. There are major obstacles, however, to translating satire that is over 150 years old. It is difficult enough to convey humor to one's contemporary audience by means of the printed word. It is even more difficult for a later audience to get the point of the humor; satire depends on a readership that is aware of the contemporary scene because the humor is developed from allusions to people and events of the day. In my attempt to solve these problems, I tried to demonstrate the concreteness of the satirical references rather than to provide an exhaustive scholarly commentary. Thus I restricted my explanations in the notes to references to historically important figures and to the more obscure allusions to mythology.

The prose is uneven in style, ranging from formal, rhetorical, literary flourishes to loosely connected strings of unpolished, elliptical phrases. Although being extremely free in altering the German punctuation, I have attempted to reproduce this variety, in the conviction that Feuerbach's prose style is an important indicator of both the content of his arguments and the relative importance that he attached to them. For example, he can move immediately from a series of logical connections to a satirical attack that contains exaggerations of the point of the argument he wishes to make. It seems to me that other translations, although excellent in many respects, have muted such changes of emotional register and thus have contributed to the present confusion regarding just what Feuerbach was attempting to say.

Thoughts on Death and Immortality

When I was a child,
Not knowing whence or whither,
I turned my wandering eye
To the sun, as if there was
An ear up there to hear my complaint,
A heart like mine
To pity the oppressed.
—Goethe, *Prometheus*

Philosophy had plenty of room to flourish among the Greeks and Romans because pagan religion had no dogmas, but today dogmas destroy everything. Authors must set to work with a circumspection that puts constraint on the truth. *The clerical rabble takes revenge on the smallest violation of orthodoxy; people do not dare to exhibit the unveiled truth.*
—Frederick the Great in a letter to Voltaire

Humble Petition
to the
Exalted, Wise, and Honorable
Learned Public
to Receive
Death into the Academy of Sciences

Highly learned and esteemed gentlemen,
May I hereby present before you Death
In order that, in your lofty circle,
You may raise him to the doctorate.

So that you do not find it disgraceful
If he sits in consultation with you,
I hereby proclaim to you
What he might contribute to science.

He is the best doctor on earth;
None of his cures have yet failed;
And no matter how sick you become,
He completely heals nature.

iv

To be sure, he never has concerned himself
With Christian theology,
Yet he will have no peer
In understanding philosophy.

So then I implore you to receive
Death into the academy,
And, as soon as possible, to make
Him doctor of philosophy.

Editor's Foreword

At a time such as the present, which is undeniably destined to bear within itself the germ of sublime developments, at a time when contradictions are piled on contradictions, yet without totally attaining, by their rapid toppling from dizzying heights, the smashing of the antiquated, decaying forms of the present and without penetrating with melody the monotonous oscillations of its pendulum—at such a time, then, the editor of this work, written and given to him by the hand of a friend, considered it to be his unavoidable duty to withhold it no longer from the world and with a steady hand to guide it toward its fate. To be sure, it is only a fragment—though it would have been an easy task for the author to have it appear in a truly scientific form, in a word, to put on the finishing touches, had not time and circumstances intervened—but nevertheless it is of decisive value.

Whereas previously materialism and subjective idealism were the two poles toward which all examinations of death and immortality inclined, in this work that which is immortal and everlasting turns out to be the reality, objectivity, and substantiality of Spirit, the Spirit from which, in turn, the author deduces death itself. By this means he posits death and then again cancels it; thus the antitheses are mediated dialectically, and the result into which death and immortality are merged at his hands is the actual world, is substantial life, is the truly infinite, is God and Spirit itself.

However, if one wanted to discuss in more detail the relationships of the inner content and significance of this work to the present, to the current condition of the life of Spirit and science, then, instead of a foreword, one would have to write a commentary or even an apologia. Therefore it is left to an editor merely to state in general why this work differs in every respect from all previous on this subject and why the *uniqueness* of its ideas are certainly excelled by none other and, indeed, put this work in a category of its own.

If a definite aim for fixed objectives is at the basis of inexactitude in the prose of this work, this may be assumed to be all the more true in the case of the poems, because here this purpose is unambiguously expressed. For the form, or rather the formlessness, of these poems, indeed, their entire manner of expression, betrays of itself the most bitter irony. And they are intended to be nothing less than poems, but only the figurative—though totally symbolical—developments of ideas in verse. The keys to understanding the poems are to be found in the prose; as a matter of fact, according to their internal order they should have been located in the middle of the prose, where the author still exists in the position of opposition. (This comment is extremely important to keep in mind for a fair assessment of their value, Spirit, and meaning.)

The vast majority of the epigrams are prospects from the *camera obscura* of the present.[1] The misery of our times may well justify their bluntness; it was necessary. If here and there are to be found usages that are not correct in the strictest sense of the word, the editor alone bears the responsibility for their inclusion, for he could not bring himself to sacrifice their inner content to the rules of versification. Again, in no way should the author be blamed for this, for, as already stated, he was not able to apply the finishing touches. At any rate, in his construction of the verses, the author followed, not an Ovid or a Horace, but the authors of our nation—which should be stated to those who complain about the toughness of the outer shell when their delicate mouths find the kernel to be too bitter.

The editor, swept along by the living torrent of these epigrams and warmed by their ardor—in these times so rare—for eternal truth, permitted himself to introduce a few more rivulets from the same springs into their strong and deep current, presupposing that his small trickles could neither muddy the clarity of the main stream nor alter its unique course. They are too easily discernible to need a special designation, at least for the thoughtful reader who is able to grasp the ideas of the author totally and to follow them without interruption, but they are merely individual shadings that place into a still more magical light the silver waves of the substantial flow.

The only real contribution of the editor to this work consists in its actual publication, which he urged and accomplished with great eagerness. For the author never intended it for press in its present form, and not a little gift for persuasion was expended, so to speak, to tear it away from him and to have it appear as a fragment. What finally determined the editor to deposit it on the threshold of the future at precisely this time has already been mentioned. But the primary motivation was the very inner solidity of this only fragmentary but still excellent writing, in which the rarest wit and an almost devastating satire are intimately wedded to the most profound philosophical insight. These reasons alone should suffice!

The letter *W,* to be found under a few of the epigrams, is totally meaningless. It served in the manuscript merely to designate the order that a section of the epigrams was to follow and got into print only because of a mistake of the proofreader. Finally, the reader is urgently requested to read the concluding prose before the epigrams, as it clearly forms a whole with the previous prose. Because of an inexcusable error of the compositor, it was not placed immediately after the rhyming verse. For the rest, the reader can avoid those printing errors that change the sense of the arguments by using the list appended at the end.

Nuremberg   The Editor
25 June 1830

1   Within the developmental history of the Spirit of European humanity, it is possible to distinguish three main epochs in the doctrine of the immortality of the soul. The first epoch is that of the Greeks and Romans, who neither believed in nor were aware of immortality as we understand it. The Roman lived only in Rome; the Roman people were, so to speak, the one and only space that contained his soul and defined the horizon of his public life. The individual citizen's most idealized and extensive endeavor was to glorify Rome, to expand its might beyond all boundaries, and to establish it for the future, and, in respect to personal reward, to continue in the thankful remembrance of posterity. The Roman did not consider his self to be a reality over and above the actual common life and did not understand it to be something substantial and autonomous in such an exaltation beyond all determination and commonality. The Roman was the soul, the "I" of the Roman; he was something and was aware that he was something, not on his own, but only in union with his people, only in and through them. The belief in immortality in its modern meaning rests on the separation of potentiality from actuality; when these are one, this modern belief disappears. Ethical fulfillment in its determination as Roman ethical fulfillment, the perfect Roman, was the ethical ideal of the Roman. But it was in his power to attain this ideal, just as the ideal of the bud, the brightly colored and fragrant flower, is already attained in the bud by virtue of its natural tendency, capability, and potentiality. Now since the Roman knew of no separation or gap between representation and actuality, be-

2   tween potentiality and efficacy, between ideality and reality, he knew of no continuation of his self after death.

The same is true of the Greeks. Greece, where beauty was the all-ruling, all-permeating, and all-inspiring concept, where beauty was, so to speak, the public ideal, the people's mode of perception, where the understanding of beauty rested precisely on the presentability of inner spiritual reality in actual visible form—how could the modern belief in immortality thrive in

Greece? How could one encounter in Greece the belief that splits humans into an otherworldly, inconceivable, shapeless soul, which is hostile to both form and nature, and into a crude, spiritless body, which is hostile to the soul? The assertions of a few Greek philosophers that the soul is immortal and the ancient representations of Elysium and Tartarus cannot be counted as beliefs in individual immortality.

The second epoch in the developmental history of this doctrine or belief is the Catholic Christian period, the Middle Ages. Here immortality became a universal article of belief and doctrine. But it would be an extremely superficial opinion concerning the Catholic Christian age to cite the belief in, and teaching of, immortality as a characteristic moment and decisive indicator of the Spirit of this period. Rather, the characteristic and most prominent feature of the Middle Ages was the living belief in the actual existence of divine grace and of the highest supersensible goods, the unqualified, all-inclusive belief in the entire positive content of the Christian religion. The individual human had not yet attained the desolate and empty consciousness of his individuality, of his isolated autonomy, had not yet abandoned himself to himself and taken his stand on himself. He had been received and included in the holy communion of believers, and perceived and felt himself to be redeemed, delivered, in possession of the true life, but only by being included in a divine communion, a holy spiritual world, a real supersensible order. The highest being is communal being, the highest enjoyment is the enjoyment and feeling of unity. But the Catholic church was just this communal being, the gathering together of all spirits into one Spirit and one belief. Since the individual was not dependent on himself, was not confined to himself and left to his own resources, the attainment of his hereafter, that is, of his salvation and happiness, did not depend on his own inner self-determinations—his activities, convictions, and aspirations. Neither belief, nor moral disposition, nor moral action is being; they are only inner self-determinations, self-activities. From the perspective of belief, moral disposition, and moral action, being is something that is not actual but exists only in another world, is something to be believed in, to be hoped for, to be longed for. But in the Catholic Christian time, the only other-worldly being for belief and moral disposition was in the actually existing church, which was a real being standing beyond the merely natural and worldly life, a sensibly supersensible and supersensibly sensible world. Thus it was neither belief nor moral disposition but being in the church that constituted the essence of the individual. However, since the church as the communion of believers was the actual kingdom of God, no room was allowed for the separation between this world and the next, hope and attainment, activity and being, ideality and reality, potentiality and actuality. Therefore, the belief in immortality was only one article of belief among others, not an illuminating indicator and moment that defined and characterized the medieval Spirit. In fact, if this matter is considered with more care and exactitude, it must be asserted that, not so much the individual as such, but rather heaven and hell were the essential objects of this article of belief and doctrine.

4   The belief in heaven and hell must be distinguished completely from the belief in individual immortality. The essential mark of the belief in heaven and hell is not belief in the eternal continuation of the individual but belief in the recompense for good and evil—in other words, belief in the reality of the good and in the nothingness of evil. Indeed, heaven is nothing but a sensuous picture of the good and of the bliss united to it, while hell is nothing but a sensuous representation of evil and of the nothingness and misery that is inseparable from it. The true meaning of this belief, purged of its pictorial element, is this: good follows the good, evil follows evil, and the results of good and evil do not cease together with the end of sensible existence. Moreover, purged of all admixture of temporal metaphors, the meaning of this belief is this: there exists not only an external, sensible unhappiness, but also a pure, spiritual, moral unhappiness, which is evil itself; and there exist not just external, sensible goods, but also eternal, moral goods, which come from the good itself and which consist solely in enjoyment of the good.

Good and evil do not have only sensible consequences, do not result in just external reward and punishment; there also exist inner moral reward and punishment. Although the joys of heaven and the pains of hell have been vividly painted in sensuous form, heaven really means the realm of the good, and hell really means the realm of evil, and the meaning of this statement is as follows: good humans are rewarded with the good; evil humans are punished with evil.

If one wishes to find somewhere in the belief system of early Christianity the idea of the immortality of the individual as such, of individual continuation after death in the modern sense, one will be able to find it only in the belief in the resurrection of the body. For this belief means precisely that the body, the individual as individual, is immortal. In nature, the shadow follows the reality, but in history, the shadow precedes it. So, too, whereas in art, the copy follows the original, in history, the copy precedes it. The belief in the resurrection of the body was the symbol, the enigmatic picture, the shadow of the belief in the immortality of the individual as such. When history, which solves all enigmas and reveals all secrets, solved this enigma, when history brought forth and manifested the meaning of this belief, the belief in the picture disappeared. To confirm: the belief in the resurrection of the body is found already in the holy religious texts of the ancient Zends. But no religion of the ancient world is joined as closely in Spirit to the Christian religion as the religion of the ancient Parsees, for it proceeds from *moral principles* alone. As the whole ancient Persian religion was but one luminous, transparent symbol, was but one idea, that of the good symbolized by light and of evil symbolized by darkness, and as the whole ancient Persian religion can be called a symbol, a silhouette, of the Christian religion, so, too, was the belief in the resurrection of the body nothing but the belief in the immortality of the individual as such, its idea in picture and symbol, which only became articulated in the modern Christian age. (Thus, too, the ancient Persian representation that each reality has its heavenly guardian spirit was a likeness, a picture, of the Platonic and Christian doctrines of the ideas and essences of all things in God.)

6   The belief in the immortality of the individual as such emerges on its own grounds and without disguise only in the modern age, which therefore constitutes the third and most important epoch of this doctrine and belief, and, thus, only in this age does it form a characteristic historical moment that is determinate and determining, that should be grasped and brought to prominence for its own sake. The trademark of the entire modern age is that the human as human, the person as person, and therefore the single human individual in his own individuality, has been perceived as divine and infinite. The first shape in which the character of the modern age was expressed was Protestantism. Its highest principle was no longer the church and being in unity with the church but was belief, individual conviction. No longer was the church the principle of belief, but belief became the foundation and the principle of the church. Now the church possessed the power and the basis of its existence, no longer in the authority of unity and universality, but in the power of individual belief. The focal point of the Protestant believer was Christ, the God-man, or the essence of humanity unified with the essence of God in the shape and form of Christ. Thus already the focal point of Protestantism was the person, but not yet the concept of the person as person, within which each person is included without distinction; it was the person only as the single, world-historical person of Christ. In certain sects within Protestantism, such as those of the pietists, this veneration of the person of Christ was pressed to such extremes that even the sensuous individuality of Christ became an object of veneration; in turn, the veneration of his individuality was extended to the veneration of his corpse. This assertion can be sufficiently confirmed by the following pietist utterances from the previous century: "Those who wish to be and to

7   remain blessed must be kissed by the pale, dead, icy lips of Jesus, must smell the dead corpse of the Savior, and must be penetrated with the breath of his grave."

Now Protestantism developed further to the point that, no longer the person of Christ, but the person as person was the focal point of individual belief; thus each person in himself and in his own interior reality became a focal point to himself. Accordingly, Protestant evangelicalism became rationalism and moralism. Thus pietism must be recognized as the point transitional to these latter forms. For, in the mind of the pietist, the true and essential Christ is no longer the actual person of Christ in and for himself, as he exists in God, but is the shape that Christ assumes in the interior of the subject, the Christ who is taken up into the heart, who exists only in feeling and disposition, the Christ who has become the very I of the believing individual. Meanwhile, the only elements of the external Christ in which the pietist remains interested are his specifics, his subjective particularities. But because only that which is personal to the individual Christ—such as the painful experiences that Christ endured out of love for others—becomes an object of representation, only the subjective becomes an object for the subject, and the subject truly becomes his only object. In this sense, pietism led to rationalism and moralism, for these are precisely the forms of Spirit in which the object of the subject is solely the subject himself, in which the person alone is everything, is the essential and infinite reality. Thus the belief in individual immortality as an infinitely important and essential moment, as a specifically distinguishing, characteristic indicator of the modern point of view, first emerged in the standpoint of pietism, but then became especially prominent in moralism and rationalism. The reasons for the importance, significance, and necessity of this belief for these standpoints can be comprehended and expressed in various ways.

1. Pure, naked personhood is considered to be the only substantial reality. But for the person who grasps himself in this manner, this life is a highly inadequate condition. There is no pure personhood in this world; here, personhood is restricted on all sides, is determined, oppressed, depressed, and bothered by all kinds of conditions and painful qualities that contaminate

and tarnish it. But if the person is the only substantial reality in this world, and yet this life is a determined life, a life made agonizing by the boundaries of qualities, then this life is insubstantial, is a life that is inadequate to the essence of the person. Therefore, there must exist a second life, a life that is not determined and restricted by the conflict and dissimilarity of any qualities, a life that is lived out in an element as bright and transparent as the purest crystal water, in order that the pure light of personhood may penetrate and shine through this element without limitation, without coloration, without resistance. In earthly life, the pure person is only a represented person, only an ideal person; thus there must additionally exist a being in which the represented person is actual, possesses the ideal reality.

2. More exactly, the pure person is the sinless and stainless person, the person who is totally good, who is identical with virtue itself. Morality, perfectly virtuous personhood, is the essence of the person. But determined persons, limited by qualities and sensible properties, are not totally and perfectly good; they only strive for the essence of perfect morality. Unity with pure personhood, whether it is understood apart from individuality as goodness itself, virtue itself, or perfection itself, or whether it is understood as an absolutely perfect, holy individual, as God, is only a distant, otherworldly goal; only the one and all, the universal, the totality, being itself, the Absolute, can be perfect and complete. Therefore, if individuals as such wish to be complete, that is, to be absolute, then, in addition to the present life, they need a time that is unbounded, that disappears into eternity. However, there are two possible relationships between the individual and the object that is his goal in the hereafter. On the one hand, his striving is continued in the hereafter; in this case, it will and must be continued without end. For if the individual were to attain his goal, if he became complete, at that point he would cease to be an individual person. Only a finite measure, a determinate quantity of perfection leaves room for self-consciousness in the determined individual;

if the measure of his perfection were filled, the individual would drown, like Glaucon in the honeypot, in the overflowing well-springs of perfections. Only as long as the measure is not full does the certainty and consciousness of the individual hold out. But since the individual clings to his particular individuality as an absolute, the attainment of perfection must be put off into an unattainable future. On the other hand, individual striving ceases in the hereafter; the individual instantaneously attains his goal in the enjoyable contemplation of the good or of God. But in this case, the individual still remains distinct and separated from the object that is his goal, for only in this distinction does he maintain the certainty, representation, and perception of himself. He is a self only as long as he is distinct; his distinction cannot and should not be surrendered, for only the self is the essence of the self. For the individual, it is a matter not so much of unity with the object as of distinction from it.

3. Since the essential object of individuals is only the subject, since only personhood has absolute reality for them, they have placed themselves at a standpoint where the one thing important in every object, that is, the universal, the totality, the truly actual and substantial, disappears from sight. Because in the innermost depths of their souls, only the subject is their object, they also see outside of themselves only subjects, the subjective, the individual, and therefore only that which is defective, negative, finite. To be sure, they call the history of philosophy by its proper name; they even call it "the history of thinking reason." But, to them, it is really nothing but a history of opinions, of peculiar, paradoxical whims, of superfluous endeavors and subjective experiments. Again, they grant to the history of the church the title "Church History" (but it is nothing more than a title; for these individuals, that which is universal and substantial exists only in titles and names), but, to them, it is really only a history of popes, of orthodoxy and heterodoxy, of religious enthusiasts, of pietists, atheists, simple believers, and so on. So if church history is not quite a history of human folly, still it is a history of monstrous aberrations, of contaminations and dis-

10

figurements of the pure Gospel. Through this labyrinth of corruption is drawn a barely noticeable thread of providence,
which is at best slender and delicate. In fact, it is so thin and
frail that it is torn apart by every heretic and philosopher, and,
till now, could be observed and analyzed only by certain spe-
cially graced persons. World history is called "universal history," "world history," "history of humanity," but they know
only of humans and not of humanity, of one Spirit or one totality; world, humanity, Spirit, to them, are only titles or names.
Thus, in their minds, world history is only, on the one hand, a
history of individual humans, on the other, a history of situations, circumstances, details. The Indians thought that ele-
phants were the bearers of the cosmos, but these persons think
that the secret whims of the cabinet ministers, the parrots and
hunting puppies of princesses and queens, the fleas and lice that
nest on the heads of the great lords and heroes, are the bearers,
the movers, and the exalted pillars of the cosmos. They even
speak of a nature, yet they have no knowledge of one nature,
but only of an aggregate, of a collection of the countless single
stars, stones, plants, animals, elements, things. They even say
that God *exists;* indeed, they swear to it most solemnly; they
certify that the being of God is the being that is the most certain
being of all. But, to them, "being" is really only a word, a title;
God exists only in their hopes, their beliefs, their representations; they grant to him only a subjective, represented being.
Thus, if someone comes along and points out to them that God
really exists, that his being is not merely a represented, unreal
being, but that nature and world history are the existence
(though not the nature) of God, to their minds, one who gives
credence to an actual God, precisely because he asserts that God
exists, is an atheist and a naturalist.

Accordingly, once all that is truly actual, universal, substantial, once all Spirit, soul, and essence have disappeared from
real life, nature, and world history, once everything has been
massacred, has been dissolved into its parts, has been rendered
without being, without unity, without Spirit, without soul,
then, upon the ruins of the broken world, the individual raises

the banner of the prophet and stations the abominable sacred watchman of the belief in his immortality and in the pledge of the hereafter. Standing on the ruins of the present life, in which he sees nothingness, all at once there awaken in the individual the feeling and consciousness of his own inner nothingness; and in the feeling of this double nothingness there flow from him, as from a Scipio on the ruins of Carthage, the compassionate teardrops and soap bubbles of the world of the future. Over the gap that lies between the present life as it really is and his perception and representation of it, over the pores and gaps in his own soul, the individual erects the fools' bridge of the future life. After he has allowed to wither the fruit trees, the roses and lilies of the present world, after he has sickled away grass, cabbage, and corn and has transformed the whole world into a desiccated field of stubble, there finally springs up, in the empty feeling of his futility and the impotent consciousness of his vanity, as the weak semblance and faint illusion of the living, fresh time when flowers bloom, the nondescript, pale red, faded autumn crocus of immortality. Because nothing exists in the subject but the truthless subject itself, and because nothing exists outside of the subject but the temporal and the transitory, the finite, nothing but that which is *false* and *unreal* in the real world, it stands to reason that for the subject the *real* world is an unreal, future, otherworldly world. For the hereafter is nothing but the mistaken, misconceived, and misinterpreted real world. The subject knows only the shadow, the superficial external appearance of the real world, because he is only shallow and hollow in himself. He mistakes the shadow of the world for the world itself; and his idea of the really true world must be only a shadow, the illusion and fantastical dream of the future world.

12

One who understands the language of the Spirit of world history cannot avoid the recognition that our present time is the keystone of a great period in the history of humanity and the point of origin of a new spiritual life. To be sure, we see how a great multitude of our contemporaries, unconcerned for the exalted teachings of history, paying no attention to the strenuous deeds and painful works of humanity, scorning and insulting the rights and claims that reason has earned over a thousand years of battles, has turned back to the old ways and is concerned to restore them unchanged. They attempt their restoration as if the rivers of blood of past ages had rushed by to no purpose, or, at most, had only poured forth so that certain individuals could swing all the more unconcernedly in the hammocks of the ancient faith, and, in the stream of centuries that had passed in vain, could possess a mirror of the splendor, solidity, and durability of their own particular possessions, their belief and piety. But just this phenomenon proves that soon a new Spirit will bless humanity with its appearance and will deliver it from the miserable oppositions and contradictions to which it is presently reduced. For history teaches us that just when something stands at the verge of its total destruction, it once again raises itself with all its force, as if it wished to begin anew its already finished course of life.

To be sure, we also see how innumerable people seize the present as an absolute and hold fast to the contemporary Spirit, the current opinions, representations, perceptions, systems, maxims, and principles. But one can meet this phenomenon in every age. Nothing is more dear to the commonsense man than to regard the present as an insuperable, absolutely final period with which to arrest the flow of history. But only that person who knows how to swing himself above the planet to contemplate the heavenly forces can apprehend planetary motion. It is granted to only a few to see the end of the present, to be raised beyond its boundaries, and to feel through the hard skin and crust of the currently secure maxims and principles to the eternally bubbling spring of everlasting life. It is granted to only a few to go beyond the superficies that everywhere presents the appearance of something that is unchangeable and self-identical, to press into the depths and to perceive the pulsebeat of the creative new time. For the oncoming Spirit, which will be the bright and excellent day of the future, at first always appears only in individuals, in dark presentiment and longing, in disgust with and repugnance toward the absolutes, the idols of the present day, and in the conscious insight into their nothingness. Perhaps even the spirit of the present writer is a fleeting drop out of the spring of eternal life, which bubbles under the crust of the present; perhaps his thoughts on death and immortality are sparks that ascend through the smokestacks of the present from the subterranean forge and fireplace of the creative Spirit.   14

If a new Spirit, a new being, is again about to enter the breast of contemporary humanity, at present filled only with emptiness and vanity, then it is of the utmost necessity that the human being, after he has reveled long enough like a true Muhammedan in the paradisaic dreams of his immortality, after he has lived long enough in rapturous self-contemplation and in intoxicating enjoyment of his individuality, that the human being recalls his true and total transitoriness and mortality, and, in this recollection and reflection, awakens in himself the need for seeking the sources of life and truth, the determining basis of his actions, and the abode of his tranquillity, but in a place that is different from his own individuality and the belief in his own immortality and infinity. Only when the human once again recognizes that there exists not merely an *appearance of death,* but an actual and real death, a death that completely terminates the life of the individual, only when he returns to the awareness of his finitude will he gain the courage to begin a new life and to experience the pressing need for making that which is absolutely true and substantial, that which is actually infinite, into the theme and content of his entire spiritual activity.

I

True religion, true humility, true and complete surrender to and submersion in God is possible only when the human recognizes death as true, real, and entire. The entire pietistic or modern mystical theology rests only on a game of ball. The individual throws himself away only in order to have God throw him back   15
again; he humbles himself before God only in order to be

reflected in him. His self-loss is self-enjoyment, his humility is self-exaltation. He submerges himself in God only to surface again intact, and, refreshed and renewed, to sun himself in his own excellence; he sinks himself only in order again to fish out of God the pearl of his precious self. As certain herbs give off a pleasant smell only when they are crushed, so the individual crushes himself only to smell himself; and as certain things are tasty only when they are dissolved on the tongue, so the individual boils and dissolves himself like sugar in the blood of the Savior only in order to gain a taste of himself. How sweet must such a pulverized, slimy, and dissolved individual taste!

If you were to watch a child biting a nut, how you would admire him, even before he bit off a few teeth or before he left off cracking the nut, if you were unaware of what was hidden in the nut, of the purpose of this difficult and painful effort. But how quickly your admiration would change into the opposite emotion if you recognized the goal and the real object that the child strove to attain by his trouble. Now consider our pietists; see how the individual bites and cracks himself to pieces only to expose the sweet kernel of his self. Indeed, will not a person stand gazing at the ground in admiration when he hears these people speaking of their nothingness and corruption, of humility, of submission to God, of dying in Christ, and when he sees with what Spirit and with what heartrending movements they bite off from themselves their best possession, their reason? But into what emotion will his admiration be changed when he has recognized what is to be bitten to pieces? For this is nothing but the individual. When they talk of their sinfulness, of their corruption, do they not at the same time talk of their essence, of the significance and reality of their individual selves? Is he who always inspects his faults and defects in the mirror less vain and self-satisfied than he who only thinks of his virtue and handsomeness? Is it not precisely the sign of the greatest vanity always to talk of one's vanity? Religion should be a matter of God, of the will of God, of God in and for himself. Yet does not everything seem to turn only on *their* deliverance and reconciliation, on *their* salvation and immortality? God is only on the periphery of their religion; individuals themselves are its focal point. Individuals acknowledge a God beyond themselves only in order to possess in him a boundless space in which they can spread out and expand for all eternity their limited, particular, pitiable individuality, without disturbance, without a reciprocal encroachment and restriction, without the push and shove that are inescapable in real life. Their God is nothing but the atmosphere in which individuals can evaporate and spread out like gaseous vapors rising from the earth, unobstructed in their fascinating diversity from one another. If it should be unbelievable to you that for them nothing but the very same individual is produced from this kind of death, then only reflect on natural death. For these people, it is merely the room behind the theater of the world where one's clothes are changed! They hear even in the most terrifying trumpet call of world judgment only the tedious clanging of a postilion who orders up fresh horses in order to reach the postal station of the future curriculum vitae. What a heavenly enjoyment that must be, to be freed from the burden of earth (i.e., from reason), to evaporate in the atmosphere of higher being, to spread oneself out of the small shop of one's spiced and tastily glorified human uniqueness, and to soar like an airy little snow cloud over the stifling rational sphere of earthly existence! What rapture, what enjoyment that will be, to reflect back on one's past sins, to have behind one, as if it was a joke, the sour life of history and reason, and now to pacify oneself world without end!

17

God

God is love. The human loves, but God is love. When the human loves, he remains a subject; he still maintains his own being outside of his love. For the human, love is an attribute; human happiness—for love is happiness—is a transitory, momentary condition. If you think of that which is partial in the human as the whole, of the human attribute as subject, person, substance, if you think of that which is momentary as abiding being, you then have a perception of God. God is total love. Yet love is not tranquil but is pure activity; love is consuming, sacrificing, burning; love is fire. It is wrath on that which exists singly and selfishly. The human, a particular being, is inflamed by consuming wrath on his natural selfishness and singleness; in love, the human surrenders himself, surrenders everything that is particular and finite. But God surrenders everything. He offers up to himself the natural, selfish existence of all creatures; he is the love that consumes all and that dissolves all into itself.

God is person. But he is more, infinitely more than person. He is person who is pure love. Therefore, there must be a place, so to speak, in God where all particular beings, all creatures, become one, where they are consumed and abolished. Actually, all particular beings pass away, not directly in time, but in God himself. God is the ultimate ground of all transitoriness. It could be said that the only real proof that a God exists is time, for time proves than there exists an infinite being in which everything is consumed, before which everything that exists is finite, and by which alone everything is limited, transitory, and perishable. Time is but the manifestation of the fact that everything has perished in God from all eternity. Finite reality would have eternal existence if there were no eternal being. But just as a luminous heavenly body that has already ceased to exist many years previously can appear to cease to us only when it disappears from our sight, because of the enormous distance of the heavenly bodies from our vision, so, too, that which has perished in God from all eternity seems to perish to the sensuous human only when he sees a being die with his own eyes. For temporal death presupposes a death beyond time; sensible death presupposes a supersensible death. And this eternal death, this supersensible death, is God himself. Only the shell of death is hard; its kernel is sweet. Sensible death is, as it were, nothing but the tone by which the temporal thing gives voice to and proclaims its timeless death, is nothing but a light that shines in the darkness to make visible and manifest the hidden and secret death. That in which the divine reality did not dwell could not die. Thus, to wish, to long for something after death is bound-less error. For death is produced by an inner longing of nature, an inner longing that preys on nature as long as it exists to mani-fest what it is out of its impulse and striving, or, what is almost the same thing, to express the inner depths of nature out of its drive to truth. And that which nature longs to manifest, the inner drive that nature expresses, is that its being is consumed by and dissolved in God. You die only because all that you imagine to attain after death already exists before death; death does not approach because of need and poverty, but because of fullness and satisfaction. The weight of eternal existence and the fullness of the divine being force the shrine of your own being, which the divine encloses in itself, to burst asunder. Before death and over it lies eternity.

The best that you as an individual can attain, your ultimate and utmost accomplishment, is contemplation of God and sub-mersion in God. And what in this life could differentiate you from God and be inserted as a partition between you and the contemplation of God? Is death alone going to raise this parti-tion? But natural death is only the manifestation of a higher and different kind of death. You die only because, from eter-nity, you are known as you are in God, only because you, by your nature as a finite being, are already consumed forever in the eternally loving flame of the divine substance, only because you have died beyond time. Your present reflective and con-scious submersion in God is but a renewal of and return to your eternal submersion, is but a bringing to awareness, a disclosure, of your original, substantial, unconscious, involuntary submer-sion in him. You could not submerge yourself in God had you not already been submerged in him, were you not already, by your very nature, submerged in God by God himself. Natural death, like your reflective and conscious submersion in God, has but one root, has as its source the original, the essential, the preconscious and superconscious submersion and dissolution in God. Thus, you can expect nothing after death, for death is pre-cisely a result of that which you wrongly expect after death.

Because of your understanding, which distinguishes into temporal sequence, you believe that that which has already taken place before death and from all eternity takes place only after and at the point of natural death. To correct this impression, you need only to recall to yourself this eternal occurrence, to transform acts of essence into those of thinking and consciousness, and to renew in your knowledge and reflection the nature of eternal reality.

20   If, dear reader, you have taken up these pages by accident, and, whatever position you hold, be it pietistic or rationalistic, if these thoughts appear mystical to you, and you therefore want to reject them, still you should reflect that at least once, if not in life, then at the close of life, at the moment of death, you will be forced to become mystical whether you like it or not. For in death nature itself is totally mystical. There exists no half death, no bifurcated and ambiguous death; in nature, all is true, total, undivided, complete. Nature is not bifurcated; it does not equivocate. Death is the total and complete dissolution of your entire being; there exists only one death, which is total. Death does not gnaw something off of the human, does not leave a remainder. Totality, entirety, is the radical form and character of nature; if you die, you die totally; all of you is dead. Therefore, just by the consideration of natural death, this mystical act of nature, you should at times be stirred and moved to become a mystic, even during life, for you must become a mystic at least once. And yet it is certainly an objective of reasonable men to be intentionally, consciously, and freely that which they are forced to be eventually. Moreover, you should consider that God is the greatest of all conceivable *mystics,* that he is not a rationalist (but certainly not a pietist either), is not a superficial, barren, and stale essence, but is an infinitely profound essence.

If God is only conceived and defined as person (a definition that is not changed by the predicates of infinite, supreme, absolutely perfect, holy, etc.), if nothing is apprehended and expressed concerning God beyond self-consciousness, freedom, will, decision, purpose (and, indeed, in the very meaning that those who contemplate God only under these determinations attribute to them), then God will be conceived as a *superficial essence.* God so conceived is without depth, is only a smooth surface that reflects the human back to himself, is the prototype but also the exact image of human personhood. For just as the genuinely artistic portrait of me is not merely my image, but is truly my prototype, because it beautifies, idealizes my natural self, because it highlights the Spirit, the essence of my individuality, because it accentuates my essence as opposed to the obstructive and limiting impurities, the blemishes and flaws of natural existence, and presents it for contemplation for its own sake, so too God, conceived only under these determinations, is, although prototype, at the same time, exact image. There is nothing in this definition of God that does not exist in finite personhood; the same reality, the same content that is attributed to God exists in humanity. As those thinkers who asserted that there exists nothing in the understanding that has not existed previously in the senses established a merely formal distinction between spiritual and sensible content, so, too, there is only a formal distinction, a distinction of degree or quantity, between humanity and this definition of God. The same determinations that are in God are in humans, only they are in him infinitely, in humans finitely—in other words, they are realized in God in an *infinitely greater degree.* And if, as one must grant, a quantitative distinction raised to the highest degree becomes a qualitative distinction, still the fundamental essence, the concepts that determine and distinguish both God and humanity, remain identical.

Accordingly, death, which shines into the depths of all essence and knowledge, will be grasped only as a *superficial,* external negation, produced by the external necessity of all natural existence and touching only the outer shell of the individual, but not as an inward negation that presses and rises into the heart. Death is then nothing but a nutcracker that bites through only the external surrounding shell of the individual so that the meaty, savory kernel of the individual emerges on its own. For the human recognizes only himself in God, finds in God only his self-assurance, only recovers himself in and from God; God is to the individual only the inviolable sanctuary, the holy authority, the sacred certificate and guaranty of himself and his own individual existence. God is to the individual only the daddy of his house, his watch master and night watchman, his guardian Spirit, his patron saint. And how else could the individual think his way into his end, since he always thinks only of himself even in the infinite, since he finds in God, not his end and the principle of his death, but only the principle of his existence, only the principle of his selfish reality, since to him God is only the beginning of his finitude and not also its end? How could he be expected to be capable of looking into the depths of death when he sees in the most profound reality only the gleaming surface that mirrors and reflects him?

Therefore God is not yet defined as Spirit when he is defined only as absolute person, who is in himself distinguished from nature and who knows himself in this distinction. For in this case nature, the otherness of God, will be thought of as existing independently, outside of God; although God is now distinct from nature, he does not distinguish himself from it, and is therefore only person and not Spirit. He is Spirit only when he is what he is through himself, when his being is the product and result of his own activity. But if God is grasped only as person, only as distinguished from nature, then, as already established, nature falls outside of God, and only the distinction falls into God. But distinguishing, or the activity of distinguishing, is proper to the finite subject existing outside of God. Then God as the absolute person is distinguished from nature only because the finite person makes the distinction. God is then only a subject; but subjectivity itself, the principle and the effective ground of subjective being, does not exist in him. God's distinction from nature is the result of his own activity of distinguishing, and God distinguishes himself from nature only if he is distinguished from himself within himself, not when he is thought of as just absolute person, that is, as just a "who" without a

23

"what," a person without essence, but only if he is both person and essence, only if he is all essence and nature within this essence that is distinct from him as self-conscious person. Where there is no opposition, no otherness, there is no distinction. (For in opposition there is distinction, and in distinction there is opposition; the things to be distinguished say to one another, "I am *not* what you are, you are *not* what I am; as much as you are, so much am I not; where I am, there you are not; where you end, there I begin; my beginning is your end.") But where there is no opposition and distinction, there is neither joy nor pain, no drive, no stimulus, no spur, no impulse. Where these are not found in an essence, there exists in it no basis for activity; an essence that lacks self-activity is a dull and dead essence, an essence without drive and stimulus. Thus, if the distinction from God is not within God himself, if he does not include within himself an essence that is distinct from his person (which is the only name by which most people call him), and if his essence does not include his opposite, then he is indeed distinguished from nature, but this distinction is not a result of his own activity. For the only self-active essence is one that is distinct from itself within itself, one that is dual in itself.

Why is the human a spiritual being? Not just because he is distinct from nature, but because his distinction from nature is a result of his own activity of distinguishing. The human by nature is distinguished from nature; but his Spirit and the work of his Spirit consist in the fact that he activates this distinction from the outset, acts as if he were not distinguished, allows the distinction to develop and result out of his activity of distinguishing. But in what lies the possibility of the activity of distinguishing? In the fact that he is not just person, self-conscious, but he is and possesses in himself that from which he distinguishes himself, that in distinction from which he is self-distinguishing person, self-consciousness; he is, and possesses within himself, nature, soul, essence. If there were no nature in him, or rather, if he were not nature, then the impulse, the beginning, and the initiative to activity and distinction would lie outside of him; he would be a spiritless essence, activated only from without. Mere personhood on its own is just as spiritless as mere nature on its own; Spirit is only the unity of soul and consciousness, or—what is the same—the unity of nature and personhood. For nature is pure and total soul; it is not just a kind of matter or a dead collection of dead things and essences that are suspended from, and strangled on, the chain of external necessity. You cannot distinguish the true concept of nature from that of soul. If God were nothing more than personal being, the human truly would be more exalted and more profound than God, for even the human is not just person, not without soul. Therefore, to make personhood into the only determination of God is to make spiritlessness and soullessness into determinations of God.

You say, "Personhood is being-in-self and knowing-of-self." But what is it that this knowing knows? You certainly do not want to take self-knowing to be the object and content of self-knowing. What kind of an empty and finite person would he be who knew nothing but himself, who knew only that he knew of himself, or in whom knowing and that which is known was only himself, the person? God is person, is knowing; but that which he knows is not again knowing, is not he himself as person; that which he knows is his essence, his soul. In his knowing, God is within and for himself, but in his soul and essence he is everything. Thus, that which he knows, the content and object of his knowing, is not God as he is self, but is God as he is everything. As God knows himself he knows and is everything. God is distinguished from everything by the fact that he is not something but is everything; his specificity is totality, his distinction is universality. Whatever you might like to distinguish from him, God is not distinguished from everything by the fact that he is a being that is distinguished, that is, particular—this is the distinguishing mark of the finite being—but he is distinguished from everything by the fact that he is everything from which he distinguishes himself. That from which he distinguishes himself as self-knowing is not his own distinction but is his essence, in which he is everything. He is one with himself and one for himself insofar as he is one with everything. In any case, God's distinctness is included not just in his knowing, but also in his essence. For his essence is *his* essence, the essence that is *proper* to him, his being is *his* being, the being that is *proper* to him, precisely because his essence and his being are all essence and being, and not the being of something, of the particular, of the single, all of which we distinguish from God. A God who is something only in the fact that he is something, whose distinction consists only in distinction, whose being-for-self consists only in being-for-self, is no longer a God but an idol, for the idol is distinguished from God by the fact that the idol is something while God is everything. You have made it your only object to distinguish and to separate God, to make him into a something, a particular and distinct reality. But by these distinctions do you not in the worst possible manner confuse and mingle God with things and finite essences, not to mention with nature itself? If God is only a distinct being, he certainly is not nature, but he is like a single natural essence, for natural essences are distinguished from God by the fact that they are only distinct and particular. You accuse pure pantheism of making everything into God, but the accusation of the worst pantheism of all, of "particular-pantheism," fits you. For because you think of God only under the determination of being-in-self and knowing-of-self, or, better, of being-for-self, and, therefore, only under the determination of particularity and distinctness, you raise to the status of the absolute, not the totality, but only the something and the particular.

26

Do you know self-consciousness only in its driest, emptiest, and most limited determination? Are there not degrees of personhood? Is self-consciousness present only when the person knows only himself, when nothing but the person exists in the person? Is not love self-consciousness, and is it not also profound enjoyment, the greatest of all self-feeling? But is the self that you feel in love the juridical, excluding, distinguishing self, a self that is only self-contained and self-knowing? Or, rather, is not the feeling of the self in love at the same time the feeling of an essence that is distinct from and yet also at one with the self? When you love, not self but essence is object and content of your feeling, and you feel yourself because you feel and experience in you the other essence. Moreover, it is unique to love that feeling and knowing are not separate from being; you are one with the essence of which you are aware, you are truly that essence. Now can you not also raise yourself to the thought that God is everything and yet is self-conscious, that as he knows himself, he knows everything as himself and himself as everything? Can you not also fit God's being-for-self together with his being-everything? Being-everything as it is in God and is God and being-everything as it is in nature and is nature are distinguished by the fact that God's being-everything is absolute being-one, and is therefore being-for-self, while nature's being-everything is being-everything as many, as particular, as single, as separated, as being-outside-of-itself and being-in-sequence. And the distinction between unity and multiplicity is not just formal, but everything insofar as it is one is precisely a distinct content, independent from everything as it is multiple. To recognize this, only seek to grasp the mystery of love. Love is distinguished from all other experiences by the fact that it is all experiences; it is not one particular experience, but is the absolute, infinite, totally universal experience; it is at once all pains and all joys, all pleasure and all suffering. And yet, because it is all experiences simultaneously and as an indivisible unity, love is an experience that is distinct and independent from all those experiences that occur particularly, singly, in external sequence. Moreover, this distinction of love from all other experiences is not just formal, but is an essential distinction in content. In love, one is all and all is one, while in all other experiences, that which is one in love is multiple, dispersed, diverse. Not only do you experience differently in love than in the dispersed and particular experiences of your soul, you also experience something different. Thus all multiplicity as it exists in unity and is unity is distinct from the many insofar as the many exists in multiplicity and is multiplicity. A new essence arises only when one arises from many. Therefore, you have an analogy of the unity of being-for-self and being-everything in humanity, in which nature does not exclude personhood and personhood does not exclude nature or soul. In his soul the person is not-I, is not a person, as you can see, for example, in sleep, where there is soul but not consciousness, while there cannot be consciousness without soul.

When you say of God, "He loves," or, better, "He is love" (on a deeper level, even the human soul in love is, in a certain measure, identical with love itself, as it is thought itself when it thinks; to be sure, the human also eats, travels, hits, sees, smells, but love and thought are related to humanity differently than are eating, hitting, and smelling), you have already transcended your conception of the personhood of God. For the personal being as such, only as person, does not love, but only excludes and repels; the person strictly conceived as person cannot love but can only hate, divide, estrange. In order to be capable of love, the person must be able to surrender his harsh, excluding, being-for-self. But the person cannot accomplish this surrender if there does not exist in him an abode, so to speak, where he is not-person, where he is not divisive separation and expelling distinction, but in which all is one and one is all. Certainly you do not eat with eating, but with the fork, with your hands, mouth, and teeth, nor do you smell with smelling, but with your nose; yet the organ and instrument of love is love itself. You love only with and in love. But love is not being-in-oneself and being-for-oneself; love is being-together, being-in-common. Therefore, you love not with your personhood or as person, but only in and with essence, which is being-together, but not being-distinct or being-for-oneself. You love only because you are deeper and more than a person. There is no love where there is only essence, but also there is no love where there is only person. Love is the unity of personhood and essence and, therefore, presupposes both distinction and unity. Where there is only essence, there is only unity; where there is only person, there is only distinction, and love dwells only in the unity of the two. As the human who has experienced love has experienced everything, so the human who has known love

28

knows everything. Know love and you have known God and everything. Thus only the genuine pantheist knows what love is; only he can love. Apart from pantheism everything is egoism, self-seeking, vanity, greed, mercenariness, idolatry. Even the egoist, although the object of his love might be the most limited reality, yet, to the extent that he is at all capable of love, gives up his egoism and becomes a pantheist. Otherwise, he could not have attained even the most fleeting experience of love. Just as you transcend the determination of personhood when you say, "God is love," you also transcend it when you assert, "God is blessed," or "God is blessedness." For blessedness does not exist within particularity, distinctness, exclusiveness, or person-hood as such, but only in unity. But God is truly blessedness only when he is at the same time the blessedness of all things and essences, only when he is the unity of all essences as one independent essence.

Thus, if you consistently and honestly stick to and carry out the determination of personhood, while refusing to drop it and then take it up again at your pleasure, then you must admit that you cannot attribute love to God as contemplated only under the determination of personhood. You cannot say that God is love when you attribute love to him only in relation to yourself, when you acknowledge in him only determinations that are affirmations of your personal existence, when you only find yourself contained and confirmed in him, when you make room only for yourself in him while pushing out everything else. If you acknowledge in God only the determinations that constitute subjects as subjects and do not equally acknowledge the deter-minations that constitute the object as object and nature as nature, then your God is not love, essence, and substance. On the contrary, when you represent God as an independent being who is distinct from you only under the determinations that constitute subjectivity, then your God is nothing but egoism and selfishness raised to the ultimate degree. God is conceived as an objective, absolute being, and not just as a subjective being, only if you conceive him under the determinations by means of and in which a thing exists, and not just under the determinations in which you are an I. And a thing is a not-I, a thing, if you find contained in it both the beginning and ground and the end, the negation of your personhood and your personal existence. God is not just a God who affirms you, but he is also a God who negates you; he is not just the beginning and end of all *things,* but he is also the *beginning* and *end* of *your self.* Those things and essences that exist outside of you, that you distinguish from yourself, that you acknowledge as different from your I and your self, and that you order under the species-concept of object or nature, all these things are points that limit and negate your self. As much and as far as other things and essences exist outside of you, so much and so far you do not exist. And as many of these things as exist, so many edges and boundaries, in and at which you and your being cease, have you. In every tree, every wall, every table that you touch, you touch your death, as it were, you touch the boundary and the edge of your existence. To bring to mind your end, you do not need to take a walk to the cemetery; every dose of snuff that you take, since it is outside of you, can bring to mind the coffin of your self. Every punch in the ribs, every squeeze, every impact, is a living memento mori; all of nature is a cemetary of your selfishness. If you think of being as a common property that God, at the beginning of the world, dispensed to you and to all the things and essences outside of you, then you will recognize that as much being as is due to other things and essences, so much being is not due to you, that each thing that exists kills, as it were, a portion of your being, and is a deprivation, a negation, a curtailment, and a restriction of your being. But now, since God is not just a subjective being but is also an objective being, since God is not just a God of and for the self but is also a God of and for nature, since there exist in God not only the determination of personhood (therefore not you alone) but also the determination of objectivity, and, therefore, since there exist in God the things and essences outside of you, so too must there exist in God the boundary, the end, the negation of your personal existence and of your I, and you must acknowl-

30

edge God to be the ultimate and principal ground of your death as much as you acknowledge him to be the ground of your existence. If things exist in God, or at least originate in God, then the limits and the end of your I and your being also originate in him. But if the limits of your existence originate in God, then death originates in God, for death is only the result, the manifestation, of the inner limits of your self. It is these same inner limits that have external, objective existence in things; their aggregate is objectivity in general. If no object existed, the subject would be infinite and therefore immortal per se. If the personal subject existed alone, it would be impossible to conceive of its end, its limit, its death. But the existence of an objective reality is the factual proof of the finitude of subjectivity; for the existence of objective reality, as much and as far as objective reality exists and is objectivity, constitutes the not-being, the end, of subjectivity. Whatever you may want to think about nature, you state and represent to yourself that God created it. So you can twist and turn, lie and deceive, but the truth must be confirmed that God gave existence and reality to the not-being of your being, and that, therefore, he is the ultimate ground of your death.

Evidently you are so feebleminded that you forget what you have thought, said, and done at the very moment in which you grant the creation and existence of nature and thereby admit the necessity, rationality, and reality of your termination and death. And no wonder. You think that only you are the content and value of God, that only you are a matter of infinite import. Thus it is natural that, for you, death is something that should not exist, that your end is not a *true* end. Since you do not encounter your end even in God, then it is natural that you can encounter your end even less in natural death, and therefore must glue onto the end of this life the waving, tedious paper dragon tail and vaporous comet tail of a rootless immortality. But once again you are so myopic and self-contradictory that you are unaware that this admittedly glorious comet tail of the future is still only a pale, misty reflection and weak shadow of your present majesty and splendor. Because you take your moral subjective determinations to be the only absolute determinations of the content of God, and because, as just stated, you take yourself to be the content and value of the absolute, you experience and recognize, not your breaking point in God, but, rather, only the continuation and permanence of you and your moral properties, a continuation that, indeed, raises you to a higher power, that makes you perfect. But your quantitative, timelessly temporal, infinitely finite continuation into the future fits your qualitative, essential continuation and permanence in God just as little as the mildew fits the bread, the shine fits the light, the nebula fits the sun, the rose on the tapestry fits the living rose, the bad copy fits the original. Since you already were everything that you could be in this life, what is left to you after life but the pale moonlight that follows the sunlight of the present? Great Achilles, prototype of the Greek Spirit, dear day laborer on earth, who so nobly confessed to your wish to rule the realm of the shades, could you only see how today's modern subject spreads the peacock fan of his immortality, how he devours the corn of the present only in order to chew it once again in the next world as tasteless excrement, how he seeks to strangle the heroic shapes of reality with the grey rattail of his endless temporality only in order to assure himself of the necessity of an insubstantial shadow existence!

If the meaning of what has been developed so far still remains hidden from you, reflect on the subject from another simple perspective. You may possess no profound knowledge of God, but at least you know that God is the unlimited, the infinite being, and that, in order to make God the object of contemplation, one must take away, or negate, all determinations and limitations within which finite reality is enclosed, and that the person who cannot abstract from the being of here and there, now and then, this and that, this way and that way, is in no way capable of representing the infinite. But this necessity of having to press to the thought of the infinite only by means of the negation of the finite has its basis, not in you, but in the object itself. Only because the infinite *is* the negation of the finite must you negate the finite, abstract from it, in order to think of the infinite. As you strive to engender in you the representation of the infinite, your act of abstraction is only an imitative action, a copying, as it were, of what the infinite itself accomplishes. The actual and true nothingness of the finite is the infinite itself. That things are finite, vary, change, pass away, rests solely on the actual being of the infinite. If the infinite did not exist, everything, even the *most limited,* would be *unlimited,* would be unchangeable, unmoved and unmoving, would be absolutely stable, absolute reality. The finite is finite, its boundaries are set, only by and in the infinite (though with the setting of boundaries comes the drive to movement, the desire to abandon boundaries). The finite is posited as finite by the infinite, and in this finitude are posited its nothingness and its death. The eternal, infinite, and true death of all things and essences is God himself. The death that is commonly understood to be the only death is merely the finite, determinate, temporal, false death. Eternity is the basis of all temporality. If there were no eternity, there would be no time, for the eternal is the time of the finite. The finite is not its own time, but the eternal is the passing away of the finite. Temporality is distinguished from eternity or infinity only by the fact that the passing away that is simultaneous in eternity is sequential in temporality; or, to express this distinction in more temporal images, time is only the perpetual *passing away* of finite reality, which, in turn, becomes past being that is never to be satisfied, while eternity is the fulfilled *past* and restful *past being.* Time is the passing away of the existence of the finite, or of the finite according to its mode of existence. But the finite exists finitely, separately, singly, in external relationships. Thus time, because it is the passing away of the finite in its singleness, in its externality, is only a successive passing away, a passing away of one finitude after the other. Therefore, precisely as a passing away of that which exists singly, time is a passing away that is never finished with itself, that is always developing, that is without rest, without goal, without peace. But the eternal is the passing away, not of the finite as finite, but of the *finitude* of the finite. The eternal is a passing away of

34

the finite, not according to its single existence, but according to its universal essence. This passing away is not a mere passing away that is time, but is a passing away that is itself *being* and *essence,* that is completely closed past. In this sense, eternity neither is nor should be called passing away. Thus, although being in and for itself is proper to the eternal, one can correctly call time the becoming of the eternal.

But then why does not the human embryo just remain an embryo? Why do the shapes and the modes of existence that the human has while enclosed in the mother's womb pass away? Why else are they temporal, passing shapes than because the concept and the essence of the human, which are the purpose of the embryo, are also the inner essential end of the embryo and its existence? Do these shapes, having already disappeared simultaneously in essence, disappear successively in the sensible existence of time? Then why does the planet not remain where it is now, why is it always at another place, now there, but in the same moment no longer there but elsewhere? The planet, which is essentially self-moving and which, therefore, in its spontaneous, original, innate movement, is a body possessing life and soul, is the nothingness of locality, of the essence of place—in other words, the planet is the negation of spatial boundary in general. However, time is the nothingness, not of locality, not of the essence of place, but of the existing, determinate, sensible, single place. The place passes away and disappears in time. But in sensible movement, in the time of the planet, this one place vanishes, which, as it exists determinately, is separated from another place, is after that other place, as that place is after the previous, and so into eternity, these single places in separate existence disappear one after the other. But in their essence, in the essence of determined locality, which is a nothingness, not for the stone or other single bodies, but for the planet, these single places already have disappeared simultaneously (not temporally).

You say, "I cannot doubt that God, the infinite, exists, but just as little can I doubt that I and everything finite exist. God exists, nature exists, I exist.'' But, to put the proposition according to the correct order of precedence, ''I exist,'' for you are the first person, ''God, you exist,'' for he is the second person, and ''nature, it exists,'' for nature is the third and last person. Thus do you distinguish the infinite, the unconditioned, and the finite, the conditioned. But since the being of the finite and conditioned has just as much unconditional and infinite certainty for you as the being of the infinite, you cancel the distinction in being between the finite and the infinite. And even if you ascribe a greater quantity of being to the infinite than to the finite, yet this will not settle the matter. Being is the commonality that you allow both the infinite and the finite to share. But, I am sorry to say, this *contrat social* by means of which you cause the finite and the infinite to live so compatibly within the communal region of being is not ratified by the infinite itself. Infinite being is proper to the infinite; it cannot be infinite in essence but finite in being without ceasing to be infinite. Being follows essence; the infinitude of essence cancels the finitude of being. If the infinite has in its essence no end and boundary at the finite, the being of the infinite has no boundary at the being of the finite. Thus, when you place the being of the infinite next to the being of the finite, you turn the being of the infinite into finite being; it has its boundary at the being of the finite. However, if you represent being as a sphere, as a space, it is clear that the infinite does not take up one part of this sphere, does not occupy some space and leave the rest empty; rather, it fills up the entire space, without leaving room for anything else. Therefore, the being of the infinite is the not-being, the destruction of the finite, for wherever the infinite *is,* the finite is not. But the infinite exists everywhere; it does not exist in one part of the sphere of being, but in the entire space. Therefore the finite exists nowhere. But from the perspective of this consideration, which, if maintained one-sidedly, leads to a complete negation of the finite, how is the being of the finite possible? Only because you limit, determine, and distinguish being itself into pure being and determined, temporal being. Only through and in time is finite being possible. Within the sphere of infinite being, finite being is possible only as sequential being, as succession, as dwindling and passing away. As the planet in time never rests or stands still but always wanders, never maintains the same spatial point but negates one place after the other, so, within the sphere of being that the infinite takes up, the finite never comes to a resting place at which one could say, *"It is,"* but, as it were, it will always be displaced by the infinite. This displacement is time. But in order to develop further the fact that the basis and principle of death is to be sought in God himself, I shall return to the more lively and meaningful determinations of the first discussion.

God is love as subject and substance. But, as stated previously, this love, as it appears in humanity, is a consuming fire. The being of the single and the particular, of the diverse and various, which otherwise has existence and reality for you, is consumed and destroyed by love. In and before the object of love, which, to you, is one and all, everything that is distinct and separated from it, which otherwise would be something for you, becomes nothing. All multiplicity and variety are destroyed in you as love arises in you; its arising is the disappearing of all particular existence. When you love, you no longer exist in the connections and associations with things and humans in which you previously existed and which alone constitute particular existence; you no longer exist in your particular interests, in your affairs, in the many objects in which you used to exist. You *exist* now only in the one being that is object of your love. All outside of it is vanity, is nothing. The solid and secure ground on which you used to stand has been pulled out from under you; you stand at the edge of total destruction; you have sunk into a bottomless abyss. This is just as true of the object of your love; it is not this or that, not something, not particular, but everything that is separable and divisible, various and particular, is dissolved into the one object that is everything. Take the case of love of a person. As long as you are not in love with someone, only the person's particularity, which you usually can observe and distinguish in this person, still has existence for you; this person's character, properties, good and bad sides, features, and so forth, are the only objects of your perception, and they exist in your perception as spatially separated, as it were; the entire picture of this person taken together exists for you only as a spatial whole. But when you both enter into the mutual bond of love, essence becomes object of essence, essence touches essence; and, in this unity of essence, the separated individual and particular being of both of you disappears along with all distinctions and divisions in and between you. Thus, that which cannot be negated and abstracted is unfit for love and has no share in it, for the activity of love (though distinct in object and content) is, like the activity of thinking, an activity of abstraction. Without love, you are inseparable from your particular existence; in love, you and your particularity become nothing. But at the same time this perishing is a new and more excellent state of being. Accordingly, you exist and do not exist in love; love is being and not-being in one, life and death as one life. Love gives life and takes it away, destroys and engenders life. Life and existence obtain meaning only by and in the all-consuming and painful purgatory of love. But only meaning makes life into life; a meaningless existence is as nothing. Thus existence really becomes existence only when it is the existence of love; love changes being into nothing and nothing into being, and only the something that is purged in nothing means and is something.

Now, although existence begins only with and from its meaning, it is also true that existence ends with its meaning. For the meaning of that which has a meaning is present only when it ceases; the meaning of nature is present only where it ends. You find the meaning of life only when you go beyond it, leave it behind, and abstract from it. You recognize the meaning of the riddle when you solve it; you recognize the significance of the picture when you negate it as picture. If you possess the significance of the picture, you no longer need the picture. But while the meaning of a thing is its principle and its beginning as the thing is again dissolved and consumed by its meaning, still the thing has emerged only out of its meaning. Therefore, the mean-

ing of a thing is both its end and its beginning. And, therefore,   39
existence both begins and ends in love.

If you wish to pursue further the knowledge of love as the
ground of such opposed determinations, then reflect that it is
the source and the basis of all joys and pains, that both weal
and woe arise from it, and that, therefore, love contains the
opposed essential determinations of that which makes weal into
weal and woe into woe. Joy is the feeling of being; pain is the
feeling of not-being, of a limit or a negation. But the feeling of
being is itself being, the feeling of negation is itself negation.
Further, joy and pain, as they rise to existence in the experience
of the subject, are the principles and basic determinations of all
existence. Joy is the feeling of life in life; pain is the feeling of
death in life, the feeling of the deprivation of experience. Because pain is not the feeling of the pure and therefore impercep-
tible deprivation that is death, but is the feeling of a determinate
deprivation of feeling, it is therefore pain, by virtue of this very
contradiction. Joy is consciousness of one's own being as communal, as being-in-union; joy is consciousness of being in general, of the positive, and, just for this reason, joy is itself pure
being. Pain is consciousness of the separated, distinguished
single being; therefore, pain is consciousness of finitude, of limits, and, in these, is negation itself. Thus love, as source and
ground of both pain and joy, is source and ground of both
being and not-being. Be not angry, great prophet, thoughtful,
clear-sighted cobbler of Görlitz, if I append your own exalted
and immortal thoughts on love.[2]

"What is love in its power and virtue and in its heights and
greatness? Its virtue is the nothing, and its power exists through
everything. Its heights are as high as God, and its greatness is
greater than God. Whoever finds it finds nothing and everything."

"Dear Master, tell me how I may understand this?"

"You understand the meaning of 'its virtue is the nothing'   40
when you depart from all creatures, and all nature and creatures
become nothing for you. At this point, you exist in the eternal
One that is God himself, and you experience the highest virtue

of love. But you experience 'its power exists through all' in your soul and body. So this great love will be enkindled in you, so it burns greater than any fire, and you will see how love has poured forth into all the works of God and is the innermost and outermost ground in all things, inward in power and outward in shape. Further, you understand in yourself 'its heights are as high as God' because love leads you into yourself as high as God himself.³ But it is also true to say, 'Its greatness is greater than God,' for love goes even where God does not dwell. When our dear Lord Christ stood in hell, hell was not God, but love was there and conquered death. And when you are fearful, God is not the fear, but his love is there and leads you out of fear and into himself. When God hides himself in you, love is there and manifests him in you. And it is also true to say, 'He finds nothing and everything,' for he who loves finds a supernatural, supersensible groundlessness that dwells nowhere, and he finds nothing that is like love. Therefore love is completely incomparable, for it is deeper than anything. It is all things as a nothing, because it is inconceivable. And in the fact of its nothingness, it is free of all things and is the only good that is impossible to define. Finally, it is true to say, 'He finds everything who finds it.' It was the beginning of all things and it rules all. If you find love, you enter into the ground from which all things have come forth and in which they exist. You are, in love, a king over all the works of God.''

The opposed determinations of joy and pain and of being and not-being that are one in love also may be traced back to the opposed determinations of unity and distinction. Love unites just as much as it distinguishes. But it does not distinguish according to the false model of those philosophers of understanding who find distinction only in the absence of unity and unity only in the absence, lack, and defect of distinction, but love unites in distinguishing and distinguishes in unifying. The distinction into subject and object (for example, in humans) arises only in love; love is the primary and most original self-consciousness in the human. As long as the child desires the mother only for nourishment, its soul is still only this desire for nourishment, and she is not yet object to the child. Only when love awakens, only when the mother herself becomes the object of attention and therefore the object of love, only then does the distinction between subject and object arise. But this distinction is at the same time the unifying of the lover with the beloved. Love, as it is absolutely substantive, as it is God, is ground, beginning, principle of life and being, and ground, beginning, principle of death and not-being. Insofar as it is distinction, it is ground of existence. But insofar as it is unity and unifying, it is ground of not-being (i.e., of the not-being of the determined, particular, and finite—although, since both unity and distinction are one in love, life and death each has for its ground and principle both determinations together, and each determination can be conceived for itself as the ground of both life and death, of both being and not-being).

You say, in your vague metaphors and flowery language, "God created the world out of love." What meaning does this picture have other than that existence rests on the fact that God distinguishes himself from himself, that the basis of existence is distinction from God? Or can you represent love without distinguishing? And does the proposition "God created the world out of love" have any other meaning than that God created the world from his own self-distinguishing? But now, can you separate the ground of not-being from distinction from God? Is not the distinction from the infinite the ground of all that is finite, of all limitation and negation? Is negation anything else but absence, not-being? Therefore, does not love, the ground of both existence and of not-being, of both life and death, rest on the distinction? If you acknowledge God to be the author or the ground of your existence, then you must also acknowledge him to be the ground of your not-being. But if you do not acknowledge him as the ground of your death and not-being, but acknowledge only the sin of Adam, or the natural order and blind natural necessity, then you become half an atheist and half a theist. As much as you exist, so much do you believe in God, but as much as you do not exist, so much are you an atheist. But now, if you are just as much being as not-being, just as

42

much affirmation as negation (for as you negate the negation in you, so you surrender yourself; you are what you are only within the distinction from the infinite, within negation and limitation), you are therefore just as much an atheist as a theist when you posit as extrinsic to God the ground and principle of death, of your end, of your limitation, of the negation that is not-being in general. "All finite things," states one of the ancient sages, "consist of something and nothing, being and not-being, affirmation and negation. The unification of being and not-being produces a third reality that is not pure being, but also not a not-being. The human is not nothing, but he is also not pure being; he is this distinct being or something. But he is something because he is *not* all being. Thus not-being has no less effect than being in constituting him as something. Being in itself is infinite and immeasurable, as in God, in whom there is pure being. But determination and limitation come from not-being. If the human did not partake of nothing, he would be all being, and, therefore, all-powerful, all-knowing, and all-willing. But his mode of existence dictates that he cannot accomplish much, and does not know an infinite amount, and does not love to infinity. Thus he consists of ability and inability, of knowing and unknowing, of willing and not-willing. But inability, unknowing, and not-willing are not-being."

43

You take immense pride in the fact that you are not God, that you are a particular being distinguished from God. Now then, be also so good as to acknowledge death, not only as the real and true end of your existence, but also as the true and real beginning and ground of your existence. For your existence is possible only together with the condition of death. Although death appears late, is only the end of your life, and, in sensible reality, seems only to follow life, still death is not a posteriori truth, but a priori truth. Death is the presupposed and preceding condition of your existence. As you depart from existence in death, so you enter existence only in death. Is not the end of something always its true beginning? Is not the sensible end only the manifestation of the true beginning? Do you not obtain the concept of something only at its end? Do you not perceive its essence only when it ceases? Is the human seed the true beginning of the human, or rather, is the end of the seed, the human, the true principle and the beginning of the seed? The seed is possible only under the condition of its not-being, that is, only under the condition that it does not remain a seed but becomes something different. Do not even spatial realities in their spatiality present this truth? Is not the point of the penknife also its beginning? When you acknowledge the end as also the beginning and no longer separate death from existence, then you will have to face the question of how the infinite can be the ground of the finite; how can that which is conditioned, particular, and determinate come forth from the absolute being, which is absolute love and the substantial unity of all being? There is no more insuperable difficulty. But if you separate the passing away of the finite from its arising, if you separate the end from the beginning, if you separate the not-being of a reality from its being, if you grant to the finite an insuperable, a pure and absolute existence like that of the infinite itself, then you willfully and intentionally *make* this question unanswerable, because you thereby make the finite into the infinite. For you, the being of the finite is not posited, is not that which has been begun, does not end and pass away in its beginning, but is originating, unconditionally certain and reliable, immovable, and unchangeable. With this assertion, the answers to the questions of how the unconditionally certain being of the finite is at the same time unreliable and how the originating being of the finite is at the same time not primary but posited become, indeed, less conceivable than the concept of the absolute itself.

44

But then, how can arising and passing away arise out of the infinite? To put it more correctly, how can arising and passing away be grounded in the infinite? For the infinite certainly cannot arise. This difficulty will disappear if you take the trouble to grasp the already developed relationship of time to essence and recognize at the same time that, before and in the infinite, passing away and arising are simultaneous, that, before the infinite, the interval of a determined length of time does not enter to separate the point of origin and the end point of your being, as it does before you, your senses, and your sensuous representation. Inasmuch as time is distinct from essence, all that is sequential in time is one and the same time in essence. But arising and passing away are at once in time, inasmuch as time is identical with the "at once" of essence. Everything, therefore, the multiple, particular, finite, is one and at once in essence; thus, essence is negating unity. Conceived of solely as being-at-one, essence is essence; but conceived of as *negating* being-at-one (as which it must be conceived, for without negating there is no unity), precisely as negating, it is time; essence is the being-at-one of being that is sequential, which is arising and passing away at once for the very reason that essence is the being-at-one of being that is sequential. For although arising and passing away within temporality are separated for the senses, in time itself they are inseparable. Time is distinguished from essence as negating is distinguished from negation. The essence, as it negates, is time. As negation negates, it posits and creates; that is, it posits the particular, the finite, the multiple, which is one in essence and infinite in this unity; it posits everything that is one in essence as many, as externally divided; negating negation posits the particular as particular, the finite as finite. But to posit the finite as finite means nothing else than to posit the negated as negated. Thus, essence, negation as act of negating, in which positing and canceling are one, is time. Time is only essence in action. As that which exists in disposition also exists in action, so action is only the disposition in which everything that exists at once and identically is posited in succession. So, again, time is only the positing of negation as negation. But negation is posited as negation only when that which is at once in essence, that which is negated at once, is negated sequentially, thus, only when it becomes and is succession, that is, negating in action. Action is negation only when that which is identical in essence is posited out of unity and into distinction, only when the finite is posited as finite, the single is posited as single. But this passage into external relation is simultaneously passing away, this positing is simultaneously canceling, this beginning is simultaneously ending; therefore, time is only the *active* essence, the essence in action. If you ask how essence becomes action, the only answer is that essence is already action. For essence is unity, but all unity is unity of that which is distinguished, and therefore essence is unification, is activity and action. But essence is action in identity, an identical action; or it is action in the form of identity. Time is discrete action, or action in the form of distinction. Time is only the expression of the inner timeless action that is essence itself, so that only the formal distinction of inner and outer exists between time and essence. But if you object, "A timeless action is an absurdity," my only response is that love, thinking, disposition, and many other actions are absurdities, for they are timeless actions. What else is disposition than an action that, as an inner action, identical with its essence, and therefore timeless, is also temporally successive in its connection with external existence? Action arises only out of action; thus, every temporal action presupposes a timeless action. Is not disposition an action? Is it not the sequential being of external action as a simple simultaneity, and, therefore, is it not a timeless action?

As the infinite, God himself, is the ground of the finite and so the ground of existence and of not-being—for the finite is being with limitations, with negation, therefore, with not-being—and as God himself, who contains negation in general (including your negation) in his absolutely affirmative, infinite actuality, is the ultimate and primary ground of your death, you must acknowledge, further, in all the affirmative grounds and essential determinations of your existence, the grounds and determinations of your not-being. Only that which is the ground and principle of your life is also the ground and principle of your death. As the essence that is all essence contains your negation as well as your affirmation, so anything essential contains in itself your affirmation and negation. First, space and time are affirmations of your being but are also negations of your being. You *exist* only in space and time; you begin in them, but you also end in them; they are the boundaries of your being. As an individual, you cannot exist outside of time and space; therefore, you exist only in this spatiotemporal life. For, second, as a

46

being existing in space and time, you are a being that is bounded
by space and time, or a determinate temporal and spatial being;
and, in this unity of temporality and spatiality, you are ensouled and corporeal—in other words, a living individual. Body
and soul in unity constitute your life; your being is only living
being. But, also, you die just because you live; your affirmation
is also your negation. Third, not only do you exist spatially and
temporally and with life, but you are also a human, a conscious,
spiritual being. Spirit and consciousness are the being of your
being, are all essence and all being, are the true essence and
being in your essence and being, are the highest, ultimate, infinite affirmations of your being. But they are also the true negations of your being, for they are your spiritual, invisible, and
supersensible negations, in which, therefore, the determinate
negations like time, space, life, these sensible and thus subordinate, conditioned grounds of your death, are absorbed into
their true ground. The *indeterminately* infinite ground of your
death is God, the infinite. The determinate, finite, themselves
posited grounds of your death, which are therefore *sensible* and
mediate grounds, and not ultimate and originating grounds, are
time, space, and life. The *determinately* infinite grounds of
your death, which, therefore, are not only infinite but are also
the determinate grounds of your knowledge of death itself, are
reason, Spirit, and consciousness. Space and time are only sensible affirmations, and therefore are only sensible negations.
The death that is derived only from space, time, and life is only
a sensibly grounded death. Only the ultimate ground is the primary ground. Thus, if one asserts that only time, space, and life
are the grounds of death, then one asserts as the grounds of
death, not the real grounds, but only results, manifestations,
mediate occurrences. Whoever remains with this grounding of
death is an empiricist, a materialist, a naturalist. And thus the
solarism of the belief in individual immortality asserts its right
and truth in contradiction to this materialism and tellurism. The
belief in individual immortality is true and has a foundation
only as opposition and contradiction to this naturalistic grounding of death. If death is only a sensibly grounded reality, it has

no more basis and truth than all that is sensible. Thus, as little as sensible reality is true and ultimate, so little is a death that is only sensibly grounded true and ultimate; it is not the end and conclusion of life. As the sensible is not a conclusion but is only the transition to the spiritual, so, too, is the death of the individual only a transition. For the individual is not just a sensible reality; he does not exist only in the sensible, but he exists also beyond the sensible, in consciousness and reason. Thus the individual is truly justified in placing himself beyond this conception of death, in not considering to be his end the materialist conception that includes only the sensible outcome of sensible reality. But the individual who, against materialism, clings to his immortality as to a sacrosanct shrine is not different from the materialist insofar as he also assumes that only a sensible, natural limit, only a sensible end, is the end of the individual. He differs from the materialist only by not accepting the sensible limit as the true and ultimate limit; for, by this denial, he does not fix the sensible as limit. But the *true limitation* of the individual, which transcends the sensible limit that is sensible death, is *reason,* Spirit, consciousness. Reason is the spiritual limit, the supersensible end, and the true death of the individual. The limit of everything sensible, and therefore of death itself as a sensible end, is Spirit. The true ground, the determinate infinite and determinate ultimate ground of your death, is Spirit, consciousness, reason. As the highest and ultimate—that is, spiritual—negations of your single being, of your particular being, of your being-for-self, of your individuality, of your self, of your personhood, Spirit, consciousness, and reason are universal, autonomous, and distinct from you. Moreover, they are spiritual negations of you as *your* personhood is immediately united with your sensible, single, transitory individuality. Thus the sensible negations of you are only results and manifestations of these absolute, original, spiritual negations. You are an individual, a determinate person, as that of which you are conscious, as this determinate individual that is object of your consciousness, but not *as* conscious; as a determinate thinker, you are an individual, a determinate person, but not *as* thinker. As

49

conscious and as thinker, you have been *spiritually* destroyed, have been absorbed in Spirit. You are conscious of yourself only in Spirit's consciousness of itself. Only in the pure and universal light of Spirit can you, the determinate individual, see and know yourself. The external realization of this spiritual negation is death.

II   Time, Space, Life

God alone is immortal and is the universal nature and essence of the particular things and essences that are grounded, included, and contained in him. For according to the teaching of pious, God-inspired sages, God contains in his essence all things and essences in a simple, universal, infinite manner; or, rather, he himself is all the essences in things as they exist in their essence and truth. As certainly and truly as the infinite essence, the unlimited Spirit, exists eternally, so certain and true is it that that which is determined and limited in content or essence is also determined and limited in its existence, that, therefore, a determined person exists only for a determined time. If you recognize that you are a limited essence and not essence itself, that you are *one* person and not *the* person itself, then you must also recognize that you exist now but not forever. You say, "I, as conscious of myself, as an individual distinct from others, am immortal; I, this individual, will be immortal." But by this you do not mean to say that the universal, the human in this particular human, the essence in your essence, the person in your person, is immortal—for, since you alone are that which is living and real to you, the universal is for you a dead abstraction—but you do say and mean that you yourself, this entirely determined person, this totally particular subject, are immortal. But you, this particular subject, are what you are only as particular subject, as the aggregate of all of your particular and determinate properties, types, and peculiarities. Determinateness and particularity distinguish. That you are a specific subject means equally that you are a subject that is distinguished from others.

50

Thus you cannot separate and distinguish yourself as specific subject from this, your distinction and your difference. This determinateness, this distinctness, is the boundary of your being, which cannot be canceled without you yourself ceasing to exist, as little as you could deprive a certain bird, for example, the raven, of the determinations of color, shape, and so on, through which determinateness it is what it is and is distinguished from other birds, without depriving it of its existence. But all determinateness, separateness, and distinctness rest only on this determined, actual existence, are possible and actual only in this actual life. You are this human only in this life. Thus, if this life ceases, you cease to be this human; for only you, this human in this life, consider yourself to be immortal.

The most definite expression of your determinateness is temporality. That you are a determinate person, that your being is a determinate being, finds its most definite expression in the fact that your being is temporal, is present now but is also passing away. Indeed, your being is not just temporal, but is totally temporally determined, momentary being, a being that is totally split into moments. You exist only so long as you can say, "Now, at this determined moment, I exist." You always exist only now, at this moment; and, as person, your existence is totally included in this moment. One point in time, one moment, is large enough to contain within it your totally undivided individual being. Time is inseparable from you as a determinate person; when the moments run out, you no longer exist. Perhaps it is even possible that you, as this particular being, are nothing more than a moment of the infinite being.

You are an individual only as long as you experience. The individual possesses the certainty of his existence only in experience; experience is the affirmation, the assurance, the assent, the confirmation, of individual being. Consciousness is the being of being; it alone is absolutely reliable, unconditionally certain—in other words, actual, positive being. But experience is only the self-consciousness that is individual, that is identical with the individual. Thus the individual is such only in experience. Experience is not a guaranty that is separate from or

51

accompanies the being of the individual, but it is the being of the individual. I have existence only in experience. Thus experience is the absolute determinateness, the absolutely determined expression, of singleness. The proposition "I am a determinate individual, a temporal, single being" has its determinate expression and meaning only in the proposition "I am an experiencing being." But time is inseparable from experience; where there is no "now," there is no experience. I experience only by virtue of the fact that I experience in this disappearing now, in this transitory moment. Experience exists only as moment; it is an essential property of experience that it is *now*. The moment is the essential form of experience; the boundary of experience, that within which it is what it is and which it cannot transcend, is the moment, is the definite span of time. Moreover, time itself becomes determinate time, becomes a moment, only in experience. As time exists only in the moment, the moment exists only in experience. As the single "now" excludes, as it repels that which is before and after, so experience excludes; it is the single-being of the single, of being-for-itself. But the individual is a totally determinate, separate, distinguished being. Thus experience is a being that is interrupted, that is divided by single determinations; it is not pure, self-identical being, but it is time, being-in-sequence. I am a being that experiences only as single; therefore, my being is single, is momentary, is a being-in-sequence. Experiences occur only in sequence because experience, as a determinate, excluding being-now, is the total being of the individual. People usually represent temporal duration as an unbroken, flowing line. But one can also represent the excluding moment as something bounded and closed, much as a pearl, a drop of water, assumes a spherical shape when separated from the continuous flow of water. I experience only because I separate the pearl of the moment, as it were, from the self-identical and unbroken flow of time and enclose my being within its narrow space. I only feel that which is determinate, but I, the total individual, my entire being, am contained in this determinate feeling, for each feeling is at the same time a feeling of myself, is my total being in one particular determination. But I feel only

52

because my entire being is concentrated, as it were, pushed and pressed into a single point of time, only because my entire being is unified in one "now" and is present in this concentration. As sunlight ignites when it is concentrated and compressed, so the fire of experience is kindled only by the compression of my entire being into the focal point of a moment.

Thus transitoriness is the essence of all feeling. The essence of experience appears most clearly and distinctly in sensible enjoyment. Why is there no lasting pleasure? Because a continuing, an uninterrupted pleasure would no longer be experience and pleasure; pleasure is pleasure only because it passes away. Equality, proportionality, continuousness, identity are the essential forms of the universal, of thinking, but not of feeling. Experience exists only with intermissions, temporal segments, epochs; it disappears in that which is self-identical. In order to know something one must grasp it where it emerges into existence most definitely, decisively, and characteristically. Thus you can recognize the nature of experience only where it expresses its character. But the character of experience exists clearly in sensible desire and enjoyment. The individual is only being-for-self, is total separation, limit, distinction, is a totally negative being. In other words, the individual, as excluding being-for-self, is the negation of the other, of that which is distinguished from him. Thus experience, as desire and as pleasure, is only the passing away of the object; it is extinguished together with its object, as fire is with its fuel; therefore it exists only *as* passing away. But the individual experiences only in time. The single passes away in time; time is the negativity of that which is single. The individual, the single, is only the negation of the single, is only the negation of the single object of its experience, within the universal negativity of all that is single, within time. Thus time is the ground, the principle, the possibility of all experiencing. There is no experience outside of time. Only an object that exists in time can pass away in and for a subject, and it can pass away in experience, in you, only because it passes away in time. Time and temporality are united to your susceptibility to experience; in a certain measure, time is your

53

very *capacity* to experience. Where there is no time, there is no individual; where there is no individual, there is no experience, and vice versa.

Thus, when you ascribe individual existence and experience, indeed, everlasting bliss, everlasting joy, to the individual in the dark blue hereafter, which is abstracted from all time, you only pursue the fantasy that makes possible everything that is impossible in essence, truth, and concept. But you do not pursue the truth. Eternal blessedness, eternal joy, exists only when the individual exists no longer, only when the individual ceases to be an individual; thus, this eternal blessedness exists in the Spirit, which has its true, self-identical existence and reality, not in or as the individual, but only in the existence and reality that is identical with its essence—that is, in thinking and knowing. Time disappears in thinking; time has existence for the human only in experience, whereas, since thinking exists over and beyond experience, thinking exists over and beyond time. Time exists in experience; the essence of experience is time itself. But time does not exist in thinking; time is only a semblance of thinking. If you maintain that for you thoughts arise sequentially, that you take note of them one after the other, that you are aware of one thought, which is the result of another, as occurring later, and so forth, then you maintain only the semblance of thought and take the semblance of thought to be its essence. For the fact that your thoughts enter into your consciousness only in sequence does not rest on thinking, but rests precisely on your distinction from thinking, for you think only in distinction from yourself as person and individual. You are one with thinking, not as an individual and in your individual being, your properties, and the like, but only in thinking itself. If thinking were united to your individuality, it would be only experience. Time exists only on the boundary that exists between you and thinking. Thinking is an activity that exists at home with itself in both the principle, the beginning, and in the end, the result, and that remains in unbroken unity with itself in separating and distinguishing; therefore, thinking is a timeless activity. That which, in experience is succession, is being-in-sequence, in thinking is development, determination, qualita-

54

tive redetermination, but is not quantitative and temporal sequence separated into moments. Or is the "now" an inner essential determination of thought as well as of experience? Only that in which time exists, that which has time as its inner determination, exists in time. But then, is this thought actually separated in time from other thoughts, as this present experience is separated from the previous experiences and those to follow? Are there present and past in thoughts as well as in experiences? Experience passes away; do thoughts also disappear and pass away so that the next thought arises only because the first no longer exists? Do thoughts exclude one another?* In response, I must ask you whether, in thinking, you eat and drink. If you use such temporal language concerning thinking, are you related to the object of thinking in the same way that you are related to food while you are eating? Are thoughts experiences? Are thoughts, just as experiences, affirmations and reinforcements of your separate being-for-self? Thus you take thinking for experience, you take the semblance that the individual creates for thought itself, if you do not recognize that thinking is an activity that is free from time. As already stated, in experience the single subject maintains itself only as single and thus possesses only single objects. But single objects can be present only as single objects, as mutually excluding, and therefore only in sequence. Thinking is no elongated activity, but is an activity in which the focal point is everywhere; thinking is a middle, but not of extremes. Thinking is an absolutely pure middle, an infinite present, without beginning or end, which is not separation and sequence but is inward distinguishing, development, and shaping within the substance that is the basis of self-unity.

But the determinate person, the individual, must be not only a temporal being, a being inseparable from time, but also a spatial being. Thus, when you assume the existence of a life after

*Editor's note: When the author speaks of thinking, he does not mean bestial thinking, that thinking which is also proper to animals and at which level humans often remain; thus, he does not mean sensuous representation, in which pictures come and go, but the thinking that is the activity of reason, that has as its object truth, the eternal.

death in which you will be the same individual that you once were here, in which you will be the same personal being, the same subject, that you are in this present life, then however you might try to remove all sensible representations from it, and as much as you might imagine yourself to have a spiritual grasp of it, you still must locate this life after death in a place. If this is not one of your fantasies, if there actually is such a life, then it must be somewhere. As an individual, you are a being separated from others; separation belongs essentially to your individuality. Individuals must be spatially external to one another and thus must exist spatially. Thinking, reason, consciousness are nonspatial, but these are not individuals; nonspatiality excludes individuality. But it is an essential property of the individual that hc exists separately. To exist separately, however, is the same as to exist spatially. In fact, the distinction of individuals from one another is not a distinction in essence, but a distinction that is proper only to sensible existence. That which the concept, the thought, does not distinguish, the essence does not distinguish; but only the senses distinguish individuals. The many apples on this tree are not distinguished by and for the concept, but only for the senses, because they are not distinguished in essence. But that which is not distinguished in essence and concept is distinguished only in and according to sensible existence. (More properly, the many apples are separated, for distinction is related to essence and concept, while separation is related to existence and the senses.) But humans are distinguished from one another no more than apples on the same tree are distinguished from one another. Thus space and time are the absolutely inevitable, necessary forms of all individuality. You are an individual only in sensible existence, only as you exist temporally and spatially. As much as you are sensible, so much are you an individual. That which transcends the senses is of the Spirit.

Although both space and time contain the two determinations of affirmation and negation, one may ascribe the determination of negation principally to time and that of affirmation principally to space. Space is sensible existence, the external form of divine love as it is light, as it is all-engaging and all-imparting. Time is the sensible form of divine love as it is consuming fire, as it is the negativity of all that is finite and particular. Individuals are only boundaries, limits; they exist only in separation. Thus they cannot exist outside of space; space is the very existence of individuals. As time must be acknowledged, not as an enemy, but as the intimate friend and daughter of essence, so too must space be acknowledged as in and from essence. The essence of individuals is one and the same and, in this unity, is all individuals without distinction or exception. Thus true love and blessedness exist, not in the individual, but in essence alone. But in this, the plenitude of essence, in which it is everything and has everything, the being-in-itself of essence is equally imparting, as it were, overflowing goodness, is boundless being-outside-of-itself, is the existence of all the individuals that it contains as a unity. Essence is thus the space that includes in itself all individuals (though not as they exist separately). And precisely as this unity of all individuals, which is therefore not an excluding being-for-itself, which is not a finite unity (as is the unity of the individual), essence is the distinguishing of itself into individuals, is the loving, imparting, and liberating to independent existence of the individuals that it contains in unity. The unity of essence is not just contraction and concentration, but is also unbounded expansion, the ecstasy of joy, love, and plenitude. Therefore the real space, that which grants individuals within itself, the space within which they exist as individuals, is essence itself in the determination of its being-outside-of-itself. I hope that you will at least be reasonable enough to see that the apples on this tree are not distinguished in essence. But how do things that exist distinctly derive from this one essence; how are there many apples (since to exist is to be many, and to be many is to be distinct in *existence*)? Only because not just the determination of being-in-self, but also the determination of being-everything, of unity and wholeness, therefore, the determination of abundance and liberality, but not of stinginess, the determination of carefree, unstinting

58

expansion and boundless being-outside-of-itself, and with these, the determination of existence that creates the possibility of existence, is proper to essence. Thus there is contained in essence, not multiplicity, the manifold, separation, but the possibility of these.

Therefore individuals who exist after death, in order to exist as individuals, must have a place, a common space in which they can exist. But some very serious difficulties and confusions arise at this point. The life of the individual after death is in a place. But since it is inconceivable that there are two kinds of space, or a space outside of space, this place cannot be separated or distinguished from space itself, since clearly a space outside of space would be an absurdity. This place must be the place of departed individuals and thus must be a particular place that is different from the place of the living. But as one place it is separated from the place of the living, not by spatiality itself, but only by its determined locality. Thus it is totally impossible that the place of the individuals in the hereafter can be outside of the space within which sensible nature and we, the living, exist. But we, the living, this earth, this heaven, this nature, all exist before death, together constitute the life before death. Our life, our life before death, is spatial, sensible being; space belongs essentially to our life. Space is, so to speak, the property of the beings that exist sensibly; it is only the universal expression and form of our sensible present life. Space is included in the being before death. Since, therefore, immortal individuals exist in a place, their place must be included in space, and the life after death must be included in the life before death. For if these individuals exist spatially after death (and as certainly as there exists a reason and a truth, so certainly must they exist spatially if they are to continue as individuals), then, further, not only must they exist temporally—for space cannot exist for itself, separately from time, and the immortal life is thus temporal life—but they exist burdened by all the sensible attributes and properties that belongs to this temporal life—for space and time cannot be distinguished from all the other prop-

erties of this sensible life—and the life of the beyond becomes
the life here, the life that we live here on earth. But if immortal
individuals were only spatial, without the other burdens that
must be associated with space, then the only possibility remaining to immortal individuals is that they are mathematical
figures, or at least are beings that are very similar to lines and
triangles. But lines and triangles are also included in this life.

Since, therefore, individual life after death must be included
in life before death, it was fully in order that in more recent
times, after people had rejected the dark representations of a
realm of ghosts and shades, of a Hades and Sheol, of a dark
sojourn of the dead under or upon the earth, the stars were
determined to be the dwelling places of the departed. In fact, if
you wander throughout the world, you will find no place that is
better suited for the life of the dead than the stars, especially
since this dwelling place has the extra advantage of placing the
life after death at a great distance from life before death, and
since, as opposed to previous dwelling places, on the stars the
dead could no longer afflict and bother the living. To establish
this representation of the stars as dwelling places of living
beings, the individual begins from the universal principle that
these uncountable bodies would exist in vain if they were not
inhabited by living beings, and that, therefore, if they were not
inhabited, they would contradict the essence of nature, which
makes nothing in vain, and the wisdom of their Creator.
"What?" you cry out in horror, "What? So many, such enormous worlds are to exist in vain, and only on this earth, which is
lost like a little, tasteless grain of salt in the immeasurable ocean
of these worlds, only on this earth there is to be life?" And in
your zoological and philanthropic horror you forget to permit
yourself to be instructed concerning the distant world bodies by
the very nature that surrounds you. Consider the human, from
time immemorial viewed as a microcosm, a mirror of the universe, and the contemplation of this one reality will reveal to
you the whole universe. The human body consists of infinitely
many independently distinct parts. There are parts within the

60

parts, organs within the organs, systems within the systems. The smallest part is still rich in parts and independent determinations so that (apart from the unity of property, concept, or species) if you wished to divide the bare matter of the body, you could divide the smallest parts into infinity and could count them forever. Nature develops its unlimited creative power in unrestricted multiplicity, independence, separation, severing, determining, and distinguishing. But now, look at this wonder of all wonders, this great mystery! This immeasurability and innumerability, this infinity of parts, members, organs, systems, produces only one single life, one being, one individual! This wildly agitated whirlpool of material nature, which divides and distinguishes itself without ceasing or rest, dissolves itself, becomes as clear and even as the face of a mirror and peacefully folds itself together into the one feeling of one unity which is called life! This infinite multiplicity, this enormous all becomes one. All is one, one is all; this is the mystery of life, of the unity of soul and body. The one as many is the body; the many as one is the soul.

But why, in this infinity of parts, is there only one human? Why isn't the eye a human being? Why don't humans live in the bones and hair? Why are there no bone-humans, no muscle-humans, and no nerve-humans? In relation to the soul, which occupies less space than a mathematical point, which, indeed, occupies no space, the human body occupies just as much—if not greater—space than the visible universe occupies in relation to the earth. For in relation to that which is spaceless, the smallest space is infinite. Why then does the soul, which is indivisible, simple, a point, an atom, why does this single individual take up such an enormous space? It certainly seems clear to me that the entire soul would have room enough in one root of hair; then why is the poor root not also a soul, a human? "What?" the bones, the teeth would say, if they shared these zoological and philanthropic views with humans, "What? We bones, who take up the space of a Saturn or a Uranus in relation to the invisible, indivisible point of the soul, should not our essences contain essences that are at least analogous to humans? Are we to be without essence and empty of humanity? The wretched life and the lamentable purpose that the philosophers of nature and the physicians accord to us is no life and no purpose. They tell us that we teeth exist to chew and to pulverize meat, and that this, our purpose, is our activity, life, and nature. But what is the genuine, true, ultimate purpose of this purpose, the true essence of our essence? The living, willing, thinking human. Therefore, we, who have nothing in common with the human, we gigantic natures at whose material durability and solidity the thin, cometlike essence of the immaterial soul wears away with the power of a soap bubble, we, who are infinitely farther from humanity than Uranus is from the earth—for the distance of Uranus from the earth is only spatial, measurable, but our distance from humanity is a distance of nature, of the quality of essence, is, therefore, an immeasurable, infinite, disproportionate, incomparable distance—should we have our purpose in humanity, in the soul, should we have our purpose so far from us, outside of us in another nature that has nothing at all in common with us? Is our life not to be contained in us, but in another corner of the globe, in the nature of humanity, in the soul? It is impossible, it is incompatible with the wisdom of God, that we should exist in vain, that we are not our own teeth-humans, that instead of our most immediate purpose, which is a pitiable, purposeless purpose because it is directed to a foreign essence, the soul, we do not contain in us a purpose that is just as immediate to us as the purpose that the natural scientists accord to us, but which, at the same time, is just as free, as autonomous, as noble as the human purpose. Therefore, we should contain a humanity that is proper to us, that belongs to us; in a word, we should be *teeth-humans.* If there are human teeth, then why in the world shouldn't there be teeth-humans? A hollow tooth, a tooth devoid of humanity, would be a gap in world creation that cries out to heaven! Therefore we teeth must have our own citizens and inhabitants.'' What a fool I used to be when I considered myself to be only one human. Where I used to see around me only dead, selfless, and unconscious members and parts, without purpose *in themselves,* moved to

63

produce out of themselves this one individual, I now see pure humans. I myself, this one human, am now an innumerable horde of humans!

In your contemplation of the stars, you touch only sensibly independent existence, only the size and quantity of these world bodies. "But they are, they exist; to what end do these infinite worlds exist if not for something, if not for living existence; why do they exist if they have no life?" You are correct in considering life to be the purpose of a body. But you are wrong in believing that just as these bodies are independent in spatial existence, so, too, must they be independent in their purpose and essence. That is, you are mistaken in your assumption that this particular body, which you visually locate in a place, exists in vain if that which you discover and acknowledge as its goal on earth is not also contained in and on this very body, and that, therefore, this immeasurable space is without purpose if there is no life *in it*. Caught in your own error, without hesitation you "overshadow" and populate the distant worlds with the unreal shadows of your well-developed imagination. That which astounds you and leads you astray is only the sensible existence, the unbounded space of these world bodies. But I must confess to you that such superfluous, useless, purposeless existence strikes me everywhere, even here, even on earth, filled with the warmth of Spirit and life, that even in every occupied place, empty spaces confront me in such a way that, whereas the world bodies appear to you to be in vain because no life breathes on them, all space, all existence, all nature appear to me to be in vain. That is, when I bring to nature the representations with which you consider the world bodies, I find everything to be empty and desolate, I find everything to be without purpose. If you ask, "Why do these bodies exist if there is no life on them?" I respond with the question, "Why is there a being, a space, a matter, a nature, at all?" God could have melded the entire universe into one atom; thus, whatever goes beyond the realm of the atom is wasted, superfluous, purposeless being. Why is there not one single human instead of countless numbers of humans? As many humans as exist outside of me, so many substract from me, so many empty and unoccupied spaces exist in me. Every single human who exists outside of me is a hole, a void, a gap in me. I am a thoroughly perforated essence; my entire being is one pore. Every essence that is like mine and that has independent existence punctures me, inflicts a wound in me. In every human I see only that which I lack. Other humans are nothing but the objective, independent pores of my own self as viewed outside of me. And so all things are porous, full of empty, open spaces. Why isn't one single tone the entire overture? Why does a single tone exist? In just this single tone, you can find that purposelessness and that same empty space that you notice in the sensible magnitude of the stars. This one tone is totally perforated, totally porous, for all other tones do not exist in it. Why do you overlook the voids on earth? Why isn't the leaf the fully extended tree? Why is not all reality inseparably and indistinguishably one? The purpose of the tree is the flower and the fruit; then to what end are the leaf, the veins, the boughs, the trunk, and the rest, why are these so separated from one another, and why does the tree exist so wastefully in so many kinds of specific and independent parts? Would it not have been wiser if the purpose were present immediately, all at once, and without all further conditions and complications, without all digressions and deviations, if all existed as one in a simply spiritual manner? The same holds for matter, for nature, for being itself. For all being, even nature, has a purpose for its inner essence, in respect to which nature and being outwardly appear to exist in vain. If one extends to everything your representations, which, strangely, you apply only to the stars, one would finally come to the conclusion that it would have been best if nothing existed, for all lack of purpose would be avoided only in nothing, and that being itself is that which has no purpose. Or, if one carried out your representations, one would at least be forced to the opinion that only Spirit should exist, that sensible, material being is pure wastefulness, is fruitless expenditure, and that only if the simple Spirit existed in simplicity could all that now exists without purpose have been spared.

65

Thus, until you have proved that humans live in teeth, your belief in living beings on the heavenly bodies has no foundation. On the contrary, since it is absolutely certain that several humans do not live in one human, that there is only one soul in a body, so it is absolutely certain that, in all of creation, there exists but one animated and ensouled point, and that this point is the earth, which is the soul and purpose of the great cosmos.

Everything that exists has a history or a past; its present manner of existence is not attained immediately, nor is it what it is by and of itself, but it has behind its existence and behind that which it is a being that precedes and conditions it. In other words, everything that exists has behind its being another being as its ground and background. Thus the body is the background of the soul; it is, as it were, the soul of the past, the soul that was, the prehistory of the soul; in other words, the body is the condition and presupposition of the soul; the soul cannot exist without a body. Thus the body is independent to the extent that the soul cannot exist without it, to the extent that it is the body's nature to precede the soul, and the soul appears to be dependent to the extent that it must have the body as its presupposition. Yet because the condition possesses its purpose and essence, not in itself, but, rather, in that which it conditions, the apparent dependence of the soul is negated, and the condition is lowered to the status of a mere means, of an instrument. The body is determined only for the soul; the soul is the purpose, the determination of the body's existence. Thus the body and all its parts surrender their independence, their materiality, and, by this sacrifice of their own proper being, they produce one effect, the soul. Yet, again, the soul is an effect only in appearance, only for the sensible eye, to which the condition appears to be the principal and preeminent reality. In fact, the soul, as the purpose of the body, is the body's inward, concealed spiritual cause, the hidden ground and principle that makes the condition into a condition.

Now, just as the true and essential purpose always lies at a *distance* from that which exists on account of this purpose, just as the purpose does not exist immediately but is brought to prominence only as the result of a long series of intermediate terms, which, like the body and its parts, possess particular, independent existence before the actuality of the purpose, so the purpose of the heavenly bodies is not immediately connected with them, does not exist on them, but is realized at an enormous distance from them, that is, here on earth. The purpose always lies outside of and beyond existence, far away from it. To realize the purpose, nature makes use of the widest, broadest roads; it uses no simple arrangements and methods, but only the most complicated, the most intricate, the most extensive and comprehensive. Accordingly, the human body is the most involved, most colorful, most complex, most detailed, most compartmentalized institution, filled with as many members and parts as one could imagine, and yet the effect, the purpose of this enormous institution is but one feeling, one life, one soul. To clarify this truth, one need only think of the digestive process. Its purpose is to be attained only through intermediate members. This means that *it is not immediately one with existence;* it is separated from that which has a purpose and which exists for the sake of that purpose. More accurately, the purpose presupposes that which has no purpose, for that which is lowered from purpose to means is by this very fact lowered to a mere means, to a mere appearance, which has no essence, no purpose in and for itself. It is precisely the purpose that, in order to exist as a purpose, takes away the independence, value, and significance from that which appears to the senses to be independent. For example, when I set for myself the goal of reverence for God, I take away all independence from those activities that, to a sensual human, have independent value as a purpose. These activities become nothing to me for themselves; they are only means for the attainment of a goal that lies far beyond them. Every goal negates; where there is no destruction, no negation and sacrifice of independent existence, there is no purpose. Purpose is Spirit, but Spirit is the death, the destroyer, of sensible reality.

If you were to see a human embryo for the first time and were

67

to consider to be proper the same representations that you apply in your contemplation of the world bodies, how would you respond if someone said to you, "Look, this embryo is destined to become a human; look, this mute, motionless vegetable will someday be a living, strong, willing, acting human"? What a hopelessly stupid arrangement! Why doesn't this poor thing already contain its purpose in itself, why does its purpose, its essence, the human that it is to be, lie so infinitely far from it, so that that which it already is in itself, that which it already is by potentiality, that for which it exists, is not yet actually present? And why must its purpose be attained only after a long series of years, only after running through many stages and kinds of existence? If you are not amazed and annoyed that humans exist as embryos, why, if you use your common sense, are you amazed and annoyed that the heavenly bodies are only embryos of earth, that in the heavens nature is still enclosed in the maternal bosom of its creative power and has not yet stepped forth into the bright Sunday of the development of living things? Just like everything else that exists, the earth, too, must have its stages and members that mediate and make possible its existence; the earth, too, must have its background. Since the earth is living existence, is existence that contains life, the heavenly bodies, without containing life in and for themselves, are only the conditions of life, are only the presuppositions of earth, are only the preparations, the scholastic exercises, and the prearrangements for the earth, just as the body is only the preparation for the soul. Because the past moment is the condition of the present moment, the conditions of an existing reality are its past. Thus, to state the matter metaphorically, the stars are truly only the ancestral, armorial bearings of the earth; the whole heaven is only a monument of its prehistory. In the heavens, nature celebrates its Feast of All Souls; the lights that you see up there are nothing further and nothing more than the memorial candles on the graves of the past. The stars are only the annals, the records of the earth.

If your understanding does not remain permanently beguiled by the vision of the multitude and the immeasurable size of

these world bodies, then you should reflect that one must infer   69
exactly the opposite of what you conclude from their variety
and enormous size. For unlimited expansion in mass, size, and
variety proves just the lack of intensiveness. In the heavens,
nature spreads its power outwardly; it demonstrates its intensiveness not in intensive realities, but in extensive realities.
Where nature pulls itself back inwardly, where it recollects and
concentrates itself, and expresses its power in the form of power
and intensiveness, not in and as quantity, it becomes quality,
kind, animation, earth. But where the power of nature spreads
and expands itself inwardly, where it pulls itself back from the
external, it narrows and restricts its space. See how the oak
stands before you, in far-reaching roots, in an enormously
thick, massive trunk, in an uncountable multiplicity of
branches, twigs, and leaves! But the purpose, the essence of the
tree, the entire oak—which loses itself and spreads itself out in
trunk, roots, and so forth—alights and beds down in the fruit,
in the narrow room of an acorn, as if in its home—for this
acorn is, by power and potentiality, the entire oak tree. Since
every purpose is conditioned by an infinite multiplicity of
means and appearances, since every purpose has behind it a history, a process of mediating preparation, and since every purpose lies beyond and outside of sensible existence, you must recognize, from the very multiplicity of the stars, from their very
enormous size, that their purpose is realized, not in them, but
only on earth, and that, therefore, this small earth is the fruit of
the great cosmos.

It used to be an almost universal belief of humanity that all
was made for the sake of the human, that humanity was the
purpose of the world, and that therefore the center of the cosmos was here on earth. This belief contains much truth; it is
insufficient only because the purpose of the cosmos was under-   70
stood to be only the single human, his use and benefit. Thus the
purpose was understood only in a physical sense, not spiritually;
it was not understood to be humanity as humanity. In modern
times, this belief was suppressed by the opposite point of view:
that the center of the cosmos exists on every single star as well as

on the earth, that the center is everywhere, that everything, or rather nothing, is the center of the cosmos. For clearly he who considers everything to be the center considers nothing to be the center. Thus modernity has lost the perception of the true totality, of oneness and life in one unity. The modern human was and still is without focal point, for the person, the individual without center, was brought forward and viewed as center. And as humanity's perception of itself disintegrated into the perception of totally independent centers, so the world came to be viewed as without center, and the one world was dispersed into many worlds. Thus the principal task of modern humanity became that of concentrating all existence without distinction into the consciousness; the Spirit was made into a mere mirror, into a receptable, into the empty barn of the cosmos. "Everything that is worthy of being is also worthy of knowing." Spirit was driven into the width and breadth; it set forth from itself on a trip into foreign territory; full of amazement at foreign lands, it forgot its true homeland. It poured itself without measure into boundless expansion over everything, making all, without distinction, into its center. That which humans were in themselves, they saw outside of themselves in nature. In the multiplicity, in the greatness of the stars, in quantitative nature, in boundless expansion, in merely sensible, centerless existence, they saw the true picture of their true being.

71   If living things exist on the other world bodies, there are three possibilities: either the life that exists on earth, the same living beings that exist here, exist on them; or there is a higher life, there are more perfect beings on them; or, finally, there is a life on them that is lower than life on earth; there are lower, less perfect beings than the living beings of earth. But if the same life as exists here existed on them, they would be totally superfluous. When two or more realities are so alike that they contain the same life, only one of them is necessary and useful. For of two things that are completely alike, one has no purpose. If I were aware that I would once again exist on earth, or that there was a second being totally the same as me, I would immediately

hurl myself into the abyss of nothingness in the conviction that I was a useless being. I could not bear this terrible mockery and diabolical scorn of me. For without distinction there is no purpose; the purpose excludes those which are alike, the merely plural, the twice, the duplicate. The ground, the purpose, the rationality of my existence lie only in my particularity, only in my determinateness and distinctness. One being needs to exist only once; if it exists as totally the same a second time, it is purposeless. Its purpose is the seasoning of an existence and life; only through its purpose does life obtain its taste. But only when life is once and for all does it have seasoning and taste. If the earth had such an equal brother, such a double under the stars, then, full of anger at its tasteless, flat existence, it would certainly hurl itself into the gulf of nothingness, for only the purpose holds something back from nothingness. Thus the same life can exist neither on some nor on all of the heavenly bodies.

The second possibility is that on at least some of the heavenly bodies there exists a life that is lower than on earth. But now, since the totality of life on earth is already divided into higher and lower gradations of existence and life, there are only two possibilities here: either the beings on the other worlds stand at the same level of lowliness as the lower levels of life on earth, or these beings have a lower level of life than the lowest form of life on earth. But the same level of lowliness of life cannot exist on the other world bodies, for it is enough to be lowly once. A repetition of lowliness would be totally purposeless and irrational. Thus they must be lower than the lowest and most inferior beings on earth. But the lowest life and existence on earth is, for example, the life of the stone, which is elementary, mechanical existence, a life that, therefore, many hesitate to call life. So if the living beings up there are even lower than the lowest beings on earth, then they thereby cease to be living, or else one would have to assume that death is a level of life and that not-being is a degree of being.

72

There remains only the third possibility: that on the heavenly bodies there exist more perfect, higher beings, higher levels and stages of life, than on earth. It is by no means to be doubted that one can represent, or imagine, higher beings, for the imagination has no limits and is therefore irrational. But whether these imagined higher beings exist anywhere else besides the imagination, and whether they really are higher, are questions that, if one follows the limitations and laws that reality, reason, and truth prescribe, one must certainly answer in the negative. These imaginings are nothing but imaginings and are therefore irrational both in outcome and basis. For once one transgresses humanity, the actual limits of the individual living being, every limit, once posited, becomes only an arbitrarily assumed, imagined limit. For the same reason that the imagination steps beyond humanity as a finite reality, it must also go beyond the other invented higher beings, and thus there arises an endless series of more perfect, and again more perfect, and always more perfect beings, and so on, into infinity. For every level that would be established as final would always be one more limit that again is to be canceled by the boundless imagination. The measure can never be filled; there can be only a measureless, aimless, endless, and lawless, and, therefore, spiritless, irrational, and purposeless delirium from level to level, from limit to limit. There can be only a silly, childish fluctuation of posited and then once again canceled limits.

Moreover, when such a fictitious purpose is located on the other worlds, the earth disappears as a purposeless, worthless, and meaningless grain of sand in this stream of imagined perfections, which tediously flows along without rational direction. The ultimate levels of perfection should be the goal of life on earth. But, according to these thinkers, the ultimate levels neither should nor can be the last, for, as ultimate levels, they would be boundaries and limits, and, therefore, although they are the ultimate levels of perfection, yet they must be levels to be surrenderd, imperfect levels. Thus the earth has no purpose, for a purpose that does not actually exist will never be achieved, and therefore never exists. A purpose that, instead of establishing limits, as the nature of a purpose demands, causes all limits, all determinations, to disappear into nothingness is only an imagined purpose, no real purpose, and thus no purpose at all.

But this imagining is irrational precisely in its basis. For it happens that the higher and more perfect being that is beyond sensible individuals is again conceived as a limited, individual being, and that these individuals who are greater and higher than the individuals who exist sensibly on earth are grasped partly as they themselves are to be in the future and partly as other individual beings. These thinkers do not recognize that the higher and more perfect being is only Spirit, reason, or humanity as one eternally complete totality, that perfection exists only in the unity of the whole, that individuals can never be perfect or absolute, but can only make that which is perfect into the object of their Spirit.

You are perfect only in the contemplation of the totality, only   74 in thinking, only in the delightful knowledge of the perfect. As a mortal, single individual you will share in no other perfection. But the futility and vanity of your representations of the present object of this consideration will be clarified even further in the following discussion, though I think that clarification is almost impossible for you. How could you become clear on this issue, since you have the remarkable quality of letting the light darken you? Even the lovely constellations of the heavens hide from your gaze the essence and the truth.

If there existed beings other than the earthly, which, if they are not to exist in vain, would have to assume a higher level of life than humanity, there would be no religion, no philosophy, no science at all. Instead of these universal, abstract objects of knowing, instead of God, who, compared to the higher individual beings of your imagination, is highly abstract and universal, in short, instead of thoughts, knowledge, concepts, these pure spiritual beings and objects that are the present objects of our Spirit, the inhabitants of Saturn, Uranus, and the other stars would take up residence in our heads. Instead of mathematics, logic, metaphysics, religion, and so on, we would possess the most precise Uranusography and Saturnography, the most precise portraits of the heavenly dwellers, and the picture gallery of these strange sciences would be ordered according to the order

of levels and gradations of the life of these beings. That is to
say, these higher beings, if they were higher and at the same
time actual, would insert themselves between us and the objects
of thinking and knowing; they would prevent us from seeing
these objects and would cause an eternal, complete eclipse of
the sun in our Spirit. For these higher beings would be nearer
and more related to us than thoughts because they are not
purely spiritual beings, as are ideas and thoughts, nor are they
purely sensible, corporeal beings, as are the living individuals of
the wretched earth, but they are a kind of reality lying midway
between corporeal and incorporeal beings. They are not as individual as we are, but they are not as universal, not as lacking in
individuality, as thoughts are. They are not real individuals, not
real bodies, for these are exactly determined, strictly limited;
that is, in your language, they are not grossly material. They are
quasi individuals, quasi bodies; but they are not as subtle and
ethereal as thought, for the spirituality and subtlety of thought
excludes individuality. They are corporeal thoughts and concep-
tualized bodies; in other words, they are beings of the imagination. As the child begins with the imagination before he attains
thinking, so the essences of Uranus and Venus must arise in us
before thoughts; before we attained mathematics and metaphysics, we would first have to attain Uranus or Venus. Thus
we would have to break and sever one link after the other of the
chain of these quasi beings and middle members, would have to
get sick and tired of the life in and with them, and would have
to push and shove through the center of their army before we
attained the thought of the infinite being, indeed, before we
attained any thought.

But these quasi individuals neither do exist, nor should nor
can exist in reality—for reality is infamously gross, coarse,
rough, repulsive, because no "quasi" has meaning in it—nor do
they exist in thought, for thought is totally spiritual, almost
hyperbolically so. They exist in imagination alone, because neither experience, perception, perspective, nor knowing, thought,
recognition can be obtained of them, since they are objects neither of sense nor of reason (only the actual individual is an

object of sense, as only the actually spiritual, and not the quasi spiritual, is object of reason), but are objects of imagination alone. Otherwise our entire life of Spirit would be only a dream, a fantastic play and vision of the beautiful future, a portrait or concert of these high, fantastically shaped personhoods. Therefore, that person whom the weight of reason prohibits from swimming around on the surface of the boundless ocean of imagination will recognize that the being of these half-sensible, half-invisible, indecisive, characterless, middle beings is only an imagined being, which, therefore, is destroyed by the being of thought, knowledge, and religion, and will recognize that the life light of the angels and of all other spiritually sensible and sensibly spiritual beings is extinguished in the depths of our Spirit as in an atmosphere in which they cannot respire, that all these spirits can bear the light of Spirit as little as ghosts can bear the light of dawn. In fact, all these higher individual beings, be they represented as angels or anything else, are nothing but ornaments, gothic flourishes on the temple of our Spirit. Like the busts and statues of the palaces of the great, they only decorate the atrium, the vestibule, of our inmost reality. For as we raise ourselves beyond ourselves, beyond our sensible existence and life, as we return to ourselves and concentrate ourselves, we raise ourselves to Spirit, to the thought of infinite being, and to thoughts, ideas, concepts in general without meeting higher individuals. But since it is the human who comes to reason, to thoughts, to clear, purely universal, invisible realities when he raises himself beyond sensible being and essence, then it is the sensible being of humanity which is the ultimate sensible being; humanity itself is the ultimate of all individual beings, the highest of all individuals. Thus, the highest life is life in religion, science, art, in the world-historical totality of humanity. This is the life beyond the sensible and transitory life, the life beyond death. Reason, will, freedom, science, art, and religion are the only real guardian angels of humanity, are the only actually higher and more perfect beings. Infinite, everlasting life exists in these alone, but not on Saturn or Uranus or anywhere else.

76

77

But apart from the delusion of seeing the perfect and absolute only in the form of the individual, of going beyond the determinate, actual individuality of humanity, and of assuming the existence of higher beings on the stars or anywhere else, the assumption and supposition of the existence of any beings other than those of earth, be they more or less perfect than ours, contradict the unprejudiced recognition and knowledge of actual truths and facts. That is, if there existed any other beings at all, thinking and reason would never achieve existence in us. Thinking arises only at the conclusion, only at the most extreme boundary, only at the end of all nature, of all sensible life and existence; nature has arrived at its outer boundary in thinking; there it ceases. For thinking, reason, Spirit are not only not sensible, but are also supersensible and supernatural. Since we presently do think here on earth and since earthly nature already has run through an infinitely great series of stages and kinds of sensible existence and life, of air, earth, stones, up to the organic form of life in the human shape, then earthly nature already must have filled out and exhausted the entire realm of stages of possible forms of life, must have accomplished and brought to a close its entire essence through the developmental series of the different lower and higher kinds and forms of life. Otherwise the sensible life in us would not have ceased, and would not have become a new, totally different and distinct life that is life in reason, in thinking. If earthly nature had not already unfolded its entire essence, all its possible forms of life, through its history, if, when it came to humanity, it had not called out, "It is consummated, here and no farther," then the human would only live but not think, and there would exist beyond humanity and the living beings of earth still another series of possible beings, which would continue on until finally Spirit, thinking, awakened. Between us and thinking there would still exist an insuperable partition that would be just these other living beings on some other world or continent. Thinking arises out of the total fatigue and, as it were, exhaustion of nature, out of satiation and boredom with itself, just as in the individual human the impulse to thinking begins with a disgust at sensible life. Nature has terminated and ended, and with its death, there arises over it a new world, the Spirit.

If all living nature were not assembled on earth, then earthly nature would not have become satiated and bored with life, and, therefore, there would exist still other life, still other living beings. And this other life, these other sensible beings, would exist in place of our thinking, would assume, so to speak, the place that Spirit presently assumes, and thinking would exist beyond us, beyond the earth in a till-now-unknown other-worldly land. Assuming this to be true, it would be completely unnecessary, it would be completely impossible, in fact, for these other living beings to take up a particular world body or their own world. For, because Spirit, thinking, would exist beyond us, there would have arisen a gap; an empty place would have been opened in us, and, since nature has a *horrorem vacui,*[4] without a doubt, the other living beings would exist in the spaces made empty in us by the departure of reason; they would exist, as it were, in our pores. Our head, which is presently the organ of thinking, would be the world in which they would exist. Instead of these other living beings inhabiting their own world bodies, perhaps, at least very plausibly, thought itself would occupy those worlds into which we presently misplace these beings, and, instead of the brain, thought would have as its organ a star or all the heavenly bodies. And those who used to speak so much of the limits of reason and of its restriction by sensibility seem to have prophetically indicated the thought that reason, so restricted and oppressed here on earth, would have procured a freer and more suitable existence if it had obtained a Uranus or Saturn as its instrument of thinking. We have now arrived at the insight that the world or worlds that are presently taken up by Spirit, thinking, consciousness, and will could, would, and must be the dwelling places of these other living beings (if they exist), that perhaps those very beings that you fixate and imagine to be independent, particular, living, sensible beings are nothing but, in fact and truth, Spirit itself. Until you can prove to me that the human on earth does

79

not think, you will never be able to make me agree that there are living beings in the universe beyond the earth.

Everything that exists is not without end and limit, even including the infinite. The infinite is distinguished from the finite only because its limit is not another being outside of it; the infinite has itself as its limit. Thus, in the infinite, the limit does not exist as limit, is not restraint and oppression, but is delight, joy of the infinite with and in itself, is enjoyable self-knowledge, because its limit expresses its relation only to itself and not to another. Being, determinateness, limitation are posited together with one another; only nothingness is without limitations. Every reality is a demonstration of the truth of this proposition. There is only one weapon against nothingness, and this weapon is the limit; it is the only stable point of a reality, the only bulwark of its being. For the limit does not exist as externally circling, as the fence around the field; it is the middle that is proper and central to a reality. Thus, everything in nature is what it is, not because of the matter out of which it is constituted, but, rather, because of the limitation of the indeterminate matter, because of the determinate proportion, manner of unification, and degree of mixture of the matter. Just this determinateness of the proportion of the matter constitutes the limit and the essence of a thing. If the mode of unification of those realities that are called the elementary constituents of a thing changes, if this determinate mode changes together with the proportion of the elements that are limited by this determinate mode, then the thing itself changes. Thus, the essence and life of a thing is measure, form, kind, law. And this measure, by and within which a thing is what it is, is not something that extends only to a certain matter—for instance, the chemical components—but is a measure that penetrates everything, determines everything, dwells in everything. The entire life and essence of a thing is thoroughgoing determinateness, is one all-present measure. The proportion, for instance, of the chemical matter of this fish is not just something to be weighed and enumerated; but its organism, its entire body, also has its determinate form and *habitus*,[5] which

80

distinguish it from other animals. And what else is this *habitus* but measure, limit? Equally, the external relation of this fish is no boundless, indeterminate, indiscriminate relation. It moves itself, but it has a movement determined by its shape. It lives in a determinate climate, in a determinate element, water, but, again, not in any water, but in a determinate spring, river, or sea. Ocean water is as much water as that which flows in a river, and yet this fish, just because it can never escape the limit that is the center of its nature, the limit that determines and includes everything that exists in it, can live only in this and no other water.

You can experience this truth in yourself, though with spiritual modifications. You are a moral, free being. Other humans, from whom you are distinguished, are equally moral and free. The matter, as it were, the element in which you exist and of which you are constituted as a moral being is will or freedom. As matter, the will is equal in all humans; others will with and in the same will as yours; as the fish lives in water, the human lives in the universal element of will. But as the determinate fish lives in determinate water, you live also in a determinate will. By your kind of willing, the will that, as matter and element, is one and the same in all humans becomes your will, becomes specified, restricted, distinguished will, becomes character. But you, this particular subject, are now nothing outside of this specified will; this manner of willing, this limitation of the one self-equal will, is now your essence, is you. The character of a human is not his property or possession, but is one with the human as particular subject. If your character, your measure, your determinate manner of willing change, you change. You are what you are only within this measure.

Life itself has its necessary limitations, above and below which there is no life; the very place at which life resides and has its source is also its limit. Life is possible and actual only within the determinate kind and form of the elements, only within the general measure that nature on earth assumes. It is *the essence of life itself* to exist only on earth, to be possible and actual only within the limitation that nature possesses in the form and shape

81

of the earth. As it belongs to the nature of the trout to live only in this determinate water, as it belongs to the nature of a plant to be what it is only within the limit of a determinate climate, so it belongs to nature, to the essential character of life in general, to exist in nature only as it is this nature, only as it is earth, and therefore to be capable of existence only within the boundaries of a terrestrial year, and so on.

82   On the earth, there are determinate, distinct measures of life, there are stages, levels, and kinds of life that diverge from one another. Thus each species of animal and plant is its own kind and measure of life. But nature itself, as terrestrial nature, is the universal, sole, and ultimate measure of all these many particular measures; nature is the one measure that supports and embraces the different measures of life. To be sure, the measure of life, the earth, is a determined measure; but it is no finitely determined, finitely restricted measure. Rather, in its determinateness, the earth is also a universal, infinite, meaningful measure; it is a measure that imparts, engenders, and maintains within itself the most manifold kinds, distinctions, and opposites; the earth is an organic and organizing measure, a system. If the earth, the measure of life, were finitely determined, if it were not universal and infinite in its determinateness, then this measure of life might be, for example, the measure of a single species of plant or animal. Anything that is presently only one particular member in the system of terrestrial nature would be an independent whole, would be the totality itself. The terrestrial measure of life would then exclude distinction, separation, the rich manifold content that the earth possesses. And only if the earth were merely one determinate element, for example, water or one independent gold nugget, only if the earth were, as the measure of life, one determinate, limited measure, one determined kind, only under these conditions would there exist in this limited nature of earth the ground and the necessity of transcending it as a finite reality. But since there in fact exist distinct measures and kinds of life, and yet these many distinct kinds are comprehended and contained within the common measure that is the terrestrial nature itself, then the terrestrial

nature is the universal species of all life, the species that has developed all the possible modes of life as they exist on the earth; then the earth itself is the only measure, the insuperable limit of all life; then the determinateness of the measure that life on earth possesses is the absolute and ultimate determinateness of all life. Earth is the only possibility of life and its perfected actuality; the only other possibility is that of the unnatural, irrational, spiritless, and lawless possibility of the driveling imagination.

Thus the essence of life is the measure of terrestrial nature. Wherever all the conditions required for life are not completely and fully present—and not only the universal elements and matter, but also the determinate form, the measure, the determinate proportion, belong to these conditions—there is no life. Thus when, in the course of experience, you encounter no water or no atmosphere on a heavenly body, then reason, experience, and nature itself demand from you the belief and admission that there is and can be no life on it. Certainly one can imagine that just as the feathers could be plucked from the goose without it ceasing to be a goose, so indivisible life could be picked and pulled to pieces and yet still continue. And one can imagine that on the moon life consists of death, that dryness is wetness, that the bodies of lunar beings are made out of glass, that the imaginings and the little men of fantasy who drive to and fro to destruction on the massive, crude earth find delighted acceptance and secure existence on the tolerant heavenly bodies. But those who consider imaginability to be possibility, who believe that as the feathers can be taken from the goose, so the essential can be taken from the essence and the reality can be taken from the real, and yet the same essence and the same reality remain, before they instruct us of such matters in heaven, they might offer proof on earth of this separability of essence, for if it is at all possible that essence still remains essence when one takes from it that by which it is what it is, then it must be possible on earth. They also might prove to us whether life continues to be life when the marrow is torn out of the bone, when the heart is torn out of the body. They cannot object that these demands

83

84

stand in no relation to what they do. For life in general is not less indivisible than the life of the individual. Water, the determined measure of years, and the like are not less necessarily comprehended and enclosed in the universal possibility of life, in the nature of the animated world body, than the heart and the marrow are essential to, necessary for, and inseparable from the single organic body.

I already hear you reply to me, "Nature is lust for life. Such enormous spaces and so little life; how to make sense of it? What a contradiction!" But you forget to notice in your intoxication with life that the lust for life of nature is also the lust for death. The birth of one being is the death of another; the drive of self-preservation in nature is also a drive to destruction. You do not see how unfortunate existence and life are for a single being, which cannot exist without opposing and contradicting another being, or how miserably limited and conditioned life is because it can continue only with the limitation and condition that it is contradiction. You do not see that it therefore seems as if it might be, as it were, to some extent, so to speak, a misfortune to live, to be a living, single being, an individual. And you do not recognize how this condition, that life can continue only as contradiction, that every living thing has its mortal enemy, manifests a limit and the finitude of life itself. It is a shame that nature is not as lustful for life as you are, that it did not arrange reality according to your disposition, in which mere existence, sensible singleness, the living individual is the ultimate and absolute. If nature was lustful for life in the sense that you imagine, then certainly it would have separated, scattered, and 85   dispersed life. Nature would have appointed and furnished a particular world body for every particular species of animal and plant, but for every single human, who, even in his singleness, possesses a much more comprehensive, significant, and free existence than a species of animal or plant, it would have prepared a world body to be inhabited by him alone. This arrangement certainly would be more purposeful than the present one, where the hostile, mutually destructive things of life are so pressed together and piled on top of one another. How wonderful would be this arrangement! Death, this strange and serious fact in nature, which, if considered carefully, would deprive you of all hope that other beings exist on other world bodies, death would unquestionably disappear from creation. Such an independent human, inhabiting his own world, such an absolute human would never die. The human dies only by humanity; the human dies only because he exists and lives separately and at the same time in essential unity with other humans. Death is present only where there are both unity and distinction. If the state, and thus world history—for the origin of the state is the origin of world history—if language, and thus reason, originated by contract, then why shouldn't death be a product of community, of a contract, of human society, why shouldn't death, too, have its ground in the *contrat social*? Even the plants and animals have concluded an agreement and drawn up a contract among themselves to the effect that one makes way for the other, that the entrance into life of one is conditioned on the departure of the other. Thus, a particular species of plant, if transplanted to live all by itself on one world body, would possess an infinite sphere of existence there; with this infinity of the sphere of existence, and in this absolute aloneness and solitude, the ground and the necessity of death would disappear. By this dispersion of life, this multiplication of the individual to infinity, life would enter all the heavenly bodies, peace and tranquillity would exist on earth, eternal life would be present in all of nature. In this fashion two disadvantages would be removed at once, two bothersome and destructive flies would be dispatched with one blow.

86

Thus life on earth seems to you to be too little and limited for the great universe. The world seems to you to be worthy of an infinite Creator only if life is infinitely multiple, is as innumerable as the enormous horde of the heavenly bodies, is the host of the living, of those who enjoy existence and rejoice in themselves. Therefore, you expand and multiply this life to infinity. You transpose the appendixes to, the improvements and expansions on, this limited earthly life onto other bodies and into other beings, as if the spaces of the heavenly bodies stood vacant only so that you could place in them, as in a honeycomb, the sweet honey of your fantasies. But once again you stumble against the mere measure of your brain; you lose yourself at and in locality. While you imagine that creation can be made perfect and complete only by your filling out those empty spaces, while being swept away by the steam engine of your eccentric brain, you overlook a lack, a gap on earth that has not been filled. And this gap, which cries out to heaven, this most dreadful of all lacks, this empty space, which should have been a stumbling block for you before you cried out against the desolation of heaven, this great rent in creation, is the end, the limit, the negation of life itself, is death. For there is no life in death; it is the purest desolation, the most dreadful gap in life. Certainly a new being always takes the place of the dead being. But this being, which now exists, will someday be no more; this determinate being never returns, is eternally gone. The place where this being used to be remains empty forever; a being is *this* being but once; the human is this totally determinate human only now, only once. The other, newly distinguished being that replaces it does not fill the empty space of the previous being just because it is something different. To do this it would have to be completely the same as the past being. The whole world is as porous as a sponge; the whole earth is as punctured as a sieve; everywhere there are rents, splits, fissures. As many as have died, so many empty spaces and unoccupied places exist; every death is a powerful rent and crack in living nature. What is the hollowness and emptiness of the heavenly bodies, this harmless spatial lack, which is really only a lack in your imagination, when compared with the living, qualitative lack of life, when compared with the painful negation of life that is death?

You fool! In the simple lack you miss the real lack, in the imagined gap you miss the real gap! If your imaginings had a basis and reality in nature, the chain of the living would be interrupted by neither space nor death, for the living beings on Saturn or Uranus do not make up for the positive lack on earth. The other living beings would have to be the uninterrupted continuations of the beings that live here, continuations that are not distinct, but are immediately and inseparably connected to the continuation of the life of the earthly beings. The other living beings would fill up the place of death; the life of the other beings would become immediately one with the life of the earthly beings, so that the life of this plant, of this animal, would be in itself the unbroken chain of those heavenly beings. For example, this plant, which is now in bloom, according to the present melancholy and dark dispensation of nature, has a determinate end to its life. At the point where it now approaches its end, its life on Uranus, or the life of Uranus, would begin in it; as it previously developed in leaf, stem, and flower, it would now develop in the higher being of Uranus. (As in the fantastical arabesque paintings, perhaps the heavenly beings would sprout forth from stems and flowers.) After the termination of its period on Uranus, the period of another star would begin again in it, and so on into eternity. Thus, there would be no gaps in nature, no lack of life, only if the independent dwellers of the heavenly bodies (which, in your fantasy, are separated spatially from this life and which, therefore, do not fill out the gaps or still the pain of death) were periods, forms of life, and states of plants, animals, and humans, if they were prefaces and appendixes to their own earthly life. But at the same time, these heavenly periods should not be separated or distinguished from their other forms of life. Otherwise the plant in its Uranus period would be something different from the plant in its earth period, and with this change there would enter a no-longer-being, a gap to fill up, lest it become a lack in creation. Thus the world would be totally complete only if it contained no change, for in every change something passes away, and there arises with this perishing a not-being or a lack. And since all life rests on change, there would exist no lack of life in the world only if there existed in it no life at all. Only if no life is posited will you find no negation of life.

Thus, when you attempt to cancel the limits of life by populating the heavenly bodies with living beings, as the saying goes,

88

you put the plug next to the hole, because you do not animate and fill up death by this attempt. Leave death out of the world! As long as an "alas" and a "woe," a cry of death, press through my ears into my soul, I consider myself justified in asserting as bare imaginings these appendixes and postscripts living on the stars, and all your expansions, repetitions, and tedious resumptions of life. This last death rattle, even of a dying calf or pig, is the most expressive, or rather crying, proof of the empty spaces in nature, is a tone coming to us from the desolate depths of nature, which can instruct us concerning the farthest world bodies and which can reveal that death here on earth would not end life only if there existed another life, that death would not be the end of this life only if this life were not already the end and the limit of all life and, therefore, only if all possible life and forms of life were not already contained, developed, and realized in this life.

89

The representation that after death one wanders from star to star, that the stars are ready-made and comfortable dwelling places for living single beings, is empty and shallow and especially contradicts nature and Spirit because it pulls the great and serious tragedy of nature into the common realm of the bourgeois economic life of the philistine, because the bottomless abyss of nature is turned into a shallow meadow brook near which individuals pick charming forget-me-nots and relax with tea and coffee from the burning sunlight of actual life and reason, and in which they see only themselves reflected. In this representation, which transforms all of nature into a well-constructed palace or hotel in which one can stroll along from room to room, the fearful seriousness, darkness, and gloom of nature is totally overlooked. God did not create the world as a secretary of the treasury or an economist; the night in nature was produced out of the night in God. Gor forgot himself when he created the world. He produced nature, indeed *with* will and consciousness, yet not *out of* will and consciousness, but out of his nature, as it were, in the back of his consciousness. Not as cleverly reckoning head of the household or foreman, but as self-forgetting poet, he produced the great tragedy of nature.

If one asserts the more ancient principles of knowledge, one may rightly assert that that which is not the sufficient reason of the knowledge of a reality cannot be the sufficient reason of its essence and existence. But God grasped *only* as personal, only under the determination of personhood, God conceived only antipantheistically, only as an extreme that is opposed to substance, is not the sufficient reason of the knowledge of nature and thus is not the sufficient reason of its essence and existence. Only that being which is the principle of its own changes, which stands at the basis of all its changes as an all-present, essential unity, for which, therefore, changes are inward, are immanent, are determined by that being and identical with it, only that being has a history. The stone that changes hands from a beggar to a king, that travels from America to Europe and from there to Asia, still does not possess a history, for it is not the principle of these spatial changes. And, for the very reason that the stone is not the principle of these changes, they are not actual changes, not qualitative, inner changes, but are only external changes of place—in other words, displacements. But the plant has a history, for it is a principle that is identical with its changes. Change is not a superficial metamorphosis but a creation, an engendering of essential particular shapes; with every change, the self-changing reality enters a new essential determination of its concept. Thus changes are the inner life moments of a reality, and all changes taken together are the very living being of a reality. Therefore, whatever is or has a history, and thus is the principle of its changes, has life, not from something external, but from its own interior, has life of and by itself. History is life, and life is history; a life without history is a life without life. Certainly, external existence can be given and granted, but inner, essential existence, life, cannot be given. Otherwise the reality would have to exist before it was alive; the reality would have to be able to give itself. For only the reality that is in possession of its own being and essence is alive. Life is unity of essence and being; there is life only where there is absolute self-identity. Thus, whatever is alive has the ground and the principle of its being in itself; only that which exists in and from

90

91

itself has life. To live means nothing other than to be the *ground of oneself;* being-in-self, being-oneself, is the most conspicuous and least deniable determination of life. But can you separate being-in-self from being-ground-of-oneself? Not to possess one's ground in oneself means exactly being-outside-of-oneself, not to have and be one's essence inside of oneself. For the ground of a reality must be its essence, and only its essence is its ground. Where else but in its essence should the ground of a reality exist? Is not that which a reality is also that because of which it exists, and is not that because of which it exists also truly that from and out of which it exists? Take the proposition, "This essence lives; it exists in itself"; can this have any other meaning than that this reality exists in its ground and its ground lies within it? Life is present only when origin and existence are identical, only when the ground, the principle, of the being is the being itself, only when a reality does not step outside of its ground, but remains in it, while its ground remains in the reality. Existence is always original, always at the beginning. The watch is nothing but a watch, a dead mechanical product, because its principle, the ground of its existence, is not one with it, because the watchmaker, the inventive, spiritual human, and not the watch itself, is its essence. It is not being-in-itself, but rather its being-in-itself is outside of it in the Spirit in, with, and by which it is constructed and moved. The watch becomes a watch only when and insofar as it fulfills its purpose. Its most immediate purpose is to indicate the hours. But it indicates the hours only by movement, and this movement does not come from it—rather, the Spirit of the inventor is its mover, is that in and by which the watch is what it is. You, the person who winds up the watch, are only the external means of the Spirit of the inventor. In truth, though not in appearance, all watches are moved by and in the Spirit of their inventors. The watch does not exist in and for itself, is not a self, only because it has the principle from and by which it exists, not in itself, but in its inventor.

Now, to the eye of the researcher, nature presents itself totally as history. But history is incompatible with production and manufacturing; a mere product has no history. As history, nature is the ground of its own changes; nature is life, which is inseparable from history, as the ground of itself; it can be grasped and known only from and in itself. You can even persuade yourself of the truth of the thoughts just expressed by looking at yourself as a single being, as a being that is mediated, posited, and dependent. Your father and mother engendered you. As the actuality of the species in their unity of procreation, they are the ground of your being. You are a single being, therefore, a being that is posited in origin. But when you enter into life, that is, when you become independent—for independence is inseparable from life—the ground of your existence is no longer outside of you, but is one with you within you. You are no longer a child, a posited, dependent being—for that is dependent which is separated from and yet at the same time tied to its ground—your being posited, your being as mediated by others, disappears with your childhood. As a living, independent self, you are a being that is primary, original, beginning from itself, immediate, ungrounded. To be sure, you still maintain the dependence of childhood in your knowledge and preserve the relics of your descent in the sanctuary of your piety. But in life itself, in nature, all binding attachments are dissolved in the proud feeling of your originality, independence, and immediacy. Your true beginning is not your elders as determined and themselves posited individuals, but the human in these determined humans, the human species. That you become independent, a human, means nothing more than that you enter into the feeling of your immediate originality, of the ground and beginning of all humans, of the human essence itself. And your life begins only with your independence, only when your existence descends into its ground and begins anew, only when the ground of your being exists in you. A reality that has its principle and its ground outside of it is like a fabric that can be unwoven into threads that can be attached to another reality. The watch, for example, can be repeatedly divided into its threads, as it were, and woven onto other realities. But life is not a fabric; it is indivisible, infinite unity with itself. A living being is infinitely unified with itself and absolutely self-coherent. Accordingly, life is immediacy and originality, perfect self-adherence and self-ground. Thus, if you imagine that natural life is manufactured, produced, has its ground outside of itself, then you unravel life like a knitted stocking, you dismantle it like a clock, you strike life dead.

To be sure, Spirit is the ground of nature. But Spirit produces only in a spiritual manner, produces only that which is itself spiritual and living. Moreover, much more than will and consciousness belong to Spirit; will and consciousness (taken in their commonly used meanings) produce only mechanical results. But much more than will and analytical consciousness are needed for the production of living reality, or even for the works of genuine art and science; Spirit and genius are needed for them. Why do you wish to ascribe to your God only will and understanding, but not Spirit and genius? The artistic genius does not produce out of understanding, will, and consciousness, but out of the fullness of his soul, in which he is one with his productions and in which all his works are one, *with* consciousness, will, and understanding. Thus the works of genuine art are not mere works; they possess their grounds in themselves; they are therefore spiritual, inspired works. Nature is ground and principle of itself, or—what is the same thing—it exists out of necessity, out of the soul, the essence of God, in which he is one with nature. Thus even the stars must not be considered to be manufactured out of a well-constructing and well-arranging economic and financial wisdom, out of a Spirit that only manufactures machines, but they must and can be acknowledged as coming forth only out of life itself, out of nature and its history.

As already asserted, the life of the stars is defined, not by the fact that individuals exist on them, but by the fact that they are the incunabula, the primordial historical moments of nature. They are the golden youth and morning dreams of nature, in which the actual world of the future still exists only in fantasy, in enchanting brilliance. They are the fabulous and mythical Orient in nature, its paradise; they are the first pure beings; they

94

are, as it were, totally self-identical in their innocence; they have not yet been split into body and soul, into a subjective experiencing nature and an experienced objective nature, which is an act of separation and of becoming-conscious, of articulation and distinction, that takes place only on earth. In heaven nature only learns to spell; it first learns to read on earth. In heaven nature celebrates the holy night before Christmas, but Easter and Pentecost are celebrated on earth. The lofty but also subordinate position of the stars in the system of nature rests on the fact that they are the limits of all individuality; on the stars, all separating and determining being-for-self vanishes and is dissolved into indeterminate being.

Spirit exists without body and beyond body, for its existence is thinking, knowledge, and will. But the individual, who is not Spirit, but lives only by participation in Spirit, does not exist without a body. Rather, as a temporally and spatially determined being, the individual of necessity is a corporeally living or a live corporeal being; the individual is an individual only in this, his corporeal life. The individual who believes in his immortality is also convinced of this truth and, therefore, considers it to be proper and necessary to possess a body in the hereafter. However, this body is no longer such a gross, unwieldy, empirical, everyday jacket as the earthly body, but one that is woven out of very delicate, light matter, a body that is ideal, totally clear, and transparent. The individual also considers it to be very natural that, as a process of ever-ascending stages exists in the realm of Spirit, so, too, a never-ending progress to that which is finer and more perfect goes on in the corporeal world. Here again, it is indubitable that nothing but reason stands in the way of this imagining of a body that is distilled and sublimated into delicateness for all eternity, and that when one recognizes no limits, that is, no reason, one can imagine without hindrance a body that consists of nothing but light or the scent of roses and the gleam of lilies or, indeed, of nothing but Spirit, imagination, or a beautiful Mozart sonata. But here again disagreeable reason, which, because it is itself totally bound and limited, it everywhere exhibits boundaries, ends, goals, mea-

95

sure, and law, here again reason points to insuperable limitations. The ultimate in the series of bodies is the human body, which is already a spiritual, heavenly, ethereal body. A spiritual and heavenly body is nothing more than a body that is living and ensouled, that is inhabited, permeated, and activated by a soul. Earth, water, and stones are unspiritual, earthly bodies, are bodies that are bound by gravity. But the earthly body begins to approach the superterrestrial body even in the plant. In the plant, the body is already raised to heaven, and nature already experiences a resurrection and glorification of the body. In the human shape, the body finally attains its perfection, having progressed through the long series of stages of the great variety of animal shapes. The human body is inspired and illuminated no longer by a soul that is immediately identical with its corporeal shape, but by a purely ideal soul that is independent of all matter, that exists in itself, that is self-determined, that wills and thinks, that is a Spirit. Therefore the human body is the ultimate and truly beautiful shape.

The last sensible shape is the beautiful shape, for a beautiful shape is the only shape that is saturated and made transparent by Spirit, is the only shape that is illuminated by and that mirrors Spirit. And such a shape is also the highest and ultimate form of all corporeality. Something is beautiful only at the point at which it realizes its transitoriness. Transitoriness is inseparable from beauty. Transitoriness is not a result of beauty, but is the ground of beauty. Transitoriness does not approach from the outside or from behind; rather, the sensible is beautiful only in disappearing, in passing away. A being flares up into the colorfulness of beauty only in the urgency of the disappearing temporal moment, only at the end point of its existence, only at the boundary of its life. The luminous spark of beauty arises only when the beginning meets the end, only when the harsh extremes of being and not-being come together. As being possesses attractiveness, Spirit, meaning, and significance, not in persisting, but only in passing away, so a reality is not beautiful within and in the middle of its being, but where the boundary of its being meets not-being, at the ultimate boundary within which its being is still manifest, where it thus first experiences the significance of its being, and where there remain to it only reflection and recollection, as it were. Being becomes beauty only in this recollection, reflection, and mirroring; as, for example, the plant is beautiful not in its leaves, roots, or long-lasting stem, but only in the flower, the most transitory end point of its existence. The beautiful is the sensible in its transition to the spiritual. But the sensible enters Spirit only in passing away. Thus the sensible is beautiful only where it ceases to be sensible, only where it disappears. It is not beautiful after its disappearance, when there exists only the pure nothing of the sensible, its pure negation, the invisible Spirit, and it does not exist before its disappearance, when it exists and consists totally in the sensible; the sensible is beautiful only in the process of disappearing. Therefore, the human shape is beautiful only because it is the last shape, only because it is the outermost limit of all sensible individuality and corporeality, only because here nature takes leave of itself, disappears into Spirit.

97

But further, consider the living body as living, as organic; compare it to stones, water, and earth, or to a mechanical product, or even to your representations of the corporeal and the material. Is the living body constructed? Is it constructed from parts that can be placed outside of one another? As little as you can divide the light, as little as the soul can be divided, so little can you divide the organic body. It is organic only as living, but, as living, it is indivisible unity, inseparable, absolute totality. If you divide the organic body, it already has ceased to be organic and living. Because you divide it, it dies, it no longer exists. And it proves its indivisible unity just by the fact that it dies when it is divided. If it were divisible, it would still live after division. But when the organic body is divided, it is totally, indivisibly destroyed; just this unconditional not-being, this indivisible death, is the most visible testimony to the indissoluble, unconditional unity of the organic living body.

You say, "A body is that which is divisible; its parts are external to one another." Yet the parts of the organic body are not parts but members. They are not external to one another but are internal to one another. They are divisible only by external means, but they are one by their purpose, their essence, which is the soul; for, taken together, they generate only one purpose, only one activity, only one feeling, which is life itself. Because of this dissolution of the parts into members for one purpose, because of this indivisibly simple, essential, supersensible unity, the organic living body as organic is an incorporeal body, an immaterial matter, an invisible sensible reality. If you pass beyond the consideration of that which is merely material, of the mechanical, to the consideration of the organic body, you will see that it is a glorified, spiritual, supersensible body. Even nature has its heaven. And this heaven, in which the body is resurrected and glorified, is life, the soul. Thus, the resurrection and glorification of the body must be sought in nature itself, not outside of it or beyond it.

Although your representations concerning life, body, and soul are so absurd, so silly and foolish, that it would be too disgusting and too long-winded to illuminate in every particular the weakness of your mode of thinking about these objects, yet I still should take note of a few of your definitions in order to illustrate your foolishness. I defined the organic body as immaterial matter, as indivisible, as not bound to gravity. It is totally correct to say that the organic body is also material, that the arm is not where the brain is, that the brain is not where the heart is, and so forth, that, therefore, the organic body is a multiple reality with components that are external to one another. It is correct to say that the essential determination of matter is external relation and that, therefore, the organic body, inasmuch as it is included in the determination of external relation, is matter. But is this determination of external relation an essential determination, a determination that captures, that defines and characterizes the organic body? If all you are capable of saying and knowing concerning the organic body is that it is material, that it is body, external relation, then you say and know *nothing at all* of the organic body. When you consider matter to be that which determines the organic body, you do not define it by a determining and determined reality, but you make nothing itself into its determination. Certainly external relation is one determination of the organism, but it is only *sensible,* not essential; it is only superficial, not determining; it is only external, not inward; external relation is a determination that does not locate an actual reality in the organism, but only *negatively* determines it. Only that which forms the basis for your knowledge of a reality is its inner determination. But do you know anything about the organic body when you define it as material? On the contrary, when you state that the organic body is material, when you subsume it under matter, you make into its essential determination the empty abstraction and meaningless representation of a pure matter that exists nowhere in nature, and you abstract from everything by and in which it is an organic body. Is not everything member and purpose in the organic body; is not everything determined for one purpose, which is life itself? Does not this being of inner relation, this thoroughgoing unity of purpose, in which all is one, does not this absolute penetrability and transparency, in which one reality does not darken the other, in which no reality is impenetrable to the other, but in which one purpose permeates everything, does not all this demonstrate immateriality to be the inner, essential determination of the organic body? The animal is distinguished from plants, and still more from other things or essences, by the functions of eating and drinking. And humans eat and drink. But are eating and drinking characteristic, essential determinations of humanity? Is the statement that the human is something that eats and drinks a real definition of humanity? As foolish as this definition is, you are just as foolish when you subsume your body under your representation of mere corporeality and materiality, when you comprehend it only under the determination of any body, that is, of matter, and do not consider *incorporeality* to be the determination of your body. Your only concept, your only knowledge of life, of the organic body, thus consists in the fact that you have no knowledge and no concept of it. Your highest recognition arrives when you come to the recognition of your lack of concept. Thus, in relation to your own manner of thinking, you have raised yourself to the highest and true knowledge of the organic body when you know it as unknowable, when you conceive it as inconceivable. For you recognize thereby that the organic body is the actual negation of your representations of matter and soul (which, however, you still inconsistently consider to be representations that are absolutely impossible for you to relinquish), that these representations are no longer proper to it or define it, but rather disgrace and destroy it, and that, therefore, the real organic body cannot be grasped in your imaginings of a pure, naked matter and a pure, naked soul.

It is the same situation when you apply the determination of weight to the organic body. Does weight define and designate the organic body as organic? Do you define the organic body when you say that it weighs so many pounds? Doctors know life only after life, in death; they do not know life in life, the organic body as organic, but only as inorganic, as dead. In the dissolution and loss of the unity that alone constitutes the essential determination of life, thus, in death, that which is nothing in life appears to be something, appears to be a determination. If, for example, you say that the brain weighs two to three pounds, have you *defined* the brain, have you said something or nothing about it? To be sure, weight and ponderability define metal, as imponderability defines light. But the organic body is exalted over the determinations of both ponderability and imponderability; in other words, ponderability applies to the organic body but does not exist *in* it; it does not determine or define it, as the determination of a specific weight belongs to the essential definition of metal. Weight is an inner determination of a metal; thus a metal is bound to its place. But an organic body as such has within it the principle of unbounded movement; it can change its place; it is bound to no determinate place. Thus the weight of the organic body is a determination that is canceled, subordinated, and inessential to the extent that the organic body is not what it is because of its weight.

Like everything that moves in space, the living body overcomes spatial boundary only by means of time; it goes from one place to another only in time. Just by wishing and imagining, you do not move bodily to a distant place. The weight of the living body is a burdensome shackle to wishing and imagining. Therefore, since you always make your wishing and imagining into the criterion of that which exists and should exist, you are able to destroy this contrast between what is actual and your wish, so that you can say that a body that is appropriate to your wishes must exist. But I do not understand how and why you expect the existence of this longed-for, enchanted body only after the death of the organic, rational body. Any body that exists at a wished-for place immediately upon your wish is a body that is identical with your wish and therefore is a body that is itself a wish. The existence of this body is not nature, reason, reality, but is itself wish and imagination. If it were real, or if it had been real once, or if it were connected to a real world of the future, its reality and actuality would be a limit and a restriction to your wish. As an actual body, it would contradict itself as a body that is only wished for; it would no longer be as light, as gaseous, and as vaporous as the imagination. Any body that is not a real body, but is only a weeping and a wishing for a body, must, should, and can be only wishing and imagining. So why do you play such strange tricks as dating the existence of the imagined body only from the death of the organic body?

It is the same situation with divisibility as it is with weight and matter. The organic body can be struck dumb, it can lose members, arms, legs, and so forth. When a member is missing, is not this absence a defect, a lack? Lack, or defect, is a not-being that should not be. A being lacks because it should not lack; or, in other words, a lack is something that should not be lacking when it is lacking. Something lacks because it is essentially connected with, because it essentially belongs to, that from which it is missing. Because that which is missing essentially belongs to that from which it is missing, because there should exist a unity of that which is missing with that from which it is missing, because this unity alone is proper to the essence and truth of this reality, then that which is absent should not be absent. Therefore a lack exists in this contradiction between being and that

102

which should not be. Thus lack does not exist in a pure priva-
tion, a pure absence, but only where that which is absent is
essentially connected to, or is identical with, that from which it
is missing; that is, where the lack is simultaneously negated in
the true nature and inner essence of that in which it exists. Lack
and defect presuppose that which has no lack, that which is
complete.

When a human body has no eyes, this is a lack precisely because the lack that exists in this body is not present in the
organic body itself that is the essence and nature of this body.
The organic body itself is absolutely complete and without lack;
it is infinite. It is not a specific body beyond which lies an
infinite series of possible bodies, leading up to the complete
realization of the idea of body, but is the highest actual prototype and ideal, the absolutely real idea of all corporeality.
Therefore, as a body that itself is idea and prototype, that in its
existence is the true concept of the body, it is a spiritual body.
Your determinate individual body, the organic body in the
determinate singleness of its existence, as distinguished from the
organic body in its species and essence, is a mortal, lacking,
finite body, only because the organic body itself is absolutely
without lack, only because it is an immortal, divine body. The
organic body itself is the species, the essence, of your determinate, singly existing body. But the species, the essence, is no
abstraction. The essence exists, has existence; but the existence
of the essence is not existence in its singleness, is not this single
103   phenomenon, but is existence in its totality, is existence as all
single phenomena taken together, is the existence of all that is
single as an indivisible whole. Why is the missing eye a lack in
you? Because that which is missing in you exists in another. If
you add all single existences together, and if you integrate and
compensate for that which is absent in one by that which is present in another, you will discover that all phenomena taken
together constitute the adequate, pure, complete existence of
the essence itself, that, therefore, the organic body itself, which,
in relation to your single body, is species, is essence, is not an
abstraction, but is actual substance, has reality.

Finally, you will discover that actuality itself is the totally perfect essence that possesses no lack or defect. For the existence of the single being is single existence, while the existence of essence is actuality itself, because actuality itself is not single existence for itself, but is all existence together, is everything as it is one, is the unity of all mutually compensating and integrating phenomena. Therefore, because actuality is all phenomena in unity, there is no defect or lack in actuality, for negativities, particularities, lacks, and defects disappear in the unity that embraces all single reality. In every pain, the species celebrates the triumph of its unique actuality. The painful whimpering of the sick and the last moans of the dying are the victory songs of the species; in these, it celebrates its reality and victorious lordship over the single phenomenon. There are more philosophy and reason in your pains and sighs than in your whole understanding. You really philosophize only when you moan and cry out with pain. The only sounds of wisdom that come from you are the sounds of pain. For in your pain, you assent to and affirm the essence, the species, the absolutely perfect universal, the actuality of which you deny in your understanding. Your pains and sighs are the only ontological arguments that you can furnish for the existence of God. The only lecture halls of the philosophy of time are hospitals and sick bays. Why, when your eye is missing, is this a lack in you? Why do you experience pain when it is torn out of you? Because the absolutely perfect species, the essence, is the only true reality, because the existence of a defect in you, this something missing for you, is no reality, is nothing in your real substance, because the defect that exists in you should not exist, does not exist in reality and truth. Therefore, when your eye is torn out, you experience pain because you experience that the eye that is torn out cannot be torn from your substance, because you experience limit and absolute, not-being and being, all at once. In the feeling of a determinate lack, you possess at once the feeling of the nothingness of the totality of your single being on its own and the feeling of the sole lordship and reality of the substance that is perfect in itself. You die, not when just a single limb is torn from your body, but

104

when your body itself is divided. In other words, you die because the organic body itself is indivisible, absolute, infinitely one, because it is the species, the substance, the truly real. When your body is divided, the fact that your end is an immediate result of this division affords an argument for the existence and reality of the uniquely real indivisibility of the organic body itself. Such a *crimen laesae majestatis*[6] as, for example, severing the head from the torso immediately brings death with it. But the stroke of the sword that severs this head from its torso is not the ground, or cause, of the death of this living being; it is only appearance, external means, effect, occasion. Only the species, the substance of this body, is the ground of death. That which ends when it is divided is of indivisible substance. The real negation that appears as death, the true end of this single body when it is divided, is the indivisible substance; this alone is permanent reality. Thus the division of this single body is its not-being, its death, because it can no longer exist in the indivisible substance. Division is negated, is unreal, in the indivisible substance—for the substance is the negation of divisibility and of the being of that which is divided—division is the negation of indivisibility, but no division can affect or touch substance. Thus division is a self-negating negation; negation and destruction recoil, as it were, at the substance, and can only return to themselves. The negation of that which alone is real is self-negation. Thus, division and death, not-being, are simultaneous, identical. And thus division, in its inseparability from death, in its self-negation, is the solemn confirmation and affirmation of the autocratic substance.

Now as you use your representations of the hereafter only to patch up the rents and cracks in the wooden gutters of your *capitolium,* in the gutters of your concepts and knowledge, in which gutters you let escape the refreshing and animating downpour that flows from heaven onto the earth and in which you only collect the earthly parts, the mud and mire that the rain naturally brings with it, as you devise your hereafter only to stop up the hollow and empty gaps in your spiritless and insubstantial deadhead, so your transcendent, imagined body of the future, which is to be more excellent and spiritual than the organic body, is nothing but the vain haze and wind with which you fill up the hollow husks and (*sit venia verbo*)[7] swine bladders of your porous, defective representations of the most exalted and sacred objects, of the real organic body and life. Your higher, otherworldly body is nothing but the actual body here on earth as much and insofar as you do not recognize it. The actual organic body as it exists in its truth and reality is beyond the representations that you have of it. And although at certain points you hit upon their falsity, still you consider them to be basically the correct representations. And thus your otherworldly body is only the actual body as it exists in the reality of which you are ignorant and is therefore only the mistaken and misconceived present body. In fact, you have a presentiment of the real body in your representations of the transcendent body, but only in dreams, only in fantastical pictures, and thus you fill out your lack of knowledge by means of your imaginings. The imagination creates, objectifies in pictures, incarnates. The understanding takes its siesta on the smooth pillow of imagination, and in this blissful condition, by means of the magic of fantasy, the pores and gaps in its knowledge are condensed and embodied into the independent shapes of the hereafter. The pores and gaps in its knowledge, precisely because there is nothing in them, are the only bright spots in the understanding. In the sweet hour of its siesta, these many disparate points flow together into one shimmer, they condense into one gleam; the condensation presses to its heart. The understanding awakens, terrified; the vision is reality, the many bright spots, glistening together in one shimmer, constitute the starry heaven of the distant hereafter. The hereafter exists in the empty interstices of your head; it takes its beginning when your thoughts give out. And the genesis of this hereafter is so clear: your life, your manner of disposition and action, your perceptions and representations of the world and things have their beginning and ground in principles of thought that you have never questioned, or, rather, in one principle of thought that is absolutely valid for you and that you have never thought through. The true and

106

actual principle of thought is never a determinate thought, never an axiom that can be expressed definitely or in one single concept, but is the *mode of thinking* itself. All thinking begins in being and from being; this being from which thinking begins is just the mode and manner of thinking. Thus the essential being of an individual is also the mode of his thinking, for his manner of feeling, sensing, and acting, his whole existence, depends on and is determined by his mode of thinking. The world becomes for the individual what he represents it to be; as the world is to him, and what the world is to him, so it is. Your determinate and particular manner of thinking, which has never undergone the fiery test of skepticism and negation, now becomes for you the absolute foundation both of your being and of all of your representations, thoughts, and perceptions. But in the results of this principle, in its application, in the determination of the objects that follow from it—in other words, in your determinate representations, concepts, and perceptions—there dawns in you the consciousness of their lack, of their limitations, and, therefore, of the defects of their principle. However, you become aware of the limitations and lacks in your principle only within its results, only within the determinate representations, and not within the beginning, not in and at the principle of thought. And since the world that you have imagined stands for the real world, inasmuch as the determinate mode of your representing and thinking is to you reason itself, indubitably true, essential being itself, you make the lack in your knowledge into a lack in the world. And since the Spirit, the courage, the serious free will to give up your standpoint, the foundation of your manner of thinking and being, have been broken in you, then, instead of facing the crushing awareness of the emptiness and limits of your manner of thinking and knowing, you pass beyond the supposed limits of the imagined world that you maintain to be the real world, and the hereafter now stands there in its full splendor and magnificence. Your hereafter is nothing but the boundary between your representations of the world and the real actual world. Your hereafter is the true and actual knowledge of reality, which, to you, is hereafter, distant, lying beyond your mode of thinking. Where you cease to think, there thought first begins. Where you designate an object as unknowable, there it becomes an object of thinking and knowing. Where your hereafter exists, there begins the actual world. For that which you mean by your hereafter and call your hereafter is very close to you, is one with your representation and imagination. That which is infinitely distant from you, the real hereafter for you, is actual nature, the actual world, the actual body, and so forth, and, thus, where the better world begins. Your intended, imagined real world ceases where the real world begins. Where the representations of a hereafter arise in you, there *your* representations of the real world and the real world itself, as it appears according to you and exists in your representation, perishes for you. You posit another, second world, but this second world is only the first actual world, as it exists outside of and beyond your representation.

108

The noble, immortal individual does not concern himself in the least with the nature of his future body, or with how life and death are related, or with whether it is even possible that a determinate person could remain the same person when he abandons his determinate body. Rather, he considers it to be entirely beneath his dignity to inquire whether the soul is capable of departing from its body and whether it really does depart from it in death. Instead, the individual presupposes it to be absolutely true that, as the bird is confined in a cage, as water is contained in a vessel, so the soul is contained in the body, that the body is the dwelling house, the prison, of the soul, and that, in death, the soul probably rises out of the body like smoke from a chimney. But the soul neither is contained in the body nor can be excluded from it; it exists neither in the body nor outside of it and thus cannot depart from it. For in both cases, if it could exist inside or outside of the body, it would be a thing that is contained in determinate spatiality and determinate corporeality. Thus it would itself be a determinate, corporeal reality, for only that which is corporeal can exist inside or outside of a body.

Only incorporeality is the extracorporeality of the soul. Thus

109   the soul exists in the body only in a nonspatial manner, not in a
sensible mode and manner, but in a spiritual, essential mode
and manner. The soul exists in the body in the way that a painter
exists in his brush, a musician exists in his instrument. Therefore, although the soul is incorporeal, it is just as little a soul
without its body as a master is a master without his servant, as
the end is end without means, as the artist is an artist without
his instrument, for the body is an instrument of the soul. The
body is a boundary or a limit for the soul as little as his brush is
a limit for the painter, unless by chance he himself is a brush.[8]
The brush would be a limit to the painter only if, for example,
he wished to play the clavier with it, or blow the flute, or work
in stone with it. The organ has its determination and essence in
the activity for which it is an organ; it is only the external form
of the realization of the activity. As proper and adequate to this
activity, it constitutes no hindrance, no restriction to it.

If one is to express the truth in the sharpest, harshest opposition to the traditional representations concerning soul and body
—and truth is always expressed in opposition to the lie, as virtue
speaks only as a fury against evil—one must grasp the relationship of the soul to the body in the following manner: the soul is
related to the body as the fire to its fuel. The body is the wick
and candle, the nutritive fuel of the soul. Where there is no fuel,
there is no fire. One can say that to this extent the fire is dependent on its fuel and must be bound to it; the fuel is the instrument of the fire. But insofar as it consumes and destroys the
fuel, the fire is its lord and master. As the fuel that the fire
destroys is flammable, and as the fire, the actual burning, is
only the realization of the flammability of the fuel, as nothing
that happens to the fuel does not also originate from it, similarly, neither is the body external to the soul nor is the soul
110   external to the body. The soul does not come from anywhere,
but it only comes *from* the body into the body. For the body is
no pure substance, no barren matter; as the fuel that burns is
flammable, the body intrinsically, in and for itself, is ensoul-
able, determined for a soul. Ensoulability, or determination for
a soul, is the inner determination that is identical to the body;

the soul is the realization or the actual existence of this inner ensoulability. Only that which the body is in and for itself is revealed and comes to existence in the soul. But just as the fire goes out when it has consumed all the flammable material, so, too, the *determinate* soul, inasmuch and insofar as it is the determinate, particular soul of this determinate, particular body, ceases together with its determinate body.

In fact, however, only the determinateness of the soul ceases. The soul itself, as it exists determinately, also exists in itself, and, as it is determined, it is also distinguished and free from itself as determined. In this freedom from determinateness, the soul is identical with itself and, as is self-evident, is therefore immortal. That which has a species and which has this species, and not itself, as its substance and concept is mortal. But the soul, unlike the individual, is subsumed under no species; as its own concept and substance, the soul is infinite and therefore immortal. But the soul is mortal insofar as it is united with the single existence of an individual and is distinguished from itself as self-identical substance. Spirit, consciousness, reason, and soul constitute that which is absolutely self-identical substance in all variety and multiplicity. Thus, in the strict sense, one cannot speak of the single soul, nor can one speak of souls in the plural. For singleness is inseparable from sensibility, corporeality, and spatiality. Only the sensible has a plural; only that which is sensible in its existence and supersensible in its essence, only that which is subsumed under a species, exists as several, many, single. Multiplicity is inseparable from singleness, from any sensible existence. Therefore, you do not know soul when you know only souls or one single soul. You know the single soul only as the famous *Orbis pictus* represents it in a colorful painting.[9] One can feel, paint, grasp the single soul because it is nothing but the existing individual, the single human as he is totally embodied. But precisely this soul is mortal, because it is no longer soul, but the single, sensibly existing human, or soul in its determinateness. If the single soul has consumed, as it were, its body, if it no longer possesses nutritive fuel in its body, if, by continuous use, it has worn out and eaten up its body, if it

111

no longer has matter as its opposite and object, in which it actively proves itself, if it no longer possesses that which it negates, consumes, and masters in order to be what it is—soul—then death must follow. The body is the opposite and object of the soul; the soul is soul only in the continuous conquering and negation of its own opposition. Immateriality is no dead, stable, static predicate that depends on the body as a property depends on a reality; immateriality exists as such only as negating and consuming matter. Once all substance and power have been sucked out of the body—and the single body, in and for itself as single, is a finite, obsolescent instrument of limited capacity—so that it is no longer capable of being an opposite, then the determinate single soul disappears together with its body. Soul is no thing, no dead reality, no stable, fixed essence that sits in its body like an oyster in its shell; it is pure life, pure activity, sacred, supersensible fire. It is never completed, never a finished reality, never a product; static being is never proper to it. It always *becomes,* it never *is.* It is eternal arising; it remains forever in its beginning. Beginning, middle, and end exist only in finite reality, but soul remains within itself, is eternally youthful and new beginning. But this pure activity that is soul, as it is determined, inasmuch and insofar as it is identical with the single conditioned body—that is, to the extent that it is an individual—ends together with the body.

112

Most believers in an individual immortality, when they speak of a body in the future life, appear to distinguish body and soul. And yet if one puts together all of their representations and opinions, they appear to represent the soul as somewhat corporeal, as a delicate material in distinct figure and form. Like the ancient Father who asserted that the soul is a body of a unique kind and quality, a fragile body of brilliant colors and with a completely human shape, they seem to represent the soul as nothing but the inner human, the invisible individual, the mirror image, the reflection of the individual's individuality into himself. They imagine that the soul must be something vaporous, congealed into a distinct figure, and thus something that is soft, heavenly blue and shimmering with light, or at least something ghostlike and spooky. Were this not true, how else would they believe in their own immortality, how else would they refuse to acknowledge death as final, how else would they say that the soul departs from the body, how else would they speak of a real, a spatial, sensible separation of the soul from the body? When one shows them that someday they will not exist, how could they conclude from this, "Therefore, after death we blend into the world soul or the primal matter; therefore, the soul is dissolved into the World Spirit"? In such a way, caught in worse than animal selfishness, which never allows them to attain the insight of the purest of all essences, they contaminate the pure and sacred essence of soul with their sordid representations and their muddy modes of thinking. In such a way, the eternally moving and living, burning and flowing essence is petrified into the rigid picture of the individuality of the soul in the dark, cold grotto of those distressed and compulsive spirits who have crept into the charming toad skins of their selfishness, of those virtuous souls who, out of belief in God, out of virtue and piety, out of self-sacrifice, believe in that which cannot be sacrificed, in the eternal continuation of their own selves. Their belief in their immortality stems from their belief in God or virtue, which is to say that murder stems from love for humanity, that drunkenness stems from abstinence, that promiscuity stems from chastity! What incredible phenomena are your virtue and piety and your belief! Because the foundations of your virtue and belief, the exalted authorities on which you ground them, are only your sordid representations of soul, life, and Spirit, then if your false representations are destroyed, your virtue and your belief are destroyed.

113

By stripping that which is sensible from sensible and spatial expressions, such as, "The soul is in the body; the soul is outside of the body; the soul departs from the body," by extracting their conceptual meaning and by reflecting on the significant distinctions of soul and Spirit or thinking and reason, one recognizes that the representation "The soul is in the body" has no meaning other than that soul is experience, and that the repre-

sentation "The soul is outside of the body" has no meaning
other than that soul is not just soul and nothing else, but is also
freedom, consciousness, reason. Soul as experience is the
ground and origin of individuality. Insofar as soul experiences,
it is individual and, as such, one with the body. But it is one
with the body in such a way that it is the all-present unity of the
body, self-identical in all that is spatially distinct. Since experience constitutes that which is called life, since a life without
experience is no life, and since there is only as much life as there
is experience, then, insofar as soul is understood as the principle
of life, it can be said with full right that soul is experience or the
process of experiencing. "The soul is in the body," expressed
rationally, means that the soul relates itself to its body, that the
body is its object, for I exist in that which is my object. The only
way in which soul or Spirit can exist in a reality is by that reality
being its object. Now, the object of soul in experience is sensible
reality. Specifically, its object is either other sensible realities
that are mediated through its own sensible existence, its body,
as in sensory experiences; or its object is its own immediate sensible existence, as in pain and pleasure; or, finally, its object is
both the other and itself. But also, in experiencing, soul is
already in and for itself, already object to itself, for how could
it experience something, how could it be its own object or its
own body be its object if it were not at the same time object to
itself? But soul in experiencing is object to itself only insofar as
its object is its body. It is not by and in itself immediately, but it
is object to itself only by means of and in the objectivity of the
body. However, "The soul is outside the body," when separated from its crudely sensible connotations, means, in its true
thought, that soul is thought, freedom, will, reason, self-consciousness. For as Spirit and no longer as experience, soul is not
directed or drawn to the sensible and its body, but exists only
within itself and therefore outside its body. As Spirit, soul is
object only to itself; it exists, not by means of the body, but by
means of itself; it is object to itself purely by and in itself. Even
from the standpoint of reason, soul makes the sensible, the
body, into its object, but in this case the body is an object of

114

willing or thinking; soul makes the sensible into its object, not by means of the sensible, but only by means of itself, only in and by itself, and, therefore, in this sense, outside of the sensible. It is certainly natural for us, when we make the body an object of our thoughts, to mediate reflective consideration and knowledge of the body through sensory experiences. But we do not think either by means of the senses or by means of the brain. Senses are only the external means for thinking. One can think and know only by means of thinking and knowing, just as reason does not think with the brain—such an operation would indisputably belong among the greatest curiosities under the sun —but thinks with itself. The brain is only the sensible and therefore external organ that regulates, by its health or deformity, the entrance to reason of the sensible individual. The true and therefore invisible organ of thinking is thinking itself, just as the true organ of the artist is not the hand nor the brush, but the artistically gifted soul of the artist. Certainly, the artist must have hands, but they do not make him into an artist; they are only external conditions and means. The inner, absolute condition, the absolute organ of art, is art itself. The painter actually (that is, in essence and truth) paints, not with the brush, but with art. Therefore, as the sensible representation "The soul is outside the body" contains the thought that soul exists in itself, is related to itself alone, and therefore is Spirit, reason, so the sensible picture "The soul exits from the body, it separates itself from the body" expresses only the definition of the soul becoming Spirit, the arising of reason in the soul, an arising that exists only for us, but not for soul. "The soul separates itself from the body" means (though not expressed and comprehended with the meaning and representation that you attach to it, but as it is expressed and comprehended in the true concept) that soul distinguishes itself from the body, separates itself from experience, retracts itself from all sensibility into pure relation to itself, and, in this abstraction or severance from the body, in this free relation to itself, in this unity with itself which retires from and excludes the living body as mere matter, as an other that is foreign and indifferent to it, soul is self-consciousness and thinking

115

(although this exclusion of nature as mere matter is valid only as thinking self-consciousness first awakens, not in the continuation and center of thinking).

116   But if you believe that the separation of the soul from the body and its being-outside-of-the-body signify and can signify anything more than that soul distinguishes itself from the body and, in this distinction, is thinking and reason, then you must represent the relation of soul to the body as a spatial relation and represent soul itself as a spatial reality. Thus, because you really do imagine that the soul departs from the body in death, you turn the spiritual, essential, inner disembodiment of soul, its spiritual being outside of the body, into a spatial disembodiment, and you thus imagine the highest activity and essence of soul—for this is Spirit—as a particular, spatial, and temporal event that occurs only with death. If certain diseased phenomena of the soul consist in the fact that, for some people, imaginings take on external existence, that, for example, for those people who have doubles, the sensible representation of oneself, one's picture of oneself, confronts one as an independent being, that one and the same person falls apart into two persons and the person sees himself outside of himself in space, and if the madness of these phenomena rests on the fact that representations become fixed in the human, become embodied, as it were, take on sensible, spatial existence, that representations change into immediate affections, into qualities, passions, and conditions, then your belief in immortality, insofar as it is the belief and representation that in death the soul really, actually departs from the body, is a theoretical madness, a theoretical disease of the soul. For as the insane person embodies, fixes his representations, and as they take on sensible reality for him, your presumed disembodiment of the soul only embodies it. You thus change soul's liberation and freedom from the body, the becoming of reason, freedom, and self-consciousness, which is an inner, eternal, spiritual activity, which is therefore Spirit itself, the highest activity and essence of soul, into a particular condi-

117   tion, a passion, an event taking place in space and time. For according to your belief, the soul should become free from the

body only *after* death or *at* death, should really depart from the body, therefore, in a spatial, sensible manner. Thus your belief in immortality, insofar as you base it on the nature of soul, rests on extremely material representations of it. Except that your materialism is very different from the materialism that is commonly given the name.

III Spirit, Consciousness

I hope that you will at least agree that as a spatially and temporally determined, living individual, you have an essence. For if you have no essence, it is self-evident that you are the worst and lowliest of anything that even barely exists, because everything that exists has an essence. But as you assent to this (and I do not doubt that you do), you also immediately recognize that you are not your own essence. For precisely by the fact that you affirm that you have an essence, you create a separation and distinction in yourself, and you express, in this separation, that you are not your own essence. Indeed, whether or not you are aware of it, you continually make this separation and distinction throughout your entire life; that which you call your better half rests precisely on this separation and distinction. Yet, truly this is not merely your better half, but is that which is best and highest in you, is your true totality, your essence and substance. For precisely because of this free separation and distinction, you are not just a living, ensouled essence, but also a conscious, spiritual essence. Everything that lives, indeed, everything that exists, has an essence and is divided and distinguished into existence and essence, yet every reality does not divide and distinguish itself into these. But you are a conscious essence; you possess an essence that is not mere essence but is more than essence, that is Spirit or consciousness, precisely because you separate   118
and distinguish yourself from your essence, and, by and in this distinction, you make your essence into your object. Thus, as your essence is your object, you are also object for yourself in your essence. That which is your essence as an individual is

clearly the species, your species as a human, therefore, the human species. Thus, the species, humanity, is object for you as you distinguish yourself from your essence. But this distinguishing and objectifying is not a particular activity and action that is distinguished from your essence, or, indeed, that is external to it, but is an activity and action of your essence itself. You distinguish yourself from your essence only by and in your essence; that you can distinguish yourself from your essence and make it into your object is itself your essence. This activity of distinguishing that is one with your essence and is your essence is Spirit or consciousness. You are conscious because you distinguish yourself from your essence. Therefore, distinction is included in consciousness; you cannot separate distinction from your consciousness as if distinction were something particular. In other words, distinction from your essence and your essence itself constitute one essence. You can separate yourself from yourself and distinguish your essence from yourself only because your essence is distinguished from all other essences of nature by the fact that it distinguishes itself from itself, is object for itself. You are conscious of yourself as a particular individual only because the purely universal essence in you is object for you. But the essence in you is object for you only because it is also object for itself. Therefore, you are conscious of yourself in the self-consciousness of the universal essence, Spirit.

Because you are conscious, you must distinguish consciousness itself from that of which you are conscious, your object. You yourself, this determinate, single human, this particular subject or individual, or the person, are the object of consciousness, for the person is the conscious individual insofar as he is conscious; the person is singleness as and as much as singleness is object of consciousness. Thus, the object of which you are conscious as you are conscious of yourself is a single, particular object, is you yourself. But consciousness itself is purely universal; knowing is an activity of essence, of Spirit itself. Consciousness as such is self-equal, self-identical, one in all humans. Only conscious beings are various; variety belongs only to the objects that are determinate persons who know themselves in con-

119

sciousness. In their knowing, all humans are one, as if undivided, but in that which they know, they are various and separated, for that which they know in the knowing that is consciousness is just themselves, the various particular persons. Consciousness is the light; persons are the colors. I see colors only in the light, but I cannot see light in and by means of colors. If consciousness itself were one color, if it were one with the colorful particular person, I would see and know neither myself nor others, as little as I could see one color if light itself were one with that color. Colors are the objects of light as persons are the objects of consciousness. Persons are various, are colors, only in distinction from the pure essence of the light, the essence that, as self-equal and self-identical, lies at the basis of all colors. The particular is visible only in and by means of the universal; distinct realities are objects only within that which is unity; the different is object only within that which is self-identical. Persons are persons, are self-conscious individuals, only in the pure, bright, heavenly light of consciousness, which is free of all distinctions, colors, and particularities. As the light is broken up into colors only at determinate terrestrial matter, so consciousness is broken up into the colors of persons only at the objects, only at individuals.

You are conscious not only of yourself but also of other persons and other sensible objects. An infinite multiplicity and variety, the countless host of finite beings, is object for you as you are object for yourself. Since you are one determinate person, are a particular, distinct being, this infinite multiplicity cannot be your object in and through you, who are yourself one of the many, but it becomes an object only in the infinite unity and serene universality of consciousness. When you say, "I am conscious of myself, I am object for myself," do you believe that the I by which you understand yourself as this particular person is identical to that for which it is an object when you say, "I am object for myself"? If the person, this human who is object, and the I for whom this person is that object were one and the same person, there would be no possibility of knowledge and consciousness in you. This unity of your particularity

120

with itself would exclude the only distinction within which knowing is possible. But when you say, "I am conscious of myself," you create a distinction between subject and object, or between objectivity and subjectivity in you. Since distinct determinations ground distinction, they are required for the distinction between subject and object. If you distinguish into subject and object without distinguishing something, you create a bare distinction without distinction, without distinct determinations. Actually, no distinction at all is posited between subject and object when you simply say that one is subject and the other is object. What determinations that distinguish the person as knowing and the person as object should there be other than those of universality and identity and those of particularity and variety? The knowing person in you, for which you are object, is an absolutely self-identical person, distinguished from your distinct particularity, universal in all persons, the person of Spirit itself. More accurately, this knowing person in you is the self-consciousness of Spirit, autonomous and subsisting within itself. This self-consciousness of Spirit is the absolute ground and principle of your personhood and makes it possible for you to be conscious of your individuality. Spirit is conscious of itself, is object for itself; individuals or persons are themselves Spirit insofar as Spirit is object for itself. But Spirit is not object for itself as this or that individual, not as plural, not as individuals in their singleness and multiplicity; rather, Spirit is object for itself as all individuals, as individuals are one. Thus, as Spirit is itself as it is object for itself, it exists in individuals and simultaneously in itself in autonomous distinction from them. How could you be conscious of yourself, make yourself an object, if that in which you perceive yourself, the particular person, were not object for itself, were not pure self-consciousness, were not Spirit's consciousness of itself? How could you conceive yourself, if thought did not conceive itself? How could you be conscious of yourself as this individual if your essence were not conscious of itself, were not self-consciousness? What would be the source of your consciousness if consciousness were not your essence? Consciousness cannot come to you from you yourself or anywhere else. But how could consciousness originate in your essence if your essence itself were not self-consciousness? Yet this self-thinking thought, this self-conscious essence, is just Spirit itself.

Now, just as colors change, just as they arise and pass away, so too determinate persons pass away, because they are not self-consciousness itself, but only its objects; or they are only subjects but not pure subjectivity, the principle of subjects. What is death but the action whereby the subject emerges out of its principle and ground, out of subjectivity, separates itself from subjectivity, and thus becomes mere object? That which is only an object is dead. You are living and conscious—for where consciousness is bound to life, there is no longer life as such, but the consciousness is life—only as you are object for yourself. However, as already established, the I for which you are object is not the same person as you, but is the pure I of Spirit itself, which is universal and self-identical in all persons. As person, as object, you are distinguished from the I that is Spirit, and this distinction has its sensible appearance and manifestation in death, in which you become a mere object. Death is just the   122
withdrawal and departure of your objectivity from your pure subjectivity, which is eternally living activity and therefore everlasting and immortal. As you inwardly distinguish yourself from your essence, so, too, must you be separated from your essence externally, sensibly, in your existence, for everything spiritual, inward, and essential has its materialization, its manifestation, in which it enters visible existence. Death comes only from the human into the human; it is only the accomplisher and executor of humanity's own action. Only the ungodly, lowly manner of thinking understands death as an external law, as a strict natural necessity. Where there is no Spirit, no freedom, no essence and inner nature, there is no death. For where there is no inner distinction, there is no freedom; where there is no inner distinction, there is no death. Death presupposes Spirit. You die because you are a free, thinking, conscious being. Consciousness is division; only that which can oppose itself to itself within itself, only that being which can distinguish its essence from

itself, which can place its essence above itself, which can subsume itself as a determinate and single reality under its essence, and which can relate itself to itself as to its object in this manner, only that being is conscious. But you die only because you are an object, only because you distinguish yourself and are distinguished from your essence, and the inner distinction must also become external, natural departure; the inner action of objectification must also be manifested as objective being in nature. Thus, death comes only from Spirit, from freedom. The ground of your life that is consciousness and division is also the true ground and origin of your death. Thus, too, plants and animals die only because presently Spirit breaks out in them, because presently freedom takes root in them, and because there begins in them an inner breaking and distinguishing into species, universal, essence, and into existence, singleness, appearance, or, more properly, into subjectivity and objectivity.

123 Oh death! I cannot wrench myself free from the sweet consideration of your soft essence, so inwardly fused with my own! Gentle mirror of my Spirit, reflected splendor of my own essence! Conscious Spirit has arisen, this universal, self-beholding light has broken forth out of the break and division in nature's simple unity with itself. And as the moon shines by the light of the sun, so you, in your soft glow, only mirror the burning fire of the sun of consciousness. You are the evening star of nature and the morning star of Spirit. The fools of sensible knowledge consider the one star to be two. But to the wise, you light the way out of the land of dreams to the birthplace of the true Savior, Spirit. The fools imagine that they arrive at Spirit only after and by death, that spiritual life arises only after death, as if a sensible negation could lead to Spirit, as if a sensible negation were the ground or the condition of Spirit. They do not see that death already presupposes the existence of Spirit, that death only succeeds Spirit, and that the sensible end is only the manifestation of the spiritual and essential end. The morning star does not bring the morning; it is only a manifestation of the morning.

The representation that death came into the world because of the Fall is a true and profound representation to the extent that it makes death dependent on a free action; it recognizes the ground of death in Spirit. But the truth of this representation is lost because the action of Spirit is turned into the action of an individual, because a universal spiritual action is turned into a particular, fortuitous, moral action, because an eternal action is turned into a temporal action. Thus, for the other individuals after Adam, death becomes once again an external, spiritless necessity. For the moral action of an individual concerns only this individual; as moral, this action is to be imputed only to this individual, and thus its consequences can spread to individuals different from the sinner only by blind and undifferentiating necessity. It is totally inadmissible to take Adam to be the idea of humanity, its representative, in whom other humans are supposed to have sinned. For, as sinner, as moral agent, Adam is only a single being, an individual; thus, his sins and moral actions do not in the least apply to others. Therefore, other individuals can be implicated in Adam's sin only through an external, inconceivable necessity. Moreover, in this doctrine, death for other, nonhuman beings remains an external, inconceivable necessity. "Other creatures also die, but their death is nothing compared to human death. For the birds in the air, the fish in the water, and all animals on earth die, not because of God's wrath and displeasure, but by nature and by the divine ordering for the benefit of humanity. But the death of humans is a miserable, wretched death, for it comes from God's wrath and displeasure," and so on.

"Therefore, there is nothing after death?" Exactly so; if you are everything, then when you die, there is nothing after death. But if you are not everything, then after death everything that you were not remains. If you are humanity itself, Spirit, consciousness itself, then, naturally, everything is over when you die. However, I think that I can say that you are not God, but a human. And because you are not God, there are more beings that are like you. You are not the one and only human; many other humans exist besides you. Do you refuse to believe that the plurality of humans also have their ground and origin in your essence? Do you believe that it is only by chance that a plurality of humans exists? Rather, must you not be persuaded that other independently existing humans not only belong to your existence but also belong essentially to your essence? Otherwise, you must believe that you are the only human in existence. For if you can separate yourself from other humans, if they are accidental to your inner reality, then the essence of humanity is already totally realized and contained in you, then you are one with the essence of humanity. But if you exist alone in your essence, if you are not necessarily and essentially related to others, then you exist independently in your existence, for independence in existence follows from independence in essence. But now, as experience manifestly teaches me and as you seem ready to grant, since you do not exist alone, then we both are bound to be convinced that the existence that is inseparable from us is also inseparable from the existence of other humans, and that other particular individuals belong to our essence, our nature, with no less necessity than we belong to it. Also, we attest, in many actions and experiences, but especially in the act of love, that our essence demands other essences and, in fact, in such a way that love appears to be only the materialization and sensible manifestation of a more profound and lofty union, of a union that is more truthful than love itself. Thus others remain after your death, your essence remains after your death; humanity remains uninjured and undiminished by your death. Humanity is eternal; infinite Spirit guarantees it. Spirit is eternal; consciousness is everlasting and infinite; freedom and will are withdrawn from all of nature and therefore from death. Thus persons, conscious, willing, free beings, will also exist for eternity. But you as a determinate person, as only an object of consciousness and not consciousness itself, must at some time depart from consciousness, and a new, fresh person will replace you in the world of consciousness.

It is strange that humans recoil only from the abysses of the future but not from those of the past, that they turn away in distress, troubled about being or not-being only after life but not before it, that they look only forwards and not backwards. Already, before life, you were nothing. Since you seek to escape the knowledge of the truth with all kinds of imaginings, let us suppose that you existed before life, that, somewhere, you were already inserted or enclosed in individual boundary and formation. Still, nothing would be gained by this, for you are not aware that you once existed. The being of the human is only conscious, personal being; one's being is related only to knowing. The duration of being is measured by the duration of knowing; personal being is terminated with the termination of knowing. An existence without my knowing that I am is no being for me. It could be that only in this life are we unaware that we existed before life and that someday this previous existence will be revealed to us. But even if this were true, you would still never banish the nothingness from that which precedes your course of life. If at some time it will be revealed to you in retrospect that you previously existed and lived, still, that existence and that life will have been over once and for all.

But why is it necessary to go beyond this life? In the earliest time of your life, you were not yet you, this personal, determinate being. A being becomes personal only with the determinate comprehension and grasp of himself. A person has the measure of his being and duration only with and in this personhood. You know, not from yourself, but only from others, that you were once a child and that you are the same being that you were as a child. Others are entwined and woven into your inmost life, into the unity of the consciousness of your own particular personhood, to such an extent that your knowledge of yourself is mediated by others' knowledge of you. Your consciousness of yourself was originally outside of you; others were your consciousness, were the knowledge of you; your being was taken up into the knowledge of others. Only later, when you objectified yourself bodily and externally, did you also become inwardly independent. At that point the knowledge that others had of you became your own knowledge, the external consciousness of

126

you became your inner consciousness. Knowing entered you,
or, rather, you entered knowing. You now took over the place
that others occupied on your behalf. You received from the
hands of others, as it were, a consciousness that had already
been prepared for you. Just as you once lay physically enclosed
and enveloped in your mother's womb, your self's womb was
the consciousness of the others by whom you were embraced
before you enclosed yourself. But throughout life others'
knowledge of you and your knowledge of yourself through your
knowledge of others remain knowledge that is inwardly interwoven. As your first food, your mother's milk, was prepared in
your mother's body, so you suck in your personhood, as it
were, at and from the breast of humanity. Death is nothing but
the action whereby you again give back and hand over your
consciousness to others. Your knowing once again steps out of
you and into the other. As in the beginning, your own knowledge again becomes only others' knowledge of you, a knowledge that is now recollection, memory, remembrance. Consciousness is like an office that you hold for life. In death, you
resign it. As, in the beginning, you existed only in the consciousness of others, so, at the end, you again exist only in their consciousness, which, as consciousness of the past, is now recollection.

Consciousness is the universal air of Spirit and life; when you
inhale it, you become alive and conscious; when you exhale it,
you become unconscious, dead. As little as light or air is an
attribute or even a property of the body, so little is consciousness a condition or an attribute or even a property and possession of the human. Rather, consciousness is the universal, primal element and absolute foundation of the individual, the true
being, the unlimited space in which individuals exist. Thus, if
one wishes to clarify to oneself the human essence from the
point of view of sensible beings, of individuals, all humans,
insofar as they constitute one undivided totality, belong to consciousness; consciousness is their reciprocal, indivisible perception, existing and interwoven through everyone; consciousness
is everyone's knowledge of one another taken together as one
knowledge.

The person as person exists only in knowing, or, more exactly, in distinguishing. When you take away distinguishing, you take away the person's existence. You exist only while and as long as you distinguish yourself. But the others from whom you distinguish yourself and exist as person in this distinguishing belong to you as distinguishing. You are conscious of yourself only in distinction from others, therefore, only at, in, by, and through others. But this very necessity, that distinguishing from others is demanded for the existence of a person, that your consciousness is also simultaneously the undivided consciousness of other persons, that you know yourself only with and by others, is a manifestation of the fact that consciousness is the absolute, infinite unity of all persons and humans. You can learn that consciousness is related to particular bodies and, thus, to individuals, in the manner of a common natural element, from such conditions as sleep, fainting, and drunkenness, in which the human is deprived of the use of consciousness. Unconsciousness is the beginning of humanity, and unconsciousness is its end; the middle and focal point of humanity is consciousness. The human, as a single being, enters—and every human enters in this way—humanity as a totality, as a completed, fixed, already closed being. Consciousness is the absolute center of humanity; or, rather, consciousness is humanity itself, is this undivided totality in the form of knowing. Know and see the great mystery of totality and unity in consciousness. It is the absolutely complete, indestructible, immovable focal point, the sun of humanity. As well as sensible nature, consciousness is a world into which the single human enters. Like the corn in the sun, you ripen and mature into a person by basking in the sunlight of the eternally closed and eternally youthful consciousness of humanity that forever develops and creates within itself. Exhausted by the burning solar heat of consciousness, which fatigues and consumes the single human, at death you sink back into the eternal sleep and unconscious peace of nothingness. To this extent, death is not something, not a positive reality or a determinate thing, but is only the exclusion, the deprivation of consciousness, the loss of the focal point, self-forgetting.

129

But how can you now complain that you are mortal when you do not complain that you once were a child, that you once were nothing at all? How can you be frightened of death since you have already undergone and passed through it, since you have already been what you will be once again? Look back at what you were before life and at what existed before your life; no longer will you tremble before that which you will become after life, and no longer will you doubt that something will exist after your life or what will exist after your life. Or at least look into life; you will find already in life that which will become your object at the end point of life, and you will recognize that true being is proper to consciousness alone, to Spirit alone, that outside of Spirit all is in vain. Your being is always restricted to the momentary present. You exist only as long as you are present during this moment. The past, even if it still lives in your recollection, is no longer being. Being is only the present of the moment, which disappears together with its being. Your entire life is a continuous process of becoming recollected; everything in you and you yourself pass away; and with this passing away you become an object of recollection. But recollection itself is nothing but a continuous process of spiritualization, for in recollection your being becomes essentialized and universalized; it becomes impartible. You cannot impart your mere being, the being that is immediately proper to you, but recollected being, precisely as object of Spirit, can become an object for others. If, then, your entire life is a continuous process of recollection and spiritualization, can you break off this activity with death, or, rather, must you not recognize in death only the manifestation and completion of this activity? Your recollection is nothing but the continuing preparation for death. Already in life, you exist only as a recollected person; thus, your life is concluded when you go from being an actual person to being a person who is only represented, a mere object of representation, a person who is only imparted and impartible. As consciousness, the activity of recollection is a self-identical activity of Spirit that is absolutely universal in all persons; recollection is an activity of spiritualization and universalization. As such, it is not an activity that you possess, but an activity of Spirit itself.

130

You, as particular person, exist only particularly and can only particularize; but you cannot universalize. The person as such is not impartible; for and by itself, it cannot impart. Thus, recollection, as an activity of universalization, as an activity that makes impartible the personal, the particular, the individual, and the like, is an activity that is distinguished from you as a particular person yet identical with all persons without exception in the cancellation of their distinction. But, for the very reason that the process of recollection is identical with all persons in unity, without differentiation, it is a continuous, self-identical, universal activity of Spirit itself.

Clearly this must not be understood as if it were asserted that every human has the same recollections, that all individuals have the same content and the same objects for their object of recollection. Moreover, I urgently beg you not to be so foolish as to think that when it was asserted that thinking and consciousness are absolutely one, it was thereby asserted that the object of consciousness and the object of thought are one in all humans. For content and object as such must include in themselves multiplicity, distinction, and opposition. Your objects of recollection can be totally particular, can be separated from, or even opposed to, those of others. But as recollected, as universalized, as impartible, apart from the unnecessary particularity of their content, therefore, as recollection, they are one with the recollection of the other. Recollection is one; only that which is recollected is distinguished. When I remember, I remember something, something, therefore, determinate; determinateness is inseparable from distinction. But the distinction of determinateness does not divide the essence so that there is in you a different essence of recollection than in another person. Grasped as universal activity of Spirit, and not imagined as subjective capability, recollection, in its ultimate ground and essence, is inseparable from death and time. Recollection is the assimilative activity of Spirit through which Spirit transforms into itself that which is sensible, existing, externally independent. Recollection should be called the digestive process of Spirit, taking this term in its most comprehensive sense.

Although time is distinct from and independent of your

131

recollections, it is not distinct from recollection itself inasmuch as recollection is distinct from and independent of your recollections and is a universal, necessary activity of Spirit itself. Time, as the passing away of the single, particular, and individual, as the universal activity of negation of being, is the recollection of Spirit, is its assimilative activity. Time makes things inward; it leads them from being into essence. Time is itself the transition or the crossing over and back from being into essence, from the sensible into the spiritual, for in and through the passage of time, a thing changes from a sensible object into a spiritual object, an object of recollection. The living are transported into the realm of the shades, the underworld, on the river Styx of time. But at the same time, the underworld, as the realm of essence, is the true "overworld." Time only brings the world into essence, into understanding and reflection. You possess in yourself the testimony to the truth of this thought. In passing away by and in time, being in you becomes spiritual being, object of recollection, object of representation. But precisely in this passing away, by which sensible being becomes object of recollection, you arrive at reflection and thinking; you return to yourself and your essence. Recollection, as living, effective, universal activity of Spirit, in which Spirit negates single or sensibly independent existence, recollection, in this negation of independence and sensible shape, assimilates and collects itself into its self-consciousness. Thus, recollection, as something identical with time itself, is also the ground of your death; in recollection, your being is glorified and transformed into ideal being, into the being of representation.

The boundary between you and others is your personal existence, which is proper to you and immediately identical with you as a particular person. But if recollection is grasped as universal activity of Spirit (as it is in essence and truth), there is no boundary between the recollection in you and the recollection of the other. Rather, as your personal being (to which you can attribute, for example, actions, experiences, suffering, as those realities alone in which your personal being has existence and activity) passes away and is transformed, is taken up into Spirit,

132

and, as that which is personal becomes impartible and universalized, so the boundary between you and others is canceled. As
much as you are, so to speak, recollection, to that extent you
are not person, are not excluding, unimpartible being-for-self.
As much and as far as your being is recollection, it is spiritual,
represented, impartible, detachable from you, and no longer
personal being that is identical with you. When you are impartible, you are not a person, and when you actually communicate,
although the gravity of your words might arouse great respect
for your personhood, insofar as you communicate, you cancel
your personhood. Your personhood is so exalted that you cannot even speak as a person. You speak only from, in, and by
Spirit. If there were nothing but person in you, if there did not
exist in you a universal Spirit that is distinguished from you,
you would not be able to distinguish or detach yourself from   133
yourself; you could not give up your personhood, could not
communicate, could not speak. Your personhood, for the suitable existence of which you construct a proper world, the hereafter, escapes into the wind with every word issuing from you.
Thus your life, as a continuing process of recollection and spiritualization, is the uninterrupted process of canceling the boundary between you and others and therefore of canceling your personal being and with it your personhood. In death, the result of
this process, those boundaries for the cancellation of which you
have worked in and by Spirit throughout your entire life completely disappear. The last word that you speak is death, in
which you totally express yourself and impart yourself to
others. Death is the ultimate act of communication. You live
only as long as you have something to communicate, only as
long as there still remains in you something that is not yet communicated, and, therefore, only as long as there exists a boundary between you and others which is still to be canceled. When
you have communicated everything, when there is nothing left
but the last dry shell of your personhood, then you give yourself
up. This surrender is death. But permit me to interrupt the process of the argument by skipping to the moral, spiritual essence
of humanity, in order to try to show you that death comes from

the ethical essence, from the innermost heart, from love. Indeed, death comes not just from your love for another, but from love in general.

All human actions can be derived from love; love can be found and recognized in all of them. It is impossible for the human to exist purely for himself. If the human were able to endure bare, unfulfilled being-for-self, he would be able to endure that which is least endurable, nothingness. You would not be able to distinguish a bare being-for-self from nothingness. Being is abundance that is rich in relations; it is meaningful union, the inexhaustible womb of the most manifold connections. That which exists must exist with, in, and for another. Being is community, while being-for-self is isolation, is inability to share. But nothingness is precisely that which is least able to share, is the most isolated, the least compatible, the least sociable reality in the world (that is, it would be if nothingness existed as fish and trees exist). The human loves and must love. But human love has great variety, and its truth and value are measured by the content and extent of that which is loved. The human loves either that which is single, sensible (money, determinate things), or honor, fame, or, again, that which is substantial, universal, living; he loves either single persons, determinate beings (sensible love), or humanity in general, the humanity in humans, the good in humanity, or the purely universal good, God, or the pure truth. The deeper the content of the object of love, the greater is its extent. And the value of love can be determined by the extent of the beloved object in the following manner: the more you sacrifice yourself, the greater and more genuine is your love. For one cannot love without self-sacrifice. In loving, I love myself in another, I locate myself, my essence, not in myself, but in the object that I love. I bind my being to the being of another; I exist only in, with, and for another. If I am not in love, I exist only for myself. But when I am in love, I posit myself for another; I no longer possess my own being, my being-for-self; the being of the other is my being. The human, when he does not love, when he exists only for himself,

134

is still only a natural essence; his being is independent by nature, is unmediated. But the ethical, the humanity of the human essence, consists precisely in sacrificing one's purely natural self-being, in letting the ground of one's being exist through another, in having the ground of one's being in the being of another. Thus the lover makes the beloved into the ground of his being. As he loves, he has made his being grounded, or dependent; he has now found a basis of and for his life. All love, all modes of love, have in common the fact that they are self-surrender, self-sacrifice. The lover (for this is clearest in the love of humans for humans) burns his barren, dry self and self-ishness like tinder in the fire of love. But this self-surrender is more or less true, greater or lesser, according to the extent of the object. The truth of self-surrender depends on whether the object is of such an extent that it takes up and encloses in itself the total human self, or whether it is so confined that the self has no room in it, that the self is shut out, that (to divide the indivisible) one part of the self exists within the object, while one part remains outside and unsurrendered. Honor, greed, and such are passions, are terribly destructive conditions that border on madness, are diseases, precisely because the human does indeed surrender himself, but he does so to things that cannot include the human self. For the human self is infinite and of too great an extent to be able to enter into things of such a confined and restricted space. Thus, for example, the miser exists in his money and at the same time outside of it; he is dependent on it and at the same time independent of it; he surrenders himself to an object to which he cannot surrender the self and which, therefore, always returns and reflects back to him his unsur-rendered, unfulfilled self. There thus arises in him the terrible contradiction that he is poor in wealth, is empty in abundance. In this way passion, as a disordered condition, is perverted into the desire to devour the object instead of the desire to let oneself be consumed and devoured by the object.

But the genuine human, the human acting ethically, as a thinker, as a religious being, has placed his essence, not in objects that are beneath him, but in objects that are above the

135

self. He contemplates and possesses his essence neither in himself nor in things that are beneath him, but his I is an object above his I; it is an other that is infinite, that takes up and grasps within itself his entire self. The being and life of the ethical human is a continuous sacrificial feast. The life pulse of one's own self is burned away, the light of the self is extinguished. One's own self has been freed; one's I, one's inmost reality, is now one's other, is the infinite object into which one has ascended. Nature is now defined in and for itself, is now determined and moved by free Spirit, by will itself and not by one's particular will. Death is nothing but the natural negation of the human that is defined in and for itself and established by will in order that nature may submit to and may correspond to one's true will. The same will that drives and moves you to surrender yourself in ethics, in thinking, and in religion and that at the same time binds the human with others in passion, the same will presses death out of the being of nature. Thus one can say of death that its father is the Holy Spirit and that nature is only its earthly, receptive, and passive mother. You bring about death with and in the same will with and in which you will religion and truth. It is one and the same will that effects the death in nature and the death of the self that is virtue, religion, and thinking. When you love and will goodness and truth, you do so only by means of goodness and truth themselves, in the universal will that dwells within you, within *your* will. If you possessed only your own particular will, you could never surrender yourself, you could never love and will the true and good, indeed, you could not will or love anything at all, for this anything is always something other than you, an object independent of you. But if you had only your own will, you could never will something else that is separate and independent from you. With and by your own will, you could will only that which is immediately bound to it, but you never could will an object. Will itself is human expansibility, is the power of extending the self to objects. If will were only your own will, it would dry up in you and together with you so that you could no longer submit yourself to any object, and could grasp an object as little as someone whose hand had withered or been cut off. The bond, the midpoint, and the means between you and another would be torn away.

Now this universal will of Spirit, by and in which you can will and surrender yourself to goodness, truth, and anything that is other than you, that is, insofar as humanity actually wills and loves something else, has placed the other of Spirit in general—that is, nature itself—into such an intimate and inward union with the ethical and human will that there corresponds to the inner negation a negation in nature. Love would not be complete if death did not exist. The free act of humanity must exist simultaneously as necessity in nature. The spiritual surrender of the self must also be a natural, physical surrender, although, as already stated, this surrender must be willed and established, not by your own intentional, self-conscious will, but by the universal will in your will. Natural death is thus the ultimate sacrifice of reconciliation, the ultimate verification of love. Death has its focal point in Spirit; it is moved around Spirit like a planet around the sun. As you love, you acknowledge and proclaim the nothingness of your mere being-for-self, of your self. You acknowledge as your true I, as your essence and life, not yourself, but the object of your love. As long as you live, you live both in the negation of yourself, in the continuous ratification of the nothingness of yourself, and in the affirmation, in the enjoyment, in the contemplation of the object of your love. But the death sentence that you pronounce by the acknowledgment of the substantiality of the beloved object in your place would have no truth if it were not carried out in your entire natural being, in your life. This death sentence could not be carried out if the finitude that you express by the bond with the object in love did not come forth in its own right, if your being-for-self did not become manifest precisely as something solitary and destitute, if you did not die. For death is just the manifestation of your solitary and destitute being-for-self. The infinity and substantiality of the object of your love, in the binding with which and in the grounding by which alone you exist and have life, the necessity of love and the nothingness of your mere self,

138

your being-for-self, are manifested only by the fact that your
self-positing, your self, when it exists only for itself, when it is
abstracted and separated from essence and life in any objectivity, and especially in the object of love, at the moment when it
emerges for itself alone and renounces union with objectivity
and the content of its love (which, during life, is either a continuous union or a union interrupted only by relationships of
another kind), then your self is nothing and becomes nothing.
You exist as pure I, as pure self, you exist only for yourself but
once, and this moment is the moment of not-being, of death.
Thus death, precisely because it is the manifestation of your
being-for-self, is at once the manifestation of love. In death
your being-for-self steps forth on its own ground. But the nothingness, the death of the self at the moment of isolation, at the
moment when it wishes to exist without the object, is the revelation of love, is the revelation that you can exist only with and in
the object.

Thus your morality is the most immoral, the most pitiable,
the most vain, and the most futile morality in the world if it
derives from the belief in immortality, if it does not overcome
nature, if it does not recognize in death the action of the most
exalted freedom, if it allows this belief to fall upon the mass of
moral individuals in order to consume it like a voracious wolf
and then seeks to make up the injury by the mild and merciful
gift of a tedious immortality, if it wishes to overcome death
only after death, only after its arrival. For death can be conquered only before death. But this can be accomplished only by
the total and complete surrender of the self, only by the acknowledgment of universal will, the will of God, only by the
appropriation of his will and the knowledge and perception of
the essential truth of death that must be connected to this appropriation. The person who thinks and who has profound vision
overcomes death because he knows death for what it is, as an
action immediately bound with ethical freedom. He sees himself
in death, recognizes his own will in death, recognizes in death
the act of his own love and freedom. He recognizes that death

139

does not begin, but ends and concludes, in natural death, that natural death is nothing but an exhalation of the inner and hidden death, that the death that is trapped and bound (for the binding, bound, and constrained death of the self is love) is only freed, isolated, and unbound in external, sensible death, just as the plant again exhales and excludes the matter that it has inhaled and incorporated. What is the source of death if it is not your inmost reality? Does it come from the charnel house, does it arise out of the ground and break in on you like a thief in the night? Is it a skeleton or a man who has independent existence? It is none of these; it is only the manifestation of the act of inner amputation, separation, and severance, the verification of your love, the proclamation that you have made in silence throughout your entire life that you are nothing without and outside of the object of your love.

"But then is separation an act of love?" How can you ask such a question? It is the ultimate, the most extreme, and the highest act of love; only if separation were not not-being, were not death, would it not be love. Which mother has more love: she who can exist only near her children, or she who, to confirm her love, separates herself from her children?

"But then how do animals and plants die, how does death enter them?" They die only because humans die; human death is the ground of the death of plants and animals, just as the death of the person who truly loves and is ethical is the ground of the death of the person whose love is less, whose love is finite and limited; his death pulls the death of the lesser lover along with it. That which is higher is always the ground of the lower; truly ethical will is universal, infinite, all-effective, all-present will. The earthly human hollows a place for death out of the highest, out of God, and pours it into creation. This is the love that, in humanity, steps forth into the bright day of consciousness; this is divine will, the pure human, who is still present in selfish will (otherwise the human could will nothing) and who completes the act of death in nature and in humanity. The first human brought and still brings death daily into the world. The first, or the spiritual, human, the human who has fully attained

140

God and truth, the archetypal human, dies first, leads the way to death; his death is the archetypal, original, all-effecting death. All other beings, plants, animals, selfish humans, only die after him and only exhibit him. If everything has its proto-type, its spiritual essence, its divine and most exalted origin, should not death also have its prototype, its ground, in the ulti-mate ground of things and essences? Should death alone be independent, for itself, by and from itself? There must exist an archetypal and preworldly death. Seek and you will find it.

But, to continue the main theme after this long interval, recol-lection, in its meaning as developed previously, is the principle, the foundation, and the possibility of history. History is the fac-tual proof not only that individual souls, or persons and indi-viduals, exist, but also that Spirit itself exists; history is the fac-tual proof that, as is consciousness, recollection is a universal activity of Spirit. Actual events are commonly distinguished from recollection, and recollection is usually considered to be only a subsequent event, a gift to posterity that is alloted by chance and that owes its existence only to papers and stones. This is quite proper in accordance with the representations con-nected to history and recollection. Since recollection is imagined as only a subjective capacity, it is quite natural that, for us at least, the existence of history is made dependent on the exis-tence of a highly esteemed learned public, and that we separate recollection from past history, considered to be the real history, by representing it as only the subsequent recollection that per-sons have of history. It is quite correct that Rome would have been what it was, would have done what it did, that there would have been a history of Rome, even if the esteemed learned pub-lic had known nothing of it, and that, for this public, the exis-tence of a Rome depends on paper, since it knows only paper history, not spiritual and actual world history. However, paper and stone are actually only the external means of recollection; they make possible only the recollection of determinate individ-uals; they themselves have their ground in recollection itself. For determinate individuals, who exist separately, outside of and after one another in space and time, the recollection of the historical must be a mediate or mediated activity. But because individuals are not the essence, the true, Spirit, this mediation is only a manifestation of the unity and universality of recollection, just as the necessity that I am conscious only through another, that my consciousness exists only as mediate and mediated consciousness, is only a proof and manifestation of the unity and universality of consciousness. History rests on an absolute unity of consciousness and recollection, on the unity of Spirit with itself. This unity in essence is mediation in existence, mediation for conditioned individuals who exist separately. But the external means and mediation are possible only with the presupposition and on the basis of the immediate unity of a universal Spirit and a universal recollection. History, as the life of single beings, is a continuous process of recollection, in which Spirit transforms into itself individuals, independent existences; in history is realized that which individuals already were in themselves—objects of the consciousness of Spirit. Thus, without death there is no history, and there is no history without death. History is consciousness, Spirit, the essence itself as process, the essence in action or consciousness as recollection.

142

The individual dies because he is only a succeeding moment in Spirit's process of recollection; the individual dies within history because he is only one member of the historical totality. Because its principle is one Spirit, one consciousness, humanity is not a totality or unity like a herd of sheep, which consists only of single sheep and which is actual only in single sheep, each of which exists only in its unity for itself, only as a single sheep, which satisfies its particular needs only for itself, and which suffers no loss, injury, or negation by this unity. Humanity is a totality that has independence as a totality, that has actuality as a totality in its individuals, is a unity that is thorough and penetrating, that is living, consuming, that absorbs individuals into itself. The sheep exist in their unity because it is an externally containing unity, a unity that is not independent in itself but is porous, selfless, and spiritless, because it is nothing but a herd; the unity of the sheep is only their spatial proximity. But precisely because they are not sheep or geese, precisely because they are distinct from these animals only because their unity has independence for itself, is actual essence, do humans exist in a history, in temporal sequence.

The essential, engaging, and thorough unity has its core and its taste in itself, is as dense as a diamond, as sharp as aquafortis, as consuming as zeal, as all-powerful as the sunlight, as burning as pain, as agonizing as guilt, as fearful as revenge, as clear as heaven, as deep and dark as hell. The essential unity is the inner essential negation of individuals. History is the realization of consciousness, the manifestation of unity in time, the actualization of essential negation, and, therefore, its actualization in existence. Individuals exist externally to one another as individuals. Thus, the actualization of the essence in their existence is the arising that is inseparable from their passing away, is their being-in-sequence; its result is that the existence of individuals is continuous succession, is history. Time is nothing but Spirit in zeal and wrath, the essence in fury, the *furor divinus,* the Spirit that sweeps away and inspires the world in the stream of its own inspiration.

But those who sustain nothing but a touch of moral compunction from the symposium of history (which is spiced with Attic salt), those who are incapable of accepting and approaching the sacred flame of inspiration nevertheless might still expect a hereafter in order to be cured in it from their compunction and their own pitiableness by the briny pickles and anchovies of the present life (for the hereafter receives its determination, its matter and content, its taste and salt, only from the present life). They might still wander around on the exalted Alps of history, seeking single herbs in order to trample and crush them and thus to prepare out of them the nutritive substance for a future life. Their life hereafter melts like butter in the sun of consciousness. Eternity itself is the ground of history, is its inner basis and its permeating foundation. Like the organic body, humanity is contained in constant movement, continuous renewal, creation, and transformation of the individuals who are its members. But the totality that is consciousness itself lies beyond time.

Time lies, as it were, only in the middle between the totality   144
and individuals; time is only the relation, the connection of the
totality to the members, of the unity to the individuals. Consciousness is a continuous present that is immutably constant in
and beyond historical change; for consciousness, one time is
attached to the next, immediately, continuously, timelessly.
From the most distant historical times up to those that the
vision of the historical, temporal researcher can penetrate, and
where history itself is lost in darkness, in its eternal yet still present beginning of essence (which, therefore, can no longer be
mediated historically or temporally), from all these times down
to our own, consciousness is one present, one unity that is interrupted by no course of time or temporal division. If humanity
as totality, if consciousness itself, were divided and interrupted
by temporal intervals, not only history but also the existence of
each distinct age would be impossible. Similarly, it would be
impossible for me as an individual to have a history if my individuality, and thus consciousness in me, were subjected to time,
if, just as my perceptions, passions, experiences, affairs are separated by time, are temporal, so consciousness in me were separated from itself, were interrupted by time. Beyond the alterna-
tions of times and individuals, beyond the fluctuation of arising
and passing away, consciousness is a present that is present to
itself in peaceful self-identity, in undivided unity, and in continuous rest. And humanity exists in constant activity, movement,
and development only within this unity of consciousness, which
enlightens, unifies, and embraces all peoples, times, and individuals.

But history, as the self-actualizing of the self-conscious,
thinking, rational essence, of Spirit, is no mere flow like the
flow of water, in which the same always follows the same, but is
a course that is inwardly distinguished by limits, by purpose and   145
rational determination. Thus, the historical existence of the
individual is an existence that is determined by purpose. The
individual is a determinate member of the historical totality and
has his destiny in this determination. Thus the ground of individual death is not just the indeterminate ground that the individual is a member of a totality, but is the ground that is deter-

mined by the fact that he is a determinate member of the totality. Every human has a destiny, a purpose and rational determination of his existence. This is principally manifested in the
individual as drive, desire, talent, inclination; the determination
of purpose of the individual's life is itself his power, his capability, his talent. The destiny of the individual is his sacred, inviolable essence, is the drive of all drives, the soul of his soul, the
principle of his life, his protecting and defending guardian
spirit, the inner necessity, the provident fate of his existence.
"You should be, you must be." Thus speaks destiny. But this
"should" and "must" are gentle and mild; destiny is not coercion but is one with inclination; it is the individual's soul, his
essence. And for the person whose essence it is, the essence is no
coercion or external necessity. The human lives as long as his
destiny is still destiny, as long as it still exists in him and is one
with him. The being of the individual, as the being of a member, is a being that is totally determined, totally posited in measure and goal. Thus, if the determinate destiny of the determinate individual has become reality, if it has become detached
from the individual, if it has stepped into the actual world as
object, then his soul, the principle of his life, has become objectified. But when one's life has become an object, then one's
subjective being-for-and-in-oneself, one's proper being, ceases;
one dies. When the destiny becomes object of reality and representation, it becomes a selfless object of representation. The
individual's capacity for something is the capacity out of which
he lives. Thus, when this capacity is expended, is used up, has
stepped into existence as an object, the capacity for life is also
exhausted. The inner goal of the human is also the goal of his
life; the inner measure is also the measure of his existence. The
determination is the beginning and the end of your being. Thus
it is irrational to separate the being of the individual from his
inner measure, to assume that the individual has an immeasurable continuation, and to seek the true life in the life hereafter,
which is the life without purpose and determination. The true
being of the human is his determination, his purpose, but the
purpose is limit and boundary. Thus the being of the individual,

insofar as it has a purpose or is purpose, is necessarily limited. A being without limits is an indeterminate and purposeless being. The purpose gathers and brings to mind. Death is the necessary result of this gathering and bringing to mind, of this delimiting.

Thus, that life in which individuals exist eternally, and therefore exist without determination, measure, or goal—for if they possessed inwardly a destiny, if they possessed limit and determination within their essence, then their existence would have to be one that is determined, limited, and ending—that life in the hereafter is a life without gathering and bringing to mind, without reason and seriousness, a life for play and appearance. Only when nothing is posited before the death of the individual must something still be posited after it (clearly, posited only for the individual). But then must arise the comical question, "Is there something or nothing after death?" Only when history is nothing, only when the naked individual, the individual who is stripped of all historical elements, of all destiny, determination, purpose, measure, and goal, only when the vain, abstract, meaningless, empty individual is something, and therefore only when nothing is something, and only when the something, the actually determined and determining life, history, is nothing, only then is there nothing after death, only if the nothing after death is not also something. Thus those peculiar beings and strange subjects who think that they live only after life do not reflect that they attain and make up nothing at all with their afterlife, that as they posit a future life, they negate the actual life. For if there is life after death, there cannot be life before death; one excludes the other; the present life cancels the future life, the future life cancels the present life. In the present life (which may be a transitory life only because all that is reasonable takes place in it), there is a commendable, age-old custom that the tailor does not sew up the holes in the coat with other holes, that people do not compensate by injuries, do not repay by debts, do not give away by burglary. Such common, empirical, earthly laws are no longer valid in and with regard to the hereafter. The hereafter—and this is its only priority and the

147

only distinction that commends it over the present life—sews up the holes with other holes, fills up by evacuation, enlivens by destruction, replaces by positing nothing, satiates by starvation, enriches by deprivation. Who should be surprised at the fact that the hereafter is the mad and insane present life? To what end does the hereafter exist if nothing that is not totally different from the events of the present takes place in it, if one does not live freed from the sins that one committed in actual life, if one does not feed off the nothingness of the present? To what end does the hereafter exist if there does not exist in it the something that is nothing in the present life?

The true hereafter, the heaven in which the individual will be free of the determination and limitation of his individuality and, therefore, of his individuality itself, is love, contemplation, knowing. Only in these can you exist in the infinite, though not in and by your individual, personal being. But your individual being, the being that is free of the burden of actuality and the limit of your individuality, is your being as represented, as object of recollection. Recollection alone is the realm of the dead, the land of departed souls. The extent and significance of the place that the individual maintains in recollection depend upon the content and extent of the determination of the individual. If the determination of the individual was limited, if the extent of the activities that realized this determination was confined, then the compass of recollection is also small and disappearing. But if the determination was universal, if it contained infinite content, and if the activities that realized this determination were therefore of universal content and extent, then the recollection is also a universal recollection, one that is truly historic. Thus, the character of recollection, whether it is judgment and curse or whether it is blessing and thankful recognition, depends on the moral character of the activities, on whether they were good or evil. Heaven and hell have their true existence and their ground only in history, in history as it articulates itself into unities and histories of peoples.

Heaven, in its most ancient meaning, is the objectification

and materialization of recollection as it is blessing, gratitude, love, and admiration. The origin of heaven and hell is to be sought only in the historical life of ancient peoples who maintained the present in continuous, inward connection with the past, peoples for whom history was not yet an accounting of that which had happened, but was actual life, for whom the past was the essential substrate and foundation of the present life, among whom, therefore, individuals were not cut off from the actual communal historical life, and who did not represent their isolated individuality as an essential reality in an all-negating nakedness, as do the individuals of the modern world. The highest life of the individual who did not negate history and reality but who lived and was aware of himself only in unity with his people and together with history was to live on in the thankful hearts of posterity, celebrated in the songs of his people. The harshest judgment for the individual was the curse and condemnation of posterity. The popular bards and the people themselves represented recollection as a real, existing realm. For the very reason that the recompense of grateful or damning recollection is real recompense, that recollection as the universal, unchangeable recollection of a people is an actual realm, it was necessary, apart from other considerations, that it be represented and portrayed as a sensibly existing realm. Even when the unities of the peoples of the ancient world were destroyed, and even when, with this destruction, the narrow concept of one people as humanity itself was broadened into the concept of humanity which destroyed the distinctions between peoples, even in Christianity, though certainly only in ancient, genuine, essential Christianity, the belief in heaven and hell was not cut off from the actual historical life or from the concepts of unity and community. For heaven was the destiny only of those who lived in unity with the church, the people and nation of God; the others were cast into hell.

To be sure, the recompense of history does not satisfy modern subjects, who take as the measure of reality only their experience, their own knowledge. If that which comes after death and their individuality is not included in their own knowledge

149

and experience, then there is nothing after death, according to them. If they do not experience the recompense for good actions, then they cry out that there is no reward, no God. For them, everything depends on their distinction from others, and nothing depends on the reality of the good in and for itself, or on essence, truth, or love, which is the unification with essence and the other that cancels distinction. If they still cannot distinguish themselves after death, then they say that there is nothing after death.

Modern subjects only know of subjective moral actions. For them, the subjective moral property is the sole and absolutely essential property of an action. Indeed, for them, the subjective moral property is that alone by which an action is an action. They know nothing of an infinite, universal action, an action of Spirit, such as history and world-historical actions. Modern subjects consider to be nonsense an action that is being in itself, an action the reality of which lies not in subjective inner action, not in moral disposition, but in itself. For them, history is only a history of moral subjective actions and circumstances, events, situations. Being, essence, and Spirit are not their object in history. They see in history only a swarm of actions that endlessly coil into and entangle one another. Thus, for them, being in the present and past is determined only for a being in the future and, with respect to the morality of actions, only for the land where recompense exists separately on its own, as actions supposedly exist separately on their own in the present life. However, once again, modern subjects, diseased in eye and Spirit, do not notice that in this manner they make nothing into the content of both the hereafter and the present life, that they destroy both at the same time. The separate existence of recompense cancels the essence of recompense; the separate existence of action cancels the essence of action. Future rewards never replace my present sufferings and pains. A recompense that exists separately, that is cut off from the life of action, can no longer be recognized as recompense when it comes along afterward, when I receive it after the sufferings are over, when I no longer have the need for and thus the experience of recompense. But as meaningless and vain as a separate recompense is, equally meaningless and vain is an action that exists separately and cut off from its essence, for the true recompense of an action is its own essence.

The true belief in immortality is the belief in Spirit itself and in consciousness, in their absolute substantiality and infinite reality. Insofar as Spirit is the principle of history, insofar as past, present, and future are canceled and are identical in Spirit and consciousness, the true belief in immortality is a belief in the reality of the past, in the reality of the future and present (as long as the present is not seen in isolation, but in its essence, in its essential connection with the future and past). Since the union of past and future with the present must be posited together with consciousness, the belief in immortality is found among almost all peoples. That which is true in the universal belief in immortality (and thus also in the modern belief, although those who maintain it are not aware of this truth, but, on the contrary, connect to it false beliefs and opinions), that which is true in this belief consists only in the fact that it is a sensible representation of the nature of consciousness, that in this belief, the foundation, element, and condition of all history— that is, the unity of past, present, and future as one essential reality—is fixed and raised to the level of an object, if not of knowledge and consciousness, then of dark representation and belief. Thus, your belief in immortality is a true belief only when it is a belief in the infinity of Spirit and in the everlasting youth of humanity, in the inexhaustible love and creative power of Spirit, in its eternally unfolding itself into new individuals out of the womb of its plenitude and granting new beings for the glorification, enjoyment, and contemplation of itself. It is a true belief only when it is the belief that the true, the essence, the Spirit, possesses an existence that is independent of the existence of all individuals and that humanity possesses an existence that is independent of these determinate, present individuals, when, therefore, it is the belief that these present, determinate

151

individuals are not immortal and everlasting, are truly not the last individuals, with which the essence of humanity is exhausted and played out.

On the contrary, your belief is not a belief in the substantiality and reality of that which is substantial, but a belief in the substantiality and reality of that which is finite, and your belief in eternal life is a belief in the most temporal life of all. Time is a daughter of truth; it manifests only nature; it is the mirror of essence. Time offends and harms nothing. Only that which is transitory in essence passes away in time. Time only lifts the veil in the temple of Isis; its total activity consists in unveiling. Thus if the present, transitory individuals are to be immortal, then that life in which the isolated present, the present individuals, are an absolutely ultimate and fixed reality, in which, therefore, the temporal has eternal existence and permanence, the transitory has everlasting existence and permanence, and determined persons have absolute existence and permanence, then this so-called eternal life is not just temporal but most temporal, absolutely temporal, the most temporal of all, the least true and most finite life, the *superlativus* of all temporality and finitude. But this present life, which you call "only" this life, as if it were only one single life, is absolute, eternal, and infinite life, for the finite passes away in it, the temporal is not eternal in it. Transitoriness exists in this life only because infinity itself exists in it. Transitoriness exists only within infinity. Death and time are themselves the present of eternity, are infinite Spirit in action. Your belief in immortality is true only when it is the belief in this life, in the transitoriness of that which is transitory, and in the eternalness of that which is eternal, in the *existence* of God.

I am dragged from this earthly life
In order that I may submit to nothingness.
To be sure, the old fable teaches
That I will draw near the angelic host;
But only theologians, who have long deceived themselves
About the truth, believe such stuff.
My tiresome existence as me,

152

My identity ceases
With my last cry.
Death is not a hollow jest,
Nature plays no practical joke;
She bears true death on her seal.
Being lives off being
And is embedded in nothingness: 153
Being cannot be divided,
So only nothingness can cure being.
I am only I, only one nature,
Only one being, one light, one whole;
I am only one unity, one center,
And well rounded on all sides.
I may not tamper with my being;
I can subtract nothing from it, add nothing to it.
Pains, joys, longing, and affliction,
Sins, guilt, torture, and torment,
All these are one unity,
Are essence itself, being, and individuality.
You cannot carve me up
Or take excerpts from me at your pleasure:
The I evaporates, the I is extinguished
If you extract my pain and torture from me.
And even if the fable were true,
And there really were an angelic host,
I would rather be at home with my pain
Than with the angles in the heavenly glow.[10]
You can fabricate a thousand angels out of a single human,
But it takes real bravado to make an excerpt out of him.
So even if the fable were true,
And there really were an angelic host,
Still, I would not find myself up there,
For an excerpt of me is no longer me.
And being totally the same in the hereafter
Makes no sense to me at all,
For such repetitions
Are never found in nature.

So farewell, dear I, farewell!
For all eternity, alas, alas!
Dear soul, grieve not
Even if the I collapses:
What good is it to soar in the heavenly halls
As an excerpted soul
With drained features?
What kind of existence is there if one is only
What one has been and is no longer?
Why do you want to fill the night of nothingness
And to quench its thirst for light
By existing like a dying ember
Subdued in fire, color, and substance,
As a merc identity
Without variety or quality?
To continue on as nothing
But a pale ghost of oneself,
This I may not, this I will not!
Grieve not when the I collapses.
I will not meet the shades,
Approach Socrates and Augustine;
I am dragged down to nothingness
By the kindler of new life:
I am driven to depart to those
Who are and were not yet,
Into the future that becomes a life,
Into the nothingness that brings forth being,
To the unknown distant beings
Who glean the fruits of my death,
And whom nothingness still quietly
Hides in its dark bosom,
To the dear little children
Who take our place
And breathe their vital air
Out of the dry skins of our death.
Surely a new life in fresh blossom
Springs forth out of death.

154

But I, I do not rise again;
Death ends my life course.
I must pass away to nothingness
If a new I is to arise.
My own I becomes a new I
That is totally distinguished from me;
My own I, torn away by death,
Has been released to a free self
That exists in itself
Separated from me.
The other being, which bears the future in itself,
Does not include me.
Dear beloved child,
My being now becomes your being;　　　　　　　155
Dear other nature,
I am transformed into you;
You are my resurrected I
When my being has long since faded into nothingness.
Death reverses mine and yours;
It encloses the one in the other.
You live here in self-identity
Only once within time.
Identity ceases;
Death is not a hollow jest.

Oh harsh life, bitter being!
Oh being full of pure struggle and pain!
Oh stern God! Oh breaking heart!
In the end a nothing, an eternal death!
Yet, dear soul, bear
With courage the mild yoke of truth;
Then you will no longer groan
And thirst for your own being.
The better I of another humanity
Before which my I vanishes into nothing,
This is the true kingdom of heaven
To which I ascend after death.

You call out in your distress,
"Give me consolation for death";
Yet behold the mild face of truth
And the sweet light of a new consolation:
Truth does not give you the rust of old fables;
It consoles you with *humans,*
With dear, better, other natures,
Who are because you have been,
With the angelic spirits of precious children,
The future masters of the present masters;
These call you away from life
And whisper you into a peaceful grave;
These lull you to your final sleep
And weave your being into nothingness.
Your own child, your own blood
156   Draws the breath of life from you;
As long as your I is not shattered
You still cloud the light of your little ones.
The father travels the road of death
To raise the child heavenward;
He casts himself into his corpse
To make a heavenly ladder for his child.
What makes the pale maiden gleam
White-hot with love?
Why does the boy's face glow
As scarlet as the fire?
Why, dear young virgin, do your eyes sparkle
With such clarity and purity?
Dear youth, you smite cleanly
As fire strikes forth from the eyes!
The eternal forth, the eternal away,
The no-more-me, the no-more-am,
They wash the eyes so clean,
And bring fire, light, and color.
The ground is light, nothingness is bright;
Nothing dims your source of life:
It does not flicker on in consciousness

Like a weak vigil light;
It imparts to you no ghostly vapor
Of the art of life and thought.
Life is not tolerant,
Death is no comedian.
Hence the gleam in your eyes,
Hence the blaze inside you.
The eternal deaths of our fathers
Engender the fiery red cheeks;
The last fevers of our dear mothers
Engender the white-hot maidenly gleam.
The ground is nothingness, the nothingness is night;
This is why we burn in such fiery splendor.
The darkness of nothing, the darkness of the ground
Perfectly sets off colors.
The power of thought and life does not expand
Its influence without limit
All the way to the dark chamber of death,
There weakly to flicker itself out,
But compresses itself in you;   157
This is why it can burn so intensely here.
The eternal forth, the eternal away
Gives such courage, gives such meaning;
The *one* light, the *one* life,
Only the one can give off such fire.

You can exist only once;
Submit your will to this.
All truth, Spirit, nature
Exist only once.
Life is life only
Because there cannot be a second life.
Only the once creates essence, power,
Live action, and property.
The once illuminates, warms, ignites,
And refines, presses, drives, binds.
The twice is only weak semblance,

An essence without bone or marrow.
The once is the true hero,
The nucleus, the Spirit, the power of the world;
This is the forge of being,
The great printing press of the universe.
All Spirit is already pressed out of
That which can be numbered or divided.
The tired, the faded, limp flab,
Sleep, death, consumptive pallor,
The rekindled coal, mush,
Tasteless monotony,
Unsalted, unleavened bread,
Sleepwalking, sentimental grimaces,
Pessimism, impotent longing,
Pious posturing, irksome gaping,
Watery soup, donkey gray,
Mysticism, pale and flat,
Swelling, vomiting, boredom,
Disease, and festering discharge,
These essences without drive and power,
Without nature, color, life, or sap,
These essences of vapor and mush
158   Come only out of the twice, out of the once-is-twice.
Number is only the ground of death;
Once is life, is healthy.
Spirit cannot be repeated,
Nor counted nor duplicated.
Life itself is already Spirit,
So it rejects all number.
Time and number end in the once;
Thus the once is eternity.

The once is the power of love,
The heartbeat, the drive of drives;
Only the once brings pain and joy
And love into the human breast.
Love has strict properties,

Has its power in contrasts;
This, its exacting character,
Does not tolerate immortality.
What else is love but one single pain
That completely fills your heart?
It is only the stress of soul,
A sweet, free compulsion,
The point where the whole Spirit
Concentrates on its dearly beloved treasure.
Oh gentle burden! Oh tender stress!
Oh mild pressure, sweet compulsion!
But how would you be able to realize
The exalted power and art of love?
How did the pressure of love arise in you,
If the time of life murmurs along
All the way to the sea of eternity
Without limit, compulsion, or drive?
Only within a short span of life
Does the heart unfold in love.
Only in the life-force, only in the drive to death
Is love pressed into motion;
Only at the highest pinnacle of life
Does love's lightning strike;
Only the heart's last thrust
Drives up the sprout of love.
If immortality lay in wait   159
For you behind this time,
You would be old even as a child;
Your heart would crawl along in a worn-down rut.
Already you would be faded here on earth,
Your heart a tasteless pulp;
The flood of ages without end,
Without the boundary and obstacle of death,
Would wash away all your power,
Would erode all your quality.
Once in heaven, this earth
Would become for you the beautiful hereafter.

You would gladly give up immortality
For this time,
And, in the land of death, you
Would long to leave the tiresome angelic state
To become a loving human
Once again on this earth.
For the most beautiful land, the best condition
For being a human is here;
Only where there are conflict and suffering,
Where pain clouds the clarity of soul,
Only there is my true fatherland;
Pain is the pledge of Spirit.
Let cowardly clerics
Fall in love with the hereafter!
Only my pain is left to me,
Only my loving, burning heart.
And if the whole world wished to be divine,
And to go to heaven—
Which I cannot believe,
For there still are some brave men—
I would stay outside,
I would not go in,
And, back in my own home,
Would beg the old pains
To burn once again in me;
I cannot separate myself from them.
For pain is not a single part
Cut off from the health of soul;
I am totally pressure, totally pain,
And will not dig under or fly over it.
Pain unites heaven and hell
In the blinding brightness of its ground.
Oh Niobe! Oh Niobe!
A stone for all eternity! Alas! Alas![11]
Truly a stone that weeps for all eternity,
In which there really are sin and pain,
Unites in itself more humanity

160

Than the misty host of all the angels.
So I would rather be such a stone
Than with the angels in the heavenly glow.

As bitter sap
Dwells in the citrus,
So death sits in your spinal cord
As if in its own park.
It is the wine of the universe
That moves and creates;
It poured Spirit with its softening moisture
Into the tough bulk of things,
And so made the old hide of matter
Tolerably spiritual;
For only the transitory
Creates quality in matter.
Only the fear, the horror of death
Puts matter into motion.
Death startled matter
And put nature on its course
So that it will always run
From place to place.
Death alone conducts the dance of the stars
And the music of the spheres.
The whole world, bag and baggage,
Dances only to the bagpipes of death;
Ah! and Oh! Adieu! Alas!
Are the only alphabet
That makes up the book of the world
In which creation is spelled out;
These are the only letters
That engrave sharp characters
Into the tasteless mush of matter,   161
Into the dull monotony of mass.
Even the sweet nightingale
Sings only at the setting of the source of life.
The heart is moved to song

When a final hour strikes.
The diamond sparkles
Only when washed by the waves of death.
Only after the sounding of the last hour,
Defined by the waning of the tone,
Does nature, with measured pace,
Shape the excellent crystal.
Truly the whole world is finally arranged
Only after the hour of death.
The loose sand of matter
Obtains the bond of form,
Obtains movement, essence, and figure
Only after the final hour has struck.
The roar of waves, the rustle of leaves,
The drifting of clouds, the shudder of wind,
The rage of anger, the bolt of lightning,
The glow of love, the haste of thunder,
These realities look up from their struggle
Only after the final hour.
One never hears theological truth
From the academic chair;
So I have never waited on the academy
Like a cow at a trough.
For me, the best of all masters,
My doctors, pastors, sacristans—
If it were not so, I would say that loud and clear—
Were the stars, the earth, the plants,
Was nature, controlled only by itself,
Constrained within unconstrained boundaries.
I was always only a poor devil,
Full of aches and pains and doubt;
I lived with elves as gentle as sunbeams,
With water nymphs, the *Rübezahl*,[12]
The earnest granddaddy of the frog;
Then I heard academic lectures
And struggled through swamp and morass,
Till a solid branch appeared to me.

162

The chirping of crickets, the croaking of toads
Set me free from error, the worst of sins.
I see the night of death
Softly illuminated in rolling waves;
I see the far edge of the ages,
The limit of the self in every tree;
In every apple seed,
I gaze at the dark remoteness of my own death,
And have even heard my death sentence
Pronounced by a waterfall.

Ah, what a miracle, what rich abundance!
The press of life, the silence of rest,
The night of pain, the brightness of peace
Have their source in death.
I read this in the great book of the world:
Death is the measure of all things.
Death is the silent inertia
In every power and difference.
The world would have burst into smithereens long ago
Had life and death been made separate.
It is in death that death is separated from life;
Therefore such a separate life is called a dead life.
The flame of life
Would explode through a thousand holes in your body
If death did not so coolly
Sit in your innermost depths,
And constantly trickle drops of melting ice
Through the lower aperture of your body.
Your blood pressure would be too high,
Its wild course too restricted,
So that the velocity of its force
Would break the lock of your body,
If death did not restrain the flow
In its subterranean progress,
And, like a surgeon,
Constantly bleed you,

And calm in eternity
The stormy period of life's struggles.
163　　More softly than even the song of Orpheus
Death sings the melody of peace
That presses all to harmony,
That penetrates even the stone and the log.[13]
In sleep the woman emerged from the man;
In sleep his body was split in two.
If the world were only one crude lout,[14]
Inflexible, hard, and obstinate,
Then death would never bend the self
And mollify tyranny to compassion,
And, by sleep, extract the fierce spite
From the crude lout.[15]
Death only lowers the eyelids
Of the self to bring on sleep
So that another comes from one,
So that the one benefits the other.
You could not bear the light,
Could not dare to take on life,
Were death not the blindfold
That subdues light and life;
Else every ray of sun would be
A dagger's thrust into the heart.
God looked first into the light
So that when you opened your eyes you would not die.
When God looked into the light
His back made a shadow;
He left it on earth
As a parasol for your vision.
Death is the shadow of God,
Which is necessary for the human eye;
God drew death over your head
Like a rainbow,
He spread it over you like a parasol,
Else you would have been burned to a crisp long ago.

But why is that which is called human
Divided into before and behind?
How does it happen that eyes and ears
Do not also embellish the back?
Why are you not filled with anger
At not being both before and behind?   164
Why are you not enraged that you can see and think
Only on the body's forward battlements?
Yet keep your vision clear
To see the deep ground of essence!
To see how all is interwoven,
How the highest lives in the lowest!
How even the backside
Is located for the praise of God!
If you want to, you can discover the truth
Even in the backside, even in the behind.
Only look backwards
To see how the candle of death burns eternally,
Fueled by the fat of your self,
Burning you like pine pitch,
Melting you, bone and marrow,
Like butter in the sun.
Do not let yourself be beguiled!
Death is only your backside;
Death is only your posterior you.
The eye in your back is now closed;
Thought and conscious will
Now sleep there in eternal repose.
You were once a child;
Thus you are presently blind toward the rear:
What you once were
Still remains in your essence;
Only what you once were apart from you and me
Is now located behind you.
Yet the ground that you, as an I, have abandoned

Still holds you.
You are never free of the source;
You always remain in your mother's womb.

Alas, only the side of the mirror facing you
Displays you and other objects.
The jovial mob of the senses, piled into
A single bundle, is also in the front:
Only at the tip of its highest branch
Does the tree of life propel you
Forth to the sweet sunlight,
To the bitter, ripe fruit of consciousness;
Only the highest point pours forth
The riot of the self.
The person is only the tip of the tree,
The final end of the thread of life.
Only the front of the knife is sharp
And useful for your household needs.
The flame of anger shoots up
Only at the rooster's comb.
With sharpened quill and biting silver nitrate,
The great stylus of Spirit
Etches its pure essence into the lump of nature
So that all flesh drips blood.
Only in wounds has nature
Found the ground of Spirit.
The banner of freedom waves
Only at the tip of nature's pole.
The Spirit, which grasps itself in consciousness,
Sits only on the masthead of the universe.
Spirit seizes Nature
Only by the top of her head,
And ironically looks down its nose
At its dear cousin;
Then Nature pays her compliments
And, smartly turning herself around,
Takes leave of his excellency;

165

At this point, your existence terminates.
Alas, a mere compliment
Brings you to the end of life!
Were Nature not such a fool
We would live eternally without fail.
Yet be not so amiss in understanding,
And see the great depth of nature!
Where his majesty, your self,
Is distended in self-knowledge,
And the floral display of your senses
Has faded in the night of death,   166
There lies the rich treasure of truth,
There essence has its place.
At the seat of death, you live
In possession of the riches of all essence.
You are not in essence a person
Once you have flown to God.
Person is only form and shape,
But essence is plenitude and content.
Only in his backside is the human himself God—
I say this to spite the pietist.
The spineless pietist knows
Only the grimace of the face in front;
Only in his engendering member,
Where human is discharged from human,
Where selfishness grasps itself
In the pretense of being natural,
Does the pietist have the anchor,
The strong prop of hope,
The fire hose of eternal life;
In his satisfaction with Athanasius,[16]
He does nothing but practice onanism.
This brute pious nature
Once read in his Bible
That when an old Hebrew woman
Looked backwards,
With lightning speed

She was turned into a stony pillar of salt.
So today, there is still a saying:
"Don't trust yourself to look backwards."
Thus the pietist knows only the tip of the human,
Only the lightning-bright pinnacle of the dome;
Astounded by the bright colors of parrots,
And holding fast to the tail of the peacock,
He props himself on his penis,
On the self in its distinction.

As tears flow from the eyes,
So death pours from Spirit;
For this reason, death is as miraculous,
As divinely lucid as a diamond.
167   When the first human began to know himself
An extreme pain seared through his soul,
And then the discharge of death
Poured forth through the portals of his burning eyes.
In nature, water always
Follows the track of heat.
So the heart burns at death
Because the human gains self-knowledge
Where the human departs from the human,
Where the human is split into I and object.
Thus people usually cry at death,
For tears lower the heat of pain.

When Adam opened his eyes
And first abandoned the condition of peaceful innocence,
At the steep pinnacle of his self
Gain or loss were not yet an issue.
He sucked in the shaft of self,
A power over all light,
So that plants and animals were almost destroyed
And almost perished for lack of light.
Only now, only when gathered into the storage barn of the self,
Did light become fire.

But then Adam's face burned
With the hot light of self.
He glowed as red as a tulip,
As a cock with red feathers.
Now indeed the golden age
Was forever lost to him.
Yet there remained a gleam of it
In his deeply distressed look;
It stood silently and softly,
A beautiful dream before his soul,
And rose like sweet aroma
Through the bright bloom of his self;
Surely there is a fragrance
Only when parts are burned away into the air.
Adam was totally transported by
The vision of this gleam;
And when Adam perceived this aroma
The smell truly did him good;
His eyes closed,   168
And he sank to eternal rest.
You would be truly insipid,
Contracted in Spirit and body,
If a part of your I
Did not constantly settle into nothingness.
There can be taste and smell
Only where there is eating and decaying.
Poor death is always hungry,
And always feeds on life.
The heart can continue to pump
Only so long as you have something to feed to death;
Circulation stops
When you have nothing more to put on the table for death.
Life is ever changing
And bartering away being for appearance;
A piece of you is always being lopped off,
And only a glimpse of it is left.
Your being is but a moment;

Toward the rear, there is only appearance;
Appearance ever presses farther,
Appearance ever becomes wider,
Until you become totally appearance
And only the glow of the fire remains.
The ground of things is as clear and pure
As a precious stone.
To be sure, Spirit engendered the world;
But death alone enlightens nature.
Being first becomes clear in death,
So being exists entirely in death.
Life by itself has only crudeness;
On its own, it is only flint;
Death alone brings the brilliance of diamond
To this crude flint stone.
Humanity can see itself in the mirror
Only in passing away.
Only in the final tears of Spirit,
Reflected in the mirror of the world
And inspired with the mournful flow,
Is the world illuminated in pure beauty.
Only the necessity of death

169   Covers the red with the gleam of white.
Being is only matter;
It is as dark, as shapeless as matter;
Matter first rose to a boil
Only with the flood of tears at Adam's death;
The salt from these tears purged the ground
So that it now shone with beauty and brightness
As diaphanous as parchment,
Transparent to its depths.
How bright is death!
No spring sparkles so clearly.
It is the most beautiful of diamonds;
It gleams with light in the hand of God.
No quality clouds it,
Neither difference nor variety.

It is still the golden age
In which distinction did not yet exist.
No forms constrict it;
Appearance is infinitely extended.
Thus all being exists only once
Because it first becomes clear in death.

I say to you, obtuse pietist,
That you have no truth in you,
That no matter how devout you are,
You do not fulfill the most exalted obligation.
You should reverently give thanks to death,
Consecrate to it your feelings, wishes, and thoughts;
You can raise yourself to song and prayer
Only because death stands at your side.
Even your ability to imagine yourself dead,
Even this fantasy of death—
For your spiritual death is only suspended animation—
Is imparted to you only by real death.
You think of your God as good and just
Only so that the bread tastes better to you;
Where there is only this goodness and justice,
Selfishness flourishes.
God for you is only the lard
And the absolute minimum of salt
With which you season the mush of your individuality   170
To give it a decent taste.
God is only your own I
Carefully dressed up and decorated.
First you work yourself into a proper sweat,
Then it gets a little warm for your dear little heart;
The self is secreted in the perspiration
And is separated from itself,
And this secreted I
Is defined as God for the self.
It turns the I into its own object—
Now you understand my whole subject.

If you wish to learn to treasure the homeland
You must distance yourself from it.
One must first become detached from oneself
If one wishes to know one's own value;
Because the self loves to fondle itself,
It separates itself from itself.
It calls this sweaty I
Comprehensibly incomprehensible.
Indeed this I has hidden,
Objectified, and covered itself;
Now it does not dare
Open its eyes.
One locks a jewel in a box
So that a thief cannot steal it.
The delicate maiden veils her face
From the sunlight.
The self is infinitely precious to itself,
So it wraps itself in a veil.
The self does not dare to look into the depths
For fear and dread of death;
Fear of death makes one beside oneself,
So the I becomes object to itself.
The self flees under cover of darkness
And the pietist brandishes his saber,
So that his excellence, the self,
Does not forfeit existence;
Now he desperately
Holds onto ignorance by the tail,
Has solidly glued himself onto the heavenly gates
171   So that death does not embarrass him.
He sucks on his precious belief
As if on a sweet grape.
One who compresses himself into a seed
And assumes the shape of a person in the firmament,
For whom the person is all that matters,
Now takes his rest in heaven
And observes the course of the world with a smile,

Enjoys himself, free of the deadly struggle
In the vapors of his individual self.
You see only the person in God;
Thus you set yourself on the throne.
You do not know essence and nature;
You know only the nearest point of God,
For the look into the bowels
Yields no welcome sight.
Even death is an essence;
You can read it everywhere;
Even death is a reality
Embossed on God's coat of arms.
I earnestly counsel you,
Do not take your pleasure now;
Fall down before death,
For death itself exists in God.
First let death, with all its crushing powers,
Rule in you;
Let yourself be shaken and convulsed by death,
Be penetrated by its fear;
Then the gentle warmth of mild peace
Will enter immediately into your bowels.
First let death make a clean cut from yourself;
Reconciliation will come along soon.

Now[17] let me once again, divine love, after I have spent   232
enough time casting a distressing look at the gloomy phenomena of the present, in opposition to which the truth itself
cannot appear as truth, but only as opposition, let me once
again sink myself in the delightful and inspiring thoughts of
your essence, in which all particular reality is enclosed and unified! You are God, essence, the essence of everything. You are
the consciousness that enlightens everything; you are thought
itself, Spirit itself, the time that negates everything, the space
that preserves everything. God, you exist as love itself, as all
essence, as all consciousness, as all Spirit, all time, all space, all
nature, as everything, both in its unity and its distinction, as my

affirmation and negation, my ground of life and death in one reality. As time, you are my passing away; as space, you are my continuance; as essence, my end; as consciousness, my beginning. As everything, as Spirit and nature, as consciousness and essence, as time and space, you are not just the unity of that which is distinguished, but you are the distinction of that which is distinguished, the independence of that which is independent, the multiplicity of the many, the existence of that which exists, the limit of that which is limited, the determination of the determined, the singleness of the single. How would you be everything, how would you be love, if you were only the unity in that which is one and not also the distinction in that which is distinguished, if you were only the universal and not also the particular and single, were only the unlimited and not also the limited and determined? You are everything; this is certain, is itself all truth. But what is this everything, how does it exist? This everything, is it all as one, or is it also this one as dispersed, as distinguished? How would you be everything if you were everything ony in its binding unity but not also in its dispersing distinction? Would you not be only something if you were everything only in its unity and therefore only in distinction from its distinction? If you were only the negation of that which is distinguished and particular, as only negation of that which is distinguished, you would be a reality that is only distinguished from distinction; as mere negation, therefore, as mere opposition to that which is distinguished, and as included under the concept of the distinction, you would not be everything. You are everything only as you yourself are the concept of everything; everything is comprehended in you alone, but you are comprehended in nothing but you yourself.

The infinite affirms as it negates and negates as it affirms. The infinite exists totally and infinitely, but it would not exist in such a manner if its negation were a reality that existed separately and apart for itself, if a partition, a boundary, existed between its negation and its affirmation, if, therefore, the negation were finite, if it ended at the affirmation and the affirmation ended at it. The finite does not exist infinitely in the finite, as the spiritless and godless mode of thinking intends and wills it; the finite exists infinitely only in the infinite. But infinity is precisely the infinity of the finite in the infinite, is the negation of the finite. In infinity, the finite exists in its end, not in and for itself; therefore, it exists in its negation; yet this negation is at once its affirmation. The finite existing in the end of the finite, in the limit of its limit, in the finitude of finitude, in the negation of its negation, only at that point exists in its affirmation.

If, dear human, you cannot grasp the nature of the infinite, that its negation is affirmation and its affirmation is negation, then at least try to grasp in analogy and metaphor how negation can also be affirmation. Is not the punishing wrath of a father, which, as wrath and punishment, is negation of the child, love for the child, the will for the child's best, and, therefore, an affirmation of the child? The father's relation to the child is like the relation of the infinite to the finite. The child is the human at the stage of his finitude and appearance; the father is the human at the last and infinite stage, at the stage of essence, from which stage, therefore, the father as a determinate individual is no longer in progress, but only in retrogression, not in growth, but only in decline, because he exists in the highest and last, the infinite stage, which has for its limit no other stage, not to speak of a higher one, because, as determinate single being, he has arrived at the end of his life. In contrast, the anger with which one child harms another child is only negation, for the one child is related to the other as finitude to finitude. Is not negation also affirmation in love? When your heart is inflamed by love for a being, you injure and deprive that being, you deprive it of its indifferent and satisfied unity with itself, you take from it its separate existence, its independence. You will and desire and strictly demand that it should exist only with and for you, should be one with you, but should not exist separately, that is, free and independent of you. Thus, if the beloved being wishes to separate from you, to take back or even not to surrender its independent existence, then love's power and activity of negation step forth alone and independently for them-

234

selves; and because negation steps forth into separate existence, love becomes destructive hatred, anger, vengeance, enmity. But now, is not love also affirmation in its negation of independent existence? Is not the negation that is love the highest, most profound, most certain, most real affirmation possible? How can you affirm a being more than by loving it? How can you esteem and acknowledge, verify and prove a being more than by loving it? But can you separate the negation of this being from this verification and affirmation of it? When love turns into hatred and enmity, these arise from nowhere else in the soul but from love. Enmity and hatred are pure negations; but how could love turn into enmity, how could enmity arise from love, if love were not already in itself negation? What is enmity but the negation that is infinite negation in love, which does not have its boundary at affirmation as a reality that is separate from negation, which is therefore affirmation itself that has been exposed as finite, as pure, as independent negation? Is not death itself (to show you an example of the truth, even in the case of love), although the negation of the individual, at the same time his affirmation?

Death is the manifestation of the fact that you are not a being without determination, without purpose, and, thus, without limitation. As death negates you, it is the manifestation, the confirmation, the affirmation of your limit and, therefore, of your purpose and determination. But since precisely this limit was the inner determination of your individuality, that which made this individuality into what it was, death, as the testimony, the factual proof, the affirmation of your limit, is the affirmation of your individuality. Or death, in the negation of your individuality, is at the same time the proof of its reality. The purpose determines. As it determines, it limits. As it limits, it takes away, it robs, it negates. But the purpose gives as it takes, for it makes the reality of which it is the purpose into that which it is. It affirms. Without purpose, there is no individual; without limit, there is no purpose and no death. Thus death, as manifestation of purpose, is at once affirmation and negation. Therefore, the purpose of the individual, actually his individuality itself, is not canceled and broken off with the negation of

235

his existence, but continues without interruption. Even the purpose of the individual, as it is the purpose of the individual's existence, has an uninterrupted continuation in the existence of a new individual whose determination is the same purpose.

Now, if it is true to say that the infinite affirms as it negates, if the infinite in its negating unity is also distinction that grants existence and subsistence, then this proposition can also be reversed to show that the limit itself is being in the infinite, that individuality is reality in the infinite, that determination, existence itself is essence, that life itself is immortality, that time is eternity, that a moment is infinity, that a point is immeasurability. May you again, love, solve for me the mystery and riddle of essence! When my soul becomes love, it collects and concentrates itself into one point; it determines and limits itself. My soul obtains quality and character only in this collection and concentration. But is not this oppression, this anxiety of soul in the limit and character of love, also the highest enjoyment, blessedness, freedom? Does pure being exclude limitation and determinateness? Is not this limitation of love infinity itself, pure being? What is the highest pure enjoyment but pure being itself as it is object of experience, as it exists in experience? But love is the highest enjoyment, and yet it is a determination, a quality of the soul. Therefore, does pure being exclude the limit or the limit exclude pure being? Love is the sense for the infinite. Love is not an experience of that which is determined and limited, or else it would be what it is not, a determined and limited experience. It is the experience of essence. And although a determinate essence might be the external object of your experience, still this object is only the occasion for you to experience pure essence. But in the experience of love, only the pure essence in and of the determinate essence is your object. But pure essence is also pure being, and the experience of pure essence and of pure being is itself pure essence and being. Therefore, love is a limit, yet it grasps infinity.

However, if the limit and whatever other expression of the limit is infinity itself in the infinite, then the end of the individ-

236

ual before and in the infinite is no end. As the past being of present individuals in and before the infinite is not something left behind, separated from their present being, so, in and before the infinite, the being of dead individuals is not separated from their past being. Individuals who exist no longer for themselves, in a finite relation to themselves, and who no longer exist for us, in a finite relation to us, still exist in and before the infinite. They are dead only in relation to themselves as determinate individuals and to us as determinate individuals, but they are not dead in relation to essence itself and to the infinite. To this extent humans die only out of relationships, die only before and for one another, and death itself rests on comparison.

Death has only as much reality as comparison and relationship. One can speak of the reality of death or immortality only by presupposing the reality of the standpoint of comparison and relationship, and only within this standpoint. You call something dead only because you compare it with what it was previously and with what you are presently. The end of an individual exists only for you and, at most, for that individual only insofar as he feels the end approaching. But as long as the individual only feels the end approaching, the end does not yet exist. The existence of the end excludes the existence of the individual. Thus the existence of the end, the end itself, the actual end, does not exist for the individual. But because the end of the individual does not exist for him, the end is end only for you, not for the individual who is at his end. The end could be an end for the individual only if the individual were not to end in his end, only if the individual were still also living in death in some inexplicable manner. The individual would possess the feeling of his not-being only if he were to exist in not-being at the same time as he still existed in being. Death is death and painful only before death, but not in death. Death is such a ghostly essence that it exists only when it is not and does not exist when it is. The negation of life that is only the end of life is no living, no actual negation of life. Thus the end of the individual, since it does not exist for this individual, has no reality for him, for only that which is an object of the individual's experience,

237

238

which exists for the individual, has reality for the individual. The individual ceases to exist only for others, not for himself. Death is death only for the living, not for the dying. Death exists for the one who is dying, and death is frightening to him only as long as he is not yet dead. But now, since death exists only for those whose end it is not, exists for those only as long as and while they live, exists only as long as and while death is an object to them and thus has reality for them, then the reality of death is merely relation. You compare the dead being with the living being as it remains in your representation; only in comparison do you fix death and oppose it as something separate to life. Thus humans die only in appearance; death itself is mere appearance, representation; death is not reality.

Death is no positive negation, but a negation that negates itself, a negation that is itself empty and nothing. Death is itself the death of death. As it ends life, it ends itself; it dies because of its own worthlessness and meaninglessness. An actual negation is that which exists within reality, is a negation that takes away the real while it allows reality to continue and imparts it, a negation that is only partial and not total, that thus robs reality only from a determinate reality and not from reality itself, that cancels certain properties and predicates of the real, but does not cancel the sphere of the real. Only the negation that takes only something is real. The determination of its reality or unreality depends upon the content and extent of that which it takes. A negation that takes everything is itself nothing. Because it takes everything, it no longer has a determination and content. Because it cancels all reality, it cancels its own reality. Thus only that which negates something determinate or actual is actual negation or destruction. Misfortune is such a negation, for it is a negation of the real within the sphere of reality that remains unnegated; it is a negation of the real through the real. For example, if I were transposed from having a superfluity of all goods into the condition of extreme poverty, this negation of my good fortune would have an actual existence; my poverty would be a determinate condition opposed to my previous situation. Thus death, as a total negation, is a self-negating negation,

239

a negation that, because it takes all, takes nothing. More properly, death is a destruction that is its own negation and destruction, that is nothing, that is a meaningless and insignificant negation. It would have significance only if it negated something. Precisely this something that it negates would be its significance, as, for instance, the negation of my goods, in the determination that it is a negation of a determinate existence, a negation of the reality of pure wealth, has its significance and means something just because it only negates something. That which negates existence itself has no existence. For when it negates existence itself, it negates that in, of, and by which it can exist. Thus death, because it negates itself in the negation of existence, because it is nothing in the destruction of what is positive, of life itself, is thereby the affirmation of existence, is the most infallible, strongest assurance and verification of the absolute reality of existence and life. Death has no value, no significance, no reality, no determination, and yet certainly its lack of value and significance, its unreality and lack of character, are the clearest testimony and verification of the value, significance, and substantiality in the character of life.

Surely this thought must appear to you to be unintelligible or even irrational if you measure the reality of death by the pain that the death of a beloved person causes for you, the living, and do not at the same time recognize in this pain the nothingness of death and the reality of life. The death of a determinate being, for you, the determinate being who was closely related to the person who has passed away, is also a determinate negation, or has determinate negations as its result. But then can you, the determinate being, the living being with his concerns and experiences, make yourself the criterion of the reality of death? But what does the fact that death has no existence other than relation and appearance mean; what does it mean that death is a self-destructive destruction, other than that existence alone is proper to existence, that life alone is proper to life? And again, what can this self-destruction of death mean other than that existence, life, the individual—for individuality is the only form in which life, or existence, is real—is unconditioned, limitless, and actual reality without negation, that life is the most certain and assured, the all-powerful, ever-present self-affirmation, is absolute truth, substantiality, infinity? Life is finite? Death is the limit, the end of life? Only something limits something. Only that being is finite which has its true essence in or at which it ends. Thus the world is finite, for the end and limit of the world is God, its true essence. Thus the child is finite, for its limit and end is its true essence, the mature human, whose existence is like the essence of humanity. Determinate things are finite because that in which they end is infinite, because in relation to them there is a higher level of reality. So, then, death is to be the limit and the end of life? If it were this, death would have to be not only an existing reality but also a higher reality, more reality than life itself. But death is a limitation of life that has no existence or reality. Thus life is infinite, for its limit is nothing.

Whatever loses its existence in its limit, whatever ceases to be what it is in its limit, as life ceases to be life in death, is infinite, as a reality that ceases to be what it is when it is divided is simple and indivisible. A reality that possesses limits that are mere, indeterminate, characterless negation, negation that, because of this lack, the absence of everything material, determinate, actual, is self-canceling negation, this reality is not a determinate affirmation, a determinate reality, but is infinite, absolute reality. The measure of not-being depends on the measure of being; the level of negation depends on the level of reality. But that which is not pure, total negation, but is only a level, a certain measure of negation, because, as a measured negation, it is not a negation of all being but of a certain measure of being, is a level of reality, is a certain measure of being, a material existence, a determinate something, a sphere of reality that is constituted in any manner, an essence that possesses its own designation and characterization. Thus if life were not pure, infinite reality, its negation would not be pure negation, but a determinate negation, existing as a real something or essence; the nega-

241

tion of life would not be death. Although life possesses its most decisive, most powerful, and most expressive actuality only in experience, still life has already proved its all-negating negation, its infinite actuality, in its lower stages. Even the life of a plant is infinite life. Indeed, this plant, which now wonderfully captivates your gaze, ceases to exist, but can you take this cessation to be the criterion of its finitude? Do you express anything about the life of this plant when you call it a finite life? Is finitude a predicate that determines? The plant is what it is in the determinate determinations and properties of its organism; these determinations express only themselves, but they do not express a characterless, indeterminate finitude. Thus, if you say that this plant is finite, you omit the determinateness of the determinations, the properties of the property; because you fix the bare, empty property that no longer affects or expresses the plant, you allow its meaningful life to disappear into the tasteless, odorless, and colorless predicate of finitude. And when this being that you call a plant ends before your eyes, when, therefore, with this end a disruption, an injury, takes place in the plant, is this end a limit? The plant ends because its life is its measure. But this measure is its very life and essence, is its affirmation. The plant does not encounter another, a foreign reality, in its end; it does not arrive at a boundary. It exists in the end of its life, both in the principle of its life and during its life; its own essence is its end as well as its beginning. The plant never goes outside of itself, never gets away from itself, but always remains within itself; it never loses its life. You again arrive at the end of the plant where you have begun when you pursue the compass of its life with the self-donation of thinking. You arrive at no end; you are always in the middle. The end of the plant gives nothing and takes nothing. Even the measure of life does not cancel the infinite self-affirmation that is life. Infinity exists even in the limit. If it is actual determination and property, the limit is the concept as well as the life of a thing, is its basis as well as its essence. Thus, as its essence is contained in the limit of a thing, so also the cancellation of the limit, infinity, exists in the thing.

242

But now, if death is only a self-negating negation, then immortality, in its common meaning as the total opposite of nothingness, is an unreal, indeterminate affirmation of the individual, of life, and of existence. If I say of you that you are a living, experiencing, loving, willing, knowing being, I express something that is infinitely more real and determinate and profound about you than if I say of you that you are an immortal being. Every good action, every knowledge and thought, every experience, even if it is sensible, is more than immortality. There exists more essence, more reality, more actuality in every action, experience, and knowing than in immortality. Mortality and immortality disappear as mere appearances before content, essence, the determinate and determining concept. Determinateness and property are not only immortality but are more than immortality, for immortality does not determine, engenders no concept, is not even a predicate. As little as I express something real about the plant when I say that it is transitory, so little do I determine a flower when I assert that it passes away, so little do the predicates of transitoriness and mortality affect, grasp, and touch a being, so little do the predicates of imperishability and immortality affect and touch the soul or the individual. But a predicate that does not affect, that is without impact, is no predicate, for the predicate strikes, inspires, moves a reality to passion. The predicate is definition and specification, and every limitation must place a reality into an emotional state. Only the determinations of a thing are its affirmations, but the determinations of a thing taken together and in unity are its content. Thus a thing's content is its affirmation, its substantiality, and its actuality. But the content of a thing is exalted over both mortality and immortality, for the thing is determined and determinable only by itself, has the measure of its reality only in itself. As death or transitoriness takes nothing away from a thing, so immortality gives nothing to a thing. The concept of the content and of some reality is a concept that is independent of both death and immortality.

The significance and the value of a content is the content

243

itself. Death does not diminish the significance, and immortality does not augment or heighten it. As death is only a negation that is appearance, in like manner, immortality is only an affirmation that is appearance. Those people who stated that it matters, not how long, but how you have lived were truly wise. The length, the duration, and therefore immortality—for if you enter into essence, if you do not allow yourself to be deceived by the illusion of mere words, immortality is nothing but the abstract representation of duration—do not determine, but the "how" determines. That you are an immortal essence means only that you are an essence of value and significance. A mortal essence is an indifferent essence; its being is of no consequence. It can exist or not exist, and whether or not it exists is immaterial. But an immortal essence is an essence that possesses essential, necessary being; its being is connected with inalienable, infinite concerns. But the "how," the content of a being is just its necessity and essentiality. The indifference or nonindifference of a thing depends only on its lack of significance or its content. An indifferent thing is a thing without significance or determination. The determination of an essence is the essential concern, the interest of its existence. Thus the true meaning of being immortal is being something, for lack of significance is canceled when there is something, and along with lack of significance are canceled indifference and contingency, and with these is canceled mortality. Property alone signifies. End and endlessness are without interest; they are without meaning and significance for the property. Be something, and you are everything. Meanwhile, end is spiritless and irrational negation; endlessness is spiritless and irrational affirmation. But life, in and for itself and apart from all its moral and intellectual determinations, is a being that has within itself infinite significance, and, as a significant, meaningful, absolutely determined and actual being, life is eternal and immortal.

That is immortal which is a purpose in itself. The purpose of a thing is its significance; its significance is its value and worth; its worth is its content; its content is its determinations. But life is the being that, in and for itself as being, already possesses its

244

worth, value, and significance in itself. In this unity with its significance, therefore, life is a purpose in itself and thus is immortal. Every moment of life is fulfilled being, is of infinite significance, exists for its own sake, is posited by itself, is self-satisfied, complete, and saturated plenitude of reality, is unrestricted self-affirmation. Every moment is a drink that drains to the dregs the cup of immortality, the cup that, like the magic goblet of Oberon, always refills itself on its own. Life is heavenly music that the exalted Artist of the universe conjures forth out of the instrument of nature. Fools say that life is a bare, empty sound, that it passes away like the breath, that it scatters like the wind. But life is music. Every moment is a melody or a fulfilled, soulful, inspired tone. The wind rushes past my ears without value and significance. Its essence is inessential and insignificant transitoriness, a blowing and drifting that is indifferent, without interest. But the tone is music, is plenitude, is filled being, is its own ground, is purpose, is content existing in itself. Musical tones also pass away, but every tone is filled being, has a significance as tone. Transitoriness disappears as a meaningless reality without significance in comparison to this inner significance and soul of the musical tone. The mere sound is comprehended only in the flow of passing away, for in sound the present moment is not distinguished from the past or future moment; because of this sameness without distinction, because of this worthless repetition of one and the same, sound is indifferent transitoriness and finitude. But the tone as fulfilled, meaningful moment is a determinate, distinguished moment of time. This fulfillment, this content, is its purpose and its significance. The indifference of its existence disappears because of its distinction, its property, its content. And with the indifference disappears its mere temporality, for the indifference of being is its mere temporality. An indifferent being is truly nothing but a merely temporal being. A merely temporal being is a being in which the being of present, future, and past are not distinguished from one another, for there is no distinction within time as such. The present moment of time, as mere moment of time, is not distinguished and separated from the past moment.

245

Only the content, but not time, distinguishes time. Only because of its property is the present moment a determinate and therefore a distinct moment. Thus every something, every content, is nontemporal and supertemporal; every limit in time is a limit, a negation, of time itself, is every fulfilled moment as fulfilled eternity and infinity.

Eternity is nothing but the fulfillment, the property, and the determination of time. As the active, actual negation of time in time, eternity is precisely fulfillment, determination of time. Eternity is power, energy, active deed, triumphant victory. But eternity is active deed only when it exists in time beyond time, only when it negates time in time. He alone is the victor who is exalted above misfortune, who negates and conquers misfortune in misfortune, but not he who slumbers beyond misfortune in the soft bosom of Fortuna. The tone is tone only because it is the negation of passing away in passing away, only because it is not merely temporal but, in its temporality, is determinate, meaningful, time-negating tone. Indeed, the tone is short or long. But is it nothing more than its length? This sonata, in which the individual tones are short or long, passes away; it will not be played for all eternity. But, I ask you, what would you call someone who, while the sonata was being performed, did not listen, but only counted, who separated the length of the tone from its content, who, in this separation, took the temporality to be his object, and, when the sonata was over, made the fifteen minutes that it took to be played into the predicate of his judgment concerning the sonata, and, who, while other people, overcome with admiration at its content, sought to catch its significance in exact words, characterized the sonata as a quarter-hour sonata? Wouldn't you assuredly find the predicate *fool* too affirmative to define such a person? Then how should one call those who take transitoriness to be a predicate of this life, who believe that they say something, that they pass a judgment on this life, when they say that it is temporal, it is transitory? That by which one says nothing, thinks nothing, defines nothing, is itself nothing. How should one designate those who take as their object that which is nothing and who, because they take nothing as their object, give to nothing such significance and reality that they destroy the something, the actually real, or at least lose sight of it? They call themselves the pious ones, rationalists, even philosophers. Leave the dead among the dead!

God is life, love, consciousness, Spirit, nature, time, space, everything, in both its unity and its distinction. As a loving being, you exist in the love of God; as a conscious being, you exist in the consciousness of God; as a thinking being, you exist in the Spirit of God; as a living being, you exist in infinite life itself; in time, you exist beyond all time; in space, you exist outside of space. God is immortal; only that which is immortal exists in the immortal. In order to comprehend and express the truth in and as truth, not in and as opposition, you exist in God, and therefore with immortality. God is consciousness, life, essence, but he is love as infinite, everlasting love for the conscious being, as everlasting love for essence and for that which lives without end. That which is eternal is the only object for the eternal.

Prefatory Admonitions and Rejoinders[1]

Satire—it is a microscope—greatly magnifies things,
But it does not change them; it only displays them with more
clarity.

My couplets are anatomical preparations
Of the vermin that damage our seeds and blossoms.

The naked eye is not enough for the investigation of vermin;
Only satire penetrates their inner reality.

To be sure, the couplets that I offer here are bitingly satirical;
But Spirit will vouch for me that they are truthful and to the
point.

If you don't want to talk hot air, then measure the marksman
by his target;
Every specific animal requires a certain kind of hunter.

It is also biting satire, if a surgeon
Amputes one's leg; but do you criticize him on that account?

I am only a surgeon, a totally empirical surgeon;
So do not take offense at the surgeon's bite.

Even the lady exposes to the surgeon that which she otherwise
conceals;
Where the surgeon begins, the aesthetician leaves off.

So, too, when I act as its surgeon, the present theology reveals
to me
Many things about which it would love to be modest.

My surgical vocabulary inevitably includes words that are un-
    acceptable
    In the evening tea circles, ladies and gentlemen.

Who is a biting satirist? The one who studies the sources
    From which evil emanates and then displays them to the
    public.

Certainly your satire is not biting; it only singes the hair off the
    head
    While leaving untouched the rotting flesh.

Whoever grasps evil by the root is biting.
    Indeed! If you just tear off the leaves, you don't hurt the tree.

173   But truly your satire tears from the tree only those leaves
    That are a burden to it and impede its growth.[2]

The Christian Orpheus

The Greeks drew human meaning even from rocks;
    Our pedagogy turns even humans into clods.[3]

Boundless Impudence

Presently a parasitic growth is damaging your sacred grove,
    Divine Pallas—lifeless, hypocritical piety.[4]

Noble Breeding

Saints Cyril and Cyprian now sleep with Pallas and Venus;
    Dear friend, don't be surprised at the rare brood.

A Wise Arrangement

Ah, these splendid times! Palm Sunday donkeys now graze on
    Parnassus[5]
    And are appointed to guard Greek gardens and pastures.

The Misery of the Pious

To water Ardnt's paradise, to drench his parched little plot,
These gentlemen now drain off the spring of Castalia.[6]

Ad vocem the Educational Prospectus[7]

Excellent! The sacred flow of the pure stream of inspiration
That once stoutly bore the ancients to deed and song
Must now be moderated by the cold sweat of affected melan-
choly,
Must be contaminated in the putrid swamp of long decayed
power,
Must be polluted and infected by the scabies of mystical sheep—
Quickly, a refreshing drink! Quench the thirst of youth!

The Latest Scholastic Inquisitors as
Interpreters of Classical Antiquity

They now rear parrots; they teach only mimicry,
But not Roman sense, not Greek Spirit.
In order to hold the portrait of heroism up to the souls of youth   174
They wash away its colors, they erase the heroic shape,
They do nothing but whiten the canvas and tear up the fabric
of the language
Choking the classical Spirit with the shreds of words.
Their philology feeds on neither the berries of Bacchus nor the
gritty maize of Ceres,
Not even on husks and straw;
It stands undecided between classical Spirit and pietist naïveté
Like Buridan's little donkey.*

---

*As is well known, this celebrated ass, tortured equally by hunger and thirst and standing equidis-
tant between water and hay, was unable to move to either side because of a condition of complete
indecision and passed away in terrible misery.

Degradation

Once Christ was the light of the world, bestower of Spirit and
knowledge;
But now he is only a night watchman for the mystic.

A Question

Has not humanity become older since the birth of Christ,
And, with the years, come further along in understanding?
Should humans still suck at the scriptural pacifier
And, having fully matured, imbibe only watered-down pap?

A Dismal Outcome

For centuries they have sucked at the udder of the Bible
So that it is now empty once and for all—even the cow died!

A Second Inquiry

Do you not believe that all the nourishing sap
Was sucked out of the Bible long ago by the age of Christi-
anity?
Did not the original Word later become the Christian world?
And did not the sap long ago congeal into our flesh and
blood?

A Humorous Recompense

Once Christ carried the sheep on his powerful shoulders;
To pay him back, I will now carry the sheep for the Savior.

175   The Historical Meaning and Destiny of Pietism

Know this! In its historical course, humanity goes through
The same process as the organic body.
When hungry, the body takes in material and consumes it;
Once it has assimilated it, it disposes of the superfluous.

The latest pietism is the eliminated waste
  Of the food that humanity long ago digested.
And, as in nature bluebottle flies, following the disposition of
    wisdom,
  Consume ordure with hearty appetites,
So the masses enjoy the excrement of humanity
  In order once and for all to cleanse the world of these messy
    droppings.

The Folly of Pietism

The simple seed becomes corn; by a complicated process
  It is changed into food, finally into the blood of an organism.
Observe! The same process exists in human history:
  Spirit actively transforms the material it assimilates.
Thus the Christian religion is of divine origin
  Because it already contained the seeds of its development at
    its beginning;
Its history only unfolded out of itself
  In unity with the human Spirit, and with humanity's freedom
    and spontaneity.
Once grown, Christianity was given as the material for the nour-
    ishment of later humans
  Who then transformed the written Word into the essence of
    Spirit.[8]
Therefore the exalted pillars on which the temple of our present
    orthodoxy
  Is supported are only shreds of straw.
Up there in the sanctuary, its head bowed, its torch all but out,
  Theology mournfully lies in repose on the tomb of the past.[9]
But now comes the pietist, who wants to bake nourishing bread,
  Not with grain and understanding, but out of discarded
    chaff;
He wants to dam up the stream of the Spirit of the times,
  To bind the wounds of the world with used paper and dis-
    carded rags;
The fool even wants to measure the man for the kiddie slippers
  That the boy wore out long ago,

To enlighten the world with wax candles, to relieve the man's
hunger
With gold-plated nuts, to frighten him with "grrr" and
"bowwow."

A Contribution to Psychological Paleontology,
along with a Prophecy

Schiller and Goethe, the divine geniuses of Germany, sang as
never before;
Thinkers like the great Plato created the world of ideas;
The everlasting Spirit, out of the fullness of pure inspiration,
Overflowed into the stream of development.
But mud must follow the course of the pure stream—
Look! Mysticism is presently the sediment of the Spirit of the
times,[10]
And pietists are fossils, archaic humans
Who were petrified into propositions in the spiritual stream;[11]
But the stream will continue to flow over the mystical bottom
mud,
Seeking a new channel, abandoning the propositions.[12]

The Sleep of Mysticism

Spirit raises itself on the wings of poetry in hexameter;
It withdraws into itself for reflection in pentameter;
So the poetry of Germania soared in hexameter,
And Germany's philosophy followed in pentameter,
And the enchanting tones of these harmonic verses—
In which the divine Spirit that penetrates the world
Sang to itself the great hymn of modern history—
Rocked the lazy masses to mystical sleep.

The Psychological Origin of Mysticism

Fever heat fills the chambers of the dear little heart,
While the cold of Siberia takes over the abandoned under-
standing.
But the humidity of passion mingles with the icy mind,

And now the little window that opens on our world is steamed
    up.
While people lie asleep at night, the window completely freezes;
    At dawn, behold the floral designs of frosty mysticism.

The Same Subject

The heartlet is surfeited with selfish goals;
    Its intoxication brings about an indisposition in the head.
Neither water, nor wine, nor even vinegar can remedy the con-
    dition,
    But hangovers make excellent prospects for the academy.

A Perilous Existence

177

Why does pietism dread the divine light of thought?
    Because its entire system is already as soft as butter.

The Rejected Summons of a Pietist

"Follow me steadfastly! I will keep you from danger
    And lead you in security and peace over the Alps of the
    world."
Only the donkey is more surefooted than the heroic steed,
    So your victory is only that of an ass. I would rather fall as a
    hero.

A Dialogue

"Tell me, why do you torture me in verse?
    Now you use the short form of pietist, now the long, when-
    ever it pleases you."
Because your whole system is as little suited to the present world
    As is the word *pietist* to melodic verse.

The Impure Philology

Once upon a time, a vestal virgin named Philology
    Protected the purity and clear meaning of the sacred fire of
    antiquity;

But soon the flame was snuffed out by a reverent sigh,
  For the pietist robbed her of her maidenhood.

The Pietists

Know this! The pietists are nothing but the loathsome worms
  Into which the moldering body of Saint Peter finally
    decomposed.

The Hypocrite in the Cassock

With dissembling countenance, he slyly deludes the credulous
    flock
  So that willing sheep seek only his fold.*

The Coward in the Pulpit

It is not to be denied: he displays overwhelming ardor.
  But is he ready to sizzle on a red-hot grate?

The Irrationality of Certain Preachers

Life requires sharp distinctions
  But knowledge and art reconcile the world to itself.
Yet, instead of being benefactors, instead of imparting attained
    knowledge and insight
  To those people who are incapable of gaining them on their
    own,
Instead of spreading reason, which lightens the burden of life
    by its reconciling power,
  They cry out from the pulpit against it.

The Rationality of These Gentlemen

What they call reason is nothing but their own stupidity;
  So if you believe their shrieks, you will certainly come to your
    senses.

*That is, his confessional.

The Three Newspapers of the World of Mysticism[13]

My goodness! They almost suffocated in their own fumes!
  Now, fortunately, three chimney flues carry away the smoke.

What Can They Still Accomplish?

They certainly can turn out newspapers, but the pious only write
    dull stuff;
  They do not achieve significant works, for the Spirit departed
    long ago.

How Do They Do It?

It takes a large crowd of these poor people working together to
    push one pen—
  How nervous they are in the present day!

Yet how can the pious bring themselves to write for contempo-
    rary papers,
  How can they pour the Holy Spirit into a profane vessel?
Well, these gentlemen can no longer hold their water,
  So three chamber pots collect their little contributions.

Interesting Variety

The Prussian pietists coo like domesticated little doves;
  The Bavarian rag cackles like a rabid goose.

The Bible Societies

If they had given them away for nothing, perhaps they would
    have made some profit;
  Certainly they have already done all the business they could
    with such a sacred text.

The *Campeadores* of Our Day

As once the knight of La Mancha battled the sails of the wind-
    mill,
  The heroes of our times wrestle with Satan's phantom.

The Errant Knights of the Present

Really, there are still a lot of them wandering around! But they
no longer chase the heathen or dragons,
And their royal beloved is now the little dove with the sacred
halo.[14]

The Metropolitans of Our Church

Are you astonished that, according to the most recent decree,
Only the orthodox will obtain parishes in the land?[15]
Yet if long ago they had fitted the gates of heaven with a com-
bination lock
That could be set only by the art of the mystic, they could
have closed that one, too.

Signs of the Times

Once again the clown gradually takes over the contemporary
stage,
While sorrow timidly keeps the home fires burning.
At the same time, fearful egoism raises its ugly head
And does its hallowed business in the robes of the pious
hypocrite.

Praiseworthy Foresight

Some find it an injustice that the pious leader never cares for
The development of our people. I do not, for he has more
exalted duties:
To secure for himself as time goes on a safe harbor
In the paradisiacal halls, parks, and heavenly meadows,
And so to make himself comfortable in the midst of millions of
angels
Who tell tall tales every time they open their mouths.

The Exploits of the Devout

They are never destined bravely and forcefully
To grasp the wheel of the times with strong masculine hands,

But they restrict the unending motion of life
  To their apathetic attempts to hatch existence from thor-
    oughly rotten eggs—
Eggs neither fertilized by the cock of might, self-moving time
  Nor engendered out of the plenitude of all-nourishing Ceres,
But laid shamelessly by a bird of the wrong species—
  And, at the finish line, they expect the palm of victory for
    this.

The Pious Armada
Afflabit Deus, et dissipabuntur[16]

Truly an awesome army! For the hypocrites make up the
    advance guard
And the host of seraphim lies proudly in reserve.
Led by the wardens of heaven, their fists tightly clenched   180
  Under the cloak of simplicity, as far as the eye can see
The cohorts of featherbrained bigots deploy for battle without
    quarter,
  for any opponent who falls is immediately damned for eter-
    nity.
Their allies are fanaticism and dissension;
  The dregs of the people make up their innumerable camp fol-
    lowers.

The Sectarian Spirit of the Pietists

The fire has long burned low, and there is no more fuel to revive
    it;
  In order to survive the cold, they press together.

The Origin of Mysticism

The thin tapers of Spirit allotted to these gentlemen are soon
    burned up;
  Then nothing but mystical gas remains in their heads.

The Perverted World

How can our contemporary pietist be a lawyer without being a
    backsliding Christian?
In his mind, the only *corpus juris* is the body of the Savior.[17]
Could he be a physician? The only nature he will observe is in
    the Bible,
Where everything is the same as elsewhere, but distorted and
    deranged.

The Universalism of Contemporary Christianity

Not only does Christianity encompass in its all-embracing unity
    Cherokees, Hottentots, Eskimos, and Negroes,
But now the devout world counts as in the fold
    Even natural history, chemistry, physics, and botany.

The Ass in the Lion Skin

Even when Spirit, which constantly changes forms in its youth,
    has long departed,
    The forms it sheds have a lasting existence as monuments in
    the world.
Thus great numbers of pagan temples still stand
    But their Spirit is departed; God no longer dwells in them.
Look! Now the mystic struts around menacingly
    Disguised in the form that the lion once assumed.
But he does not frighten us; we already know from history
    That now only an ass hides in the lion skin.

How Things Change

181

What was once most rare later becomes most common;
    It falls from the throne into the dust. Thus, too, the noble
    word.
Once mysticism signified the secret of a more profound knowl-
    edge,
    But today it stands for the gossip of old women.

The Miser

The skinflint who hoards life's involvement only for the future
    world
    Dies of starvation in the midst of present riches.

What I Have Is Better Than What I Might Have

As in the fable, the dog that, out of greed for the piece of bogus
    meat,
    Lost the real one that he already held in his mouth,
So the mystical fool cheats himself out of real life,
    Straining in futile greed after its mere semblance.

The Pietist, or the Fox and the Grapes

Because he is too feeble to reach the grapes of life,
    He goes away comforting himself: "Well, right *now* they are
    not yet ripe."

Nonsense

There are shadows only with light, but mystical fools notice
    Only the shadows of the world, and not its heavenly light.

A Prophecy

Spirit has surged to stormy heights in the river of modern his-
    tory
    And mysticism is presently the foam of the tempestuous
    flood.
But as once Aphrodite emerged from the foam of the sea,
    Glorious Spirit will now arise from the foam of time.

The Mystic's Use of Reason

If he remains close to belief he is at least passably rational,
    But if he ventures into reason, the result will be a fool.

182   **Defenseless Faith**

Nature has given everything weapons for protection,
　　Thus, horns for the bull, bristles for the hedgehog and pig.
To the noble human species she gave reason; faith alone
　　She left defenseless, because it is contrary to her.
Therefore, though mystics use reason in defense of faith,
　　Reason is really reason only when it defends reason.
So the mystic demonstrates to us, adduces as grounds
　　Only pig bristles, donkey ears, and horns.

Unattained Goals

When pietists defend the faith with reasons,
　　Reason merely grows horns on faith.[18]

Pious Sophistry

If faith does not suffice, then reason must help out;
　　But if understanding cannot come up with the answers, faith
　　has no need of it.

**The Superfluity of Deliverance
in the Pietistic Sense**

I need no deliverance from my past sins;
　　They were but stages of my life that were blotted out long
　　ago.
From now on, I will watch out for sins to come,
　　And the present has its own compensation.

To All Bible Dealers

Guilt is a result of sin; it is terrible human suffering
　　For in its fury, it robs the soul of happiness.
Tell me now, you pious promoters of the biblical trade,
　　Does even the Holy Book make us free of guilt?

Pious Quacks

Evil is specific and treated with specific methods:
  Thus speaks medicine, but not quackery.
Presently, the Bible societies think to cure the whole world
  With the Bible alone! What quackery!

The Hidden Goal of the Pious Community

Formerly they collected taxes for the edification of the church;
  Now they collect money to pull down the structure.

Doubt and Certainty

183

Once, perhaps, biblical words were cures;
  So much I know for certain: the Word heals no more.

Once Is Not Now

To be sure, religion was once the support of the state;
  But now the state is the support of religion.

The Power of Faith

"Faith moves mountains!" Certainly! Faith does not solve
  Difficult problems; it only pushes them aside.

The Fall

Do you know why Adam bit the apple?
  To do theology a favor.

Progress

Surely faith is about to be made into law;
  Soon the police will be the ground of theology.

Exponential Faith

At present, the faith of the pious is raised to the highest power
  For now even faith is the object of faith.

A Suggestion

"Forgive us our trespasses!" I am happy to retain my sins:
  Sins are only the extremes to which goodness is driven.

Insane Pride

What is humility? Nothing but pride gone mad,
  Because it relies on and brazenly boasts of the merits of another.

The *Canes Domini*[19]

In order to exalt the Lord, these beasts spit all over
  Even the most noble deed if it was not done "in the Lord."

Pious Exertions[20]

184

Our present-day pietists still search for dirt underneath the
  fingernails of heathen
In order to make balm for the wounds of the Lord.

The Pietists in Rome and Athens

In order to display to us the pagan world in all its nakedness
  They sit on the toilets of Rome and Athens
Demonstrating how once the foul heathen sh——
  And how faith now releases us from all the needs of nature.

For Th.

You revile Socrates because he eased nature?
  Don't Christians still go to the privy?

The Distinction between Nature and Grace

Indeed, the pagan world had excellent bowel movements,
  Because, in those days, the course of nature was unrestricted.
But faith plugs and stops up the lower intestines—
  The Christian world suffers from hypochondria.

The Heavenly Portals of Contemporary
Learned Pietists

In order to make room for himself in heaven, the hypocrite
  must carry out a purge
In order to sneak Plato and Socrates into h—— .

The Fall of Lucifer

What threw Lucifer down from the throne of heaven?
  You don't know? Nothing but clerical deceipt.

The God of the Theologians

Bread to eat, He still might be able to give us in emergencies,
  But does He still give us matter for thought?

A Demotion

Religion once reigned as lord of the head.
  But its realm is now restricted to the pit of the stomach.

The Theology of Feeling

185

When the play is over and the theater is closed
  There still remains a sentimental feeling.

Mutilation

Recently our professors of theology have lost both their heads
  and their eyes;
  The only hint of the light that they have left is in feeling.

How Far They Have Fallen!

This timid crowd can no longer erect temples or cathedrals,
  So now the only temple left for God is a chamber of the heart.

A Question of Conscience

Why was religion put into the heart?
  To improve respiration.

"It Is Exactly This Way, only Totally Different"

How can pietists have children?
  The Holy Ghost impregnates their wives.

An Important Conclusion of the Rationalists

At long last, by means of the critical-historical standpoint
  They have actually proved to the world that water never becomes wine.

The Reason of the Rationalists

What they call reason is only the vapor
  Collected from the economical dung of the Kantian
  philosophy.

The Historical Significance of Rationalism

Thinking Spirit is the restless, driving source of life;
  It is eternally in motion, eternally self-developing.
But only a chosen few continue to spin the inner threads
  Of Spirit's development, and few know Spirit.
When long ago Spirit soared into higher worlds
  The masses were left behind, for they have trouble concep-
  tualizing Spirit.
The Kantian philosophy was only the milk that nourished
  The maturing Spirit of a more lofty world.

But now this milk has curdled into cheese among the people: 186
  This smelly product is called rationalizing.

A Look into History

Philosophy is ever young, and never lacks means,
  So remember that she alone always has a new change of
    clothes.
If she throws away a dress, Theology puts it right on,
  As the robes of the princess later decorate the maid.
Recently the beggar folk have covered the nakedness in their
    heads
  With Kant's discarded clothes,
And have washed off a few stains that he left on them;
  Now the old rags look fine, almost like a new dress.

The Triteness of the Rationalists' Concepts

These foolish folk, who dream of being rational,
  Trap the divine essences of higher worlds
In the nets used for starlings
  And other things of nature.
They impale martyrs, even the Savior and his apostles,
  On pitchforks that have their proper use
Only in the miserable life of our collective economy,
  And ultimately reduce God and Spirit to dung!

Do the Rationalists Have Sharp Senses?

Not at all, no indeed! Rather, these gentlemen have sharp
    teeth,
  For they happily chew to bits kernel and content.

An Admonition to These Very People

In a pinch, your wisdom probably can satisfy geese,
  But never humans; they demand much more.

The Closer to the Pavement, the More Secure

The rationalists never have ventured every high;
  They take lodging in Kant's neighborhood and only on the
  ground floor.

Very Simple

Why are you amazed at the rationalists' gossip?
  Did these gentlemen ever keep a secret in their heads?

187

Enlightenment

By all means, the world gets brighter
  When people completely denude the forests and level the
  mountains to the plain.

The Peculiar Characteristics of the Rationalistic Light:

(1) It can be weighed.
"How could one collect light in sacks?"
  The rationalist now markets light like corn.

(2) It is as blind as a sickle.
The light of the rationalists enlightens only as much as it clari-
  fies
  Essences, matter, and objects that have disappeared from
  sight.

(3) It does not travel far.
Only the divine light brightens the whole world; but yours
  Fills just sheds and stables; it does not reach farther.

(4) It is transitory.
For you, understanding is critique, which means a little earthen
  lamp

That consumes itself along with its fuel.
So the rationalist standpoint is truly at a critical juncture:
  Its material has been totally gobbled up, and it is on the way
    out.

(5) It can be blown out.
Mysticism is a great bother to it
  For the light of the night lamp can be smothered by smoke.

(6) It is not autonomous.
Light lives only on itself, but the rationalist torch
  Lives only on darkness, and stands or falls with it.

(7) In fact, whether it really is light
has not been decided.
Your reasoning is a hypothetical middle term
  That is based on that disagreeable word *if*.
Only *if* belief is illusion, only *if* all history is nonsense,
  Only *if* others are stupid, only then are you feared.   188
But, unfortunately, the middle term is still in doubt,
  So your reasoning remains hypothetical.

The Natural Process

Morals only comes after critique—the process is natural;
  But am I not a sinner if I am moral without reservation?

The Elegant Table

They have overloaded their stomachs with morals;
  Then afterward, for dessert, they still serve up God.

Rationalistic Critique

This is silly! Even before it tastes food,
  Critique must investigate its flavor and smell.

The Clever Critic

"Can I see?" the critic asks in tones of wisdom, before he
    looks;
    But while he asks the question, he keeps his eyes closed.

The Slow Critique

While critique tries to ascertain whether the wine is potable,
    It has already turned to vinegar, and no one is thirsty any
    more.

"Parturiunt montes," and So Forth[21]

Whatever finally indicates its nature only after critique
    Has licked and sniffed around it, is as common as a dog.

The Diamond Is Known Only in Itself

You learn to think only by thinking, you recognize truth only in
    that which is true,
    You know love only when you really love, but you know
    nothing by pure critique.

Just How Critical Is Critique?

Critique must stand sentry at the door of the critical soul,
    Which does not have a secure feeling for truth or God;
189   Whoever enters the door must first call out, "Good friend."
    Otherwise one must leave the land, even if he were God in
    person.

The Position and Calling of Critique

Critique is a domestic maid in the kingdom of knowing—it
    sweeps things out.
    If the maid continues, we will lose everything.

Bon appétit!

Morality is stale home bread; to make it go down more easily,
They spread God and religion like butter all over it.

Religion out of Gratitude

Because they think themselves to be immortal, they believe that
they ought to return thanks
To the dear Lord only out of a sense of morality.

What Are God and Religion Presently?

For these gentlemen, religion is a life-insurance company;
Even sacrifice relates only to one's own good;
And God for them is the grease on the squeaky wagon of life
That makes the wheels turn more easily.

The Motto of the *Church History*

"*Pectus facit theologum.*"[22]
Certainly! Even if one were as dumb as an ass,
And one's head
As dead as a stone.
Thus you are Christian only by night; by day you are atheists;
The feeble ghost yet abides only in the night of feeling.

A Historical Fact

Once Christianity was substance and ruling World Spirit;
But what is it now? An affect of feeling.

A Contribution to Morphology

As plants unfold, then retract into themselves,
So religion develops.
It is first a single good; it lives silently hidden in the heart,

As yet a simple seed, at one with the individual;
190   But soon it bursts the confining abode of the heart
      And presses into the open as a mature tree;
Powerfully embracing the world, it gathers
      All peoples and races under its vaulted shadow.
Once it has borne fruit and fulfilled the destiny
      That a more transcendent Spirit places in everything,
It again draws back into a lonely chamber of the heart
      There to be compressed into nocturnal feeling,
Until what once blazed as substance of the world
      Now grows dim in the dark bedroom of the heart.

Commendable Maxims

As the youth puts off his lesson by consoling himself with the
      thought of tomorrow,
   So the pietist consoles himself with that which is beyond this
      world.
Whoever might wish to reprimand him would be unjust,
   For there are many mansions in the spacious house.

A Natural Explanation of the Eclipse of the
Sun in Theology

"God's essence is dark." Naturally! He is only the smoke
   Left when these gentlemen have exploded all their powder.
It is also natural that the existence of God is presently in the
      dark:
   Only the sympathetic heart has room for it.

If only the holes in its head
Had grown over!
Then our pious beast
Would no longer need the fodder of the hereafter.

"Tell me, where does the highly celebrated hereafter exist?"
   Only in the holes in their heads.

Applause

The hereafter is certainly an excellent institution,
   A welcome asylum for cowardice and spiritual want.

The Free Bird Views Everything Differently
Than the Bird in a Cage

191

You find riddles only in the cage of divinity;
   Go out into the fresh air, and everything will be solved for
   you.

"There Are Instances in Which Despair Is a Duty"

How will theology be freed of the evil of discord?
   When finally, out of desperation, it gives itself up.

And often a blow like that of Alexander
Is not without its reward.

How will you loosen the burdensome knots of divinity?
   Make short work of them: bravely hack them in two.

And yet only death
Ultimately delivers from need.

You cannot cure your suffering in theology;
   Only your own death is the complete cure.

The Devil, Even If No Healer of Souls,
Is an Optometrist

Poor theological scholarship! Only the devil can still heal you.
   So go to the devil! You will probably be cured forever.

Brevity Is the Soul of Wit

Life on earth is brief. But note, dear mystic, brief only in time,
   For in its value it is as infinite as God.

On Life and Death

What is life? Only Spirit's engendering spasm.
  Thus the event is brief, but the enjoyment sweet.

To the intelligent person, life is its own end;
  For that very reason, it is a preparation for nothing.

Only that person is wise who finds everything in life
  But also finds nothing in death but death.

192 Only Transitoriness grants magical charm
  To human life, for she is queen of the world.

Do not demand life from death; long and strive for only one
    thing:
  That some day the nobleman will remember you with love.

Spirit and Matter

Theological learning is as inert as matter; only the lumps
  Administered by worldly wisdom get the lout moving.

Bad Times

Not the best, but the cheapest sells like hot cakes;
  This is why faith is presently such a hot item.

Puzzling!

What is Christianity now? To help weak eyes,
  An amateur painted a lampshade on *The Birth of Christ*.

The Opposite Effect

If I think of Christ on my own, he stands before me as God him-
    self;
  If a pious cleric preaches him, he becomes a mere human to
    me.

Tempora mutantur, et nos mutamur cum illis[23]

If Christ would arise now and look at our pietists,
Even he would become the Antichrist.

The Plum on Earth Is Sweeter
Than the Fig in Heaven

The pains of earth are worse than the sufferings of hell
And the earth yields joys that no heaven could give.

The Distinction between the
Here and the Hereafter

Whatever you eat on earth you get in the hereafter;
   The food is the same in both places, only you obtain it by dif-
     ferent means.
On earth, the dove is roasted by the art of cooking;
   In the hereafter, it flies into your mouth already roasted by its
     heavenly nature.
Fork, knife, and hands are the earthly instruments of eating;
   In bringing you food, they channel your hunger.
But in the hereafter you never need such burdensome tools;   193
   There you eat just with your mouth, like the fortunate pig.

Take the Plunge!

The danger of death teaches us how to swim. So bravely throw
   yourself into the ocean;
   Then you won't need pig bladders, the air bags of the mystical world, to stay afloat.

A Cheerful Prospect

There are six workdays here on earth, followed by a single
   Sunday;
   But in the hereafter, we'll have a perpetual Holy Day.
   Hurray!

Harvest Festival

How beautiful it must be in the *Lirumlarum* of the hereafter[24]
   To do nothing but feast on the fruit that ripened on earth.

Where the Farmer Sows, He Reaps

Here on earth we have both spring and fall, both a time for sow-
   ing and a time for reaping;
Seed and fruit never live in two kinds of ground.

Because of its unimpeachable realism
The stomach continues to be an antichrist;
Thus the stomach should have been banned
From every Christian land years ago.

The hereafter helps me as much as the thought of a future Sunday roast
On Monday, when I am really hungry.

Above all, Sir Pietist,
Who always eats the sweetest cherries,
I hope you can stomach
These couplets.

The cherries that the sparrow picks are the sweetest of all;
   But the mystical bird picks at its own flesh because it has
   more appetite for it.

The Arbitrary Point Is Not Mathematical

People often fixate on certain points so as not to lose control;
   Christ is presently just such a point: the world cannot let itself
   lose sight of him.

194   ### Old and New

The really new is but Spirit together with the essence of former
   reality

Now released from the dungeon that held it captive.
But the mob believes that when Spirit is advanced in freedom
 The former reality, still present in essence, becomes
  nothing.

The Tastes of the Mob

The most hateful things become sacred merely by familiarity:
  the warts and squints
 Of the beloved are often beautiful to one madly in love.
Thus the aged are cherished even if the scab has already con-
  sumed;
 "The hell with the scratches," the masses cry in a rage.

"He wears boots with the tops folded down and trousers
  creased to the end of his tails."
 Thus the common people define the man, relying on his
  clothes.
In the same way, mystics rely on the clothes that Christ wore;
 They lose their heads if someone takes the clothes away from
  them.

A Solemn Truth

Christ himself is now a cloak; he no longer exists in the Bible,
 And he died as a person; long ago he became Spirit.

The Pietistic Hermit Crabs, or *Parasitici*

("*Bernhardus* [*Pagurus*], the Hermit." Cp. Blumenbach's
 Natural History, p. 424.)[25]
Once the essence that created and inhabited the structure has
  abandoned it
 A crab crawls in; the crab is called a mystic.

A Postscript

You inhabit only hermit cells abandoned by the Creator;
 Thus, dear mystic, you are a parasitic crab.

The Proof

If you were not a parasitic crab, you would know
    That nature alone creates, nature alone originates.

A Reflection

Crabs and snails are pathetic enough,
    But a hermit crab! What a combination!

The Rationalistic Vinegar Eelworms, *Aceti*[26]

195

("Thus these are a species of animal which has been *post-created,* as it were, long after the first universal creation. For, as is well known, they are found only in vinegar and gum spirits, both of which are late manufactured products of cultural humanity." Blumenbach's *Natural History,* p. 504, Remark.)
So you are engendered only in bookbinding paste, which is the
    Only bond and support of your entire system!
But you are not born in the divine spring of original, eternal
    life—
Poor rationalist! You are only a product of culture.

Strength and Weakness

Only strong natures can camp in the open; it is better for the
    mystic
To stay in bed under a thatched roof.

Certainly Very Beautiful!

Ah, how beautiful it must be, when it storms outside, to rest
    drowsily
In the stall of Bethlehem on fully threshed straw.

Narrow-minded Botany

It takes a narrow mind to think that the ample goddess
    Nature is restricted to the flora of Palestine!

The Unknown What

The flow of history affords the mystics
 Just enough water to wash their dirty linen,
But, to the rationalists, it merely gives a mirror for inspecting
 their shyness.
 Therefore, an ego has no idea what history means to them.

An Appropriate Symbol

Vishnu rode an eagle.[27] Surely a contemporary Christian painter
 Could choose only the starling as bearer of the Lord.

The Omnipresence of God

Jerusalem is not the only inn that offers food
 And lodging, for God stretches forth his arm everywhere.

How the Mystic Returns Home from a Foreign Land   196

The mystical goose flies over the Jordan into foreign territory
 But returns with the same old honk.

Something for the Chosen

Although to them everything works grace,
 Their food still takes its natural course to the bowels.
Thus they are conjurers for whom grace is nothing but talk,
 For every event in their lives comes to pass naturally.

Different Is Not Distinct

What distinguishes the Christian from other honorable people?
 At most a pious face and parted hair.

What once did the job well
Is now blunted by usage.

For centuries they preached grace and salvation

Until the salt evaporated out of the tasteless mash.
So now they pour all kinds of things into the mash,
   But the new mess disgusts sound natures even more than un-
      salted mash.

The Course of the World

What raised Homer and Phidias to exalted inspiration
   Descends to mockery in Lucian.[28]
And, in the course of time, even profound mysteries
   Lose their secrets, become trivial and common.
But then Spirit, in its craving for more secrets,
   Brings forth new miracles out of the depths.

Why Do Mystics Gain Access to Savages?

To the savage, the cry of ducks stands for the voice of Spirit;
   No wonder he grants an attentive hearing to the mystic.

The Little Pietistic Male Bees

"Mystics are the drones of the state."* Certainly!
   For they manifest productive genius only in the process of
      engendering.

197

The *Sustentatores,* or *Erectores,* penis of the Little Pietistic Male Bees

But nature is not their erector penis—
   No! Even this is sustained by belief alone.

A Plea for Forgiveness— Justification to Follow Immediately

How sly you are! What you first take from the human as Spirit,
   You then generously return to him as beast.

*The words of a pious natural scientist.

Refutation of the Justification

"You profane people do not understand us; in the act of engendering
Grace and nature enter into the most intimate bond."

Envious Sigh of the Remorseful Loser

So then your enjoyment is doubled, you lucky people!
How sweet nature must taste when grace fortifies it!

The Everlasting Word

Only that which is eternally valid for humanity is a Bible;
This divine Word is the history of the world.

The Long Episode

Within the human epoch, our Bible is only one episode
In which the creative Spirit almost forgot its theme.

The Fixed Idea

For our mystics, Peter the apostle is not living Spirit,
But only a fixed idea—they are incurable.
Indeed, they hold fast to this idea as once the fool held his water
In the fear that letting go would bring a world deluge.

The *Unitas essentialis* between Rationalists and Mystics

The mystic is nothing but a drunken rationalist;
If he becomes sober and alert, he becomes a rationalist.

Their Unity in Principle, Their Difference in Method

198

Both deprive humanity of its essence,
But both stuff its empty hide in different ways.

A Rough Calculation of Their Distance
from the Truly Human

Both are as divorced from real humanity
  As the stuffed bird is divorced from a live one.

The Exalted Content of Their Souls

Rags, hay, and straw—neither originating essence
  Nor living, beating hearts are found in these gentlemen.

Their Species

Both belong to the species of ruminating animals,
  But are only of a different variety—at any rate, the state can
  use them.

The Comical Ground of Their Difference:
A Parable

Both pick the same fruit from the same tree,
  But the rationalist climbs up himself
While the mystic is lifted to the branches on foreign shoulders,
  And thus feasts on the precious fruit without effort.
But, because each has picked the fruit with a different method,
  Each believes that the fruit itself is different—this is the sole
  basis for their quarrel.
Meanwhile, I am happy to admit, the rationalist
  Is somewhat more sensible and much more honest,
For he picks fruit that is homegrown
  And for purely domestic reasons; thus, he finds nourishment
  in the land in all honesty.
However, although the mystic eats the same fruit,
  It has been obtained from Palestine.
He mystifies this totally everyday fruit and offers it for sale
  As imported produce, thereby committing a pious fraud.

An Extract

You are a *formal* rationalist, dear mystic—
  Just as stale, only with more ceremony.

The Same Destination, but Different Paths

199

Both incline to the Dead Sea of triviality,
  But each flows toward it by a different route.
Look! The mystic twists and turns in a labyrinthine zigzag,
  Wriggling like a worm to his desired goal,
While the rationalist flows as straight as a string;
  He attains the goal more quickly, and thus is more withdrawn.

A Closing Remark

You are a rationalist who has been obstructed in the course of development,
  Dear mystic; maybe you are an abortion.

Another Manuscript Reads:

Dear mystic, you are only a crippled rationalist;
  You have the very same subjectivity, but twisted and distorted.

Brothers at Odds

Mystics as well as rationalists belong in our lectures on natural history.
  Hear, then, how they are described:
Both are birds of the same feather—thus experience teaches—
  Both even fell out of the same nest.
But, their parents having departed, one, who had been a fledgling for a long time,

Confidently caught his own food,
Whereas his pathetic brother, who had let his parents pour food
    into him,
Stayed close to the nest for fear of the world.
Therefore, I will once again explain clearly to you:
    Neither breeding nor diet separates this fine pair;
Dissension arises only because one still lives off grace
    And receives as a gift what the other obtains on his own.

Pars pro toto[29]

Hear how well mystics and rationalists
    Understand anatomy:
Both cut a single piece of flesh out of the human—
    It is located beneath the head, not far from the belly
On the left side (clearly the weaker in a human),
    Near enough to the arm so that one can protect it if need be;
It is the most vulnerable place, the center of one's own life,
    But only as related to the self, not to the outside world—
200   They go to market and put up for sale, as if it were the whole
        body,
    This single fragment, the sacristy in the body's sacred pre-
    cincts,
Proclaiming that humans can and should live and think
    By means of this organ alone,
And that they themselves never conduct their business
    With brains or sex organs, but only with this one.
But if someone comes along and shows that the human really
    has a brain—
    An organ that raises him to the gods,
That is not destined for service to a self-oriented life,
    But ascends on high to truth alone—
And if he shows them that the brain is an organ that reaches
    down
    To the great mystery of productive nature, even to the ground
    of creativity,
That it sinks humanity into the depths of everlasting unity,

Even to the ecstatic loss of the miserable self,
They insult him as a pan-a-theist, an antichrist, and a perverter
Of all morality, just because he manifests reality.

Empirical Psychology

If you want to know humans, take account of what they hate;
Hate always gets to the bottom of humans better than love.
Those who come together in hatred of the same object,
No matter how much they might differ in other respects, are
one at bottom.

The End

Like the mystic, the rationalist cannot put up with
A philosophy that goes deeper than his. So, again, they stand
together.

An Appendix for *Ingenia tarda*[30]

Both cling merely to the surface of essence,
In which they see only themselves;
Only the deeper reality, which obliterates their picture,
Manifests essence and substance; thus the self fears the
depths.

The Mediators between Rationalists and Mystics

Mediators are even worse than either one of them!
For bad consorts with bad and always has the worst as its
product.

A Proof from Medicine

201

It is good to combine what is good, but when you mix two different diseases
Sickness reaches such proportions that health never returns.

From the State of Holy Matrimony

The marriage of old women and men is unfruitful:
Even if they beget a child, it is a sorry creature.

From the Honorable Profession of Tailoring

You can patch together old rags as much as you wish,
But you will never come up with a durable coat.

From Good Old Logic

If you wish to combine antitheses, to take the task seriously
You must first abolish the spheres that they have in common.

But You Philistines Are Too Cowardly for This, Aren't You?

Because, if you wish to abolish the antitheses in sacred learning,
Then, my friends, you must bravely abolish theology.

The Exalted Standpoint

The standpoint to which you ascend, dear mediator, is high,
But the air up there is so thin that life has no chance.

The Philosophical *Dogmatics* from Berlin[31]

Behold the slut Dogmatics. We thought she had gone to the
    devil long ago,
    But see how she still preserves herself, how firm her bosom is!
Yet wait! Her bosom is only filled out with horsehairs
    Plucked from the backside of philosophy!
Not her own flesh? For shame! How horrible and disgusting!
    Get away from her body! What a poor attempt at seduction!

Haec fabula monet:[32]

Youth! Feast on the bosoms of the pure, eternal virgins
Philosophy and Art, but flee whores and sluts.

To the Greatest Pharisee of Our Time

Oh, M——, your *Dogmatics* is only the pocket handkerchief
That Professor —— used to blow his nose in.[33]

To the Same Person

Give us a wave! But, truly, the handkerchief of your *Dogmatics*
Will never give us a pure, refreshing breeze.

Bon voyage!

The little bark of divinity is now stuck deep in need;
Its life course is over, it can never get moving again.
But M—— arrives, the great one, and spreads his handker-
chief—
As its sail! Good luck, theology![34]

The Complete *Dogmatics*

Your *Dogmatics* lacks nothing, let me say it again;
Even you lack nothing, except maybe Christianity.

Can You Parry *This* Thrust, Sophist?[35]

The form is itself essence; thus you abolish the content of faith
If you abolish the representation that is its proper form.

Material for a Book

Christian philosophy flourished with the Fathers of the Church;
What is now called Christian philosophy is so in name only.

To Nobody Else but You

Do you expect to evoke nature from its hidden depths
When it has never been the object of Christian thought?
How can you speak of Christian philosophy? What miserable
times!
Every virtue that used to adorn humanity is gone!

A Word for the Times

Christian is now only a name; its content is totally immaterial;
  Today even the devil could pass as a believing Christian.
And Christianity is now the pass into the land of the Philistines,
  Where one can securely eat one's bread in obedience to
  authority.

The Plaintiff:

203

"The same practices are prevalent in the contemporary spiritual
  world as in commerce:
People put the Christian stamp on the most pagan goods."

The Lawyer:

"That is speculative; the firm of Hauser,[36]
  With a long-standing reputation for solidity, recommends
  these goods."

The Conscientious Historian Speaks
to the Conscience:[37]

Christianity strictly distinguished Spirit and nature;
  Thereby the Christian Spirit could have a clear grasp of Spirit
  in itself.
But the task of modern times was to prepare
  For a final reconciliation of Spirit with nature.
Bruno and Jacob Böhme and Spinoza were the noble men[38]
  Who prophetically laid the ground for this feast of reconcilia-
  tion.
So tell me, philistine, when you proclaim what these
  Noble prophets proclaimed to us, do you teach true Christi-
  anity?

To the Concept:

"Only the concept is the essence." This means that the human
  skeleton

Has more reality than the living human,
That flesh and blood are nothing but superfluous accessories,
And that life itself is only an appendix to bone.

An Argument *a posteriori et a priori*

Thus the concept will never become flesh and blood in our
   youth,
For what goes in as bone comes out as bone.

The Philosophical Dogmatist

Now he wants to drum the world out of its sleep by beating
   On the donkey hide of dogmatics with the bones of withered
   concepts.

A Rectification

Why is this *Dogmatics* proudly called the Hegelian wisdom?
Like the hyena, it is satisfied with mere bones.

To the Theological Jupiter

204

"Everything is laid down in a skeletal framework." One notices
   this in your *Dogmatics,*
For Philosophy recently broke its leg in it.

The Older and More Recent Architecture

Dear friend, do you want to know the look of present Christi-
   anity
And measure the gap that separates it from its former shape?
Just go to great Berlin to see
   That charming edifice called the Cathedral,[39]
Which, though consecrated to God, looks like an airy villa,
   An elegant inn, or even an orangery.
If you are sufficiently disgusted with this foppishness in stone,
   This dandified shape, this excellent sign of the times,

And then go to the cathedral of Cologne, to the minster of
    Strasbourg,
And wonder at the Spirit that created such exaltation,
Yet do not understand that the Christianity of today is a fop,
    A dandy, and an ape, then you too are a dandy.

A Contribution to the Doctrine of Spirits and Angels on Behalf of the Polyspiritualists

As Berlin has no beer but all kinds of biers,
    So heaven has no Spirit but all kinds of spirits.

Polytheism and Polyghostism

Many gods but one Spirit: this was the essence of pagan reli-
    gion.
The Christian has but one God, but plenty of ghosts.

The Brief Present and the Long Hereafter

Expressing profound content concisely, God, the author of the
    universe,
    Wrote on earth in laconic style.
But in the hereafter he writes plainly, broadly, boringly, super-
    ficially—
    I suspect almost like Krug here in Leipzig.[40]

An Interesting Remark

What is the most miserable chatter that one can hear?
    A gentleman of divinity talking about philosophy.

What I Would Not Like to Be

205

Three things I would not like to be: an old hag, a hack
    In the academy, and finally a pietist.

Appearance Is Not Being

Even after the sun is down, it still appears in the heavens.
Draw your own conclusions, dear mystic.

Couplets without Name or Title

All cows are black at night, so you must take it on faith
　That what is a human for you by day becomes your Venus at
　night.

"This philosophy shall pass." Therefore you like no philosophy
　at all.
　Accordingly, because you, too, will pass away, you would
　much rather not live.

In fact your doctrine does wonders for the sick.
　But, by the same token, I wouldn't prescribe it for the
　healthy.

Truly life is short. But its brevity is like that of the couplet,
　Which conceals eternal value in its fleeting form.

Thus life, like the couplet, is neither short nor long;
　Brevity and length pass away before attained significance.

Mystics ask, "How many feet and verses does life have?"
　But not, "What is its meaning?" For them, life is clearly too
　short.

The most basic precept in the aesthetics of the gentlemen of
　divinity
　Is that any comedy that does not keep us laughing forever is
　bad.

If learned divines knew the meaning of brevity and length
　Theology would soon be more reasonable.

Even a couplet can solve riddles incomprehensible
To our theology, even though it is inspired.

What is the hereafter? Only the paraphrase of this world;
Whoever understands the original language needs no translations.

Much mystery surrounds the Author of our world; as his interpreter,
The hereafter pours out the words, but elucidates nothing at all.

206 The divine Spirit is far from these gentlemen in actual existence;
Their admission of this is the ghost of the hereafter.

Humanity is the image of God; therefore nature belongs
To God as well as to humans—note well, you pastors.

If you make yourself the friend of nature, you recognize Spirit in it;
Then you will eventually subside into the earth in peace.

Divine Spirit, the Spirit of nature, and World Spirit of history—
This sacred trinity is the root of being.

The heavenly light becomes the fire of life
Only when it is concentrated on earth by the lens of time.

Humans who do not spend much of their lives in the open air
Are susceptible to sunstroke, as is demonstrated in the case of mystics.

But cold compresses drawn from the spring of life
And mixed with satire heal this disease.

Once you awaken to the light, you are destined to slumber;
The earth releases no one from its domain.

Do not be afraid of death; you will stay forever in the homeland,
　On familiar ground, which tenderly embraces you.

Brachybiotik[41]

The artist's life is brief. But remember that all humans are
artists,
　Even the senseless cleric; therefore, life itself is brief.

The God of Theology

The God of sacred erudition does not exist
　In the depths of nature, but only externally surrounding it,
Far from its inner core, spreading a nimbus around it,
　Making the external shell glitter with tinsel.
This God exists neither in the grace of artistic achievement
　Nor in the world of ideas, of number and figure.
Truly this is a totally particular little god, who exists—
　Can you doubt where?—only in theology.

Thirst Is the Best Brewer of Beer

207

A couple of glasses of plain old beer in the evening
　Revive us terrestrial day laborers, allaying our strong thirst.
But in the hereafter, people luxuriate in everlasting pleasure
　Without longing or thirst driving them to gratification.

And Hunger Is the Best Cook

Beloved earth, you send us longing
　For the sole purpose of sweetening the feeling and enjoyment
　　of life,
Only to spice food and drink, to make them tasty
　Thus to breathe essence and Spirit into the stale mash,
While the flickering jack-o'-lantern of the hereafter,

Which neither warms nor burns, which never animates or
    creates, ultimately fades before you.
This swamp growth, this thing that mimics the light,
    Which gives off a light but does not have the effect of a
      light,[42]
Grants only those pleasures that are not evoked by night, want,
    or need,
    And does not, as you do, earth, have hunger as its cook.

De gustibus non est disputandum

My stomach can hold down the bread and water of our earth,
    But not the liquor and sweets produced in the hereafter.

Absentmindedness

Often I go looking for something that is already in my pocket;
    So, too, dear pious one, you are always looking for some-
    thing that is already under your thumb.

The Fateful Short Beer

The pious one needs just a little glass of life,
    But it totally wipes him out.

A Tavern Scene

"A glass of wine!" the customer orders;
    "At your service!" answers the innkeeper.
The same scene is enacted in sacred scholarship,
    Only God is the innkeeper, while the mystic is the customer.

The Natural Redeemer

208

You mystics are always anxiously asking how to be freed from
    sins.
    You lazybones! Work your tail off! Work delivers from sins.

Christian Love

To keep the insects of sin from biting us,
    The pious one deals us a mortal blow—it scares the devil out
        of us.

A Hymn

Glorious divine Spirit, clasping all to yourself in love,
    You are both Spirit and nature, one and all,
Yet you do not disdain to dwell in the lowest things,
    You do not even fear to lose consciousness in the inert stone;
Your power in the universe is all-expanding and all-embracing;
    You extend the tiniest space to infinity itself.
You who forgot yourself in sacrifice when you became the uni-
    verse,
    Teach those humans who languish in the dungeon of self-
        seeking
To imitate you; teach them no longer to be ashamed of death,
    Of that activity by which you are all, are loving Spirit.

*"Sublatis vestimentis ostendunt id, quod reconditum vult natura"**

As women drive off a lion as soon as they
    Expose to it that which nature has concealed,
So the pietist reveals the nakedness of his heart when threat-
    ened,
    Hoping to frighten off victorious Spirit with naked feeling.
Indeed, Spirit is forced to close its offended eyes out of shame,
    But in the end Spirit alone stands victorious.

---

*See Kant's *Physical Geography,* Vol. II, Sect. 1, p. 313. [Translator's note: *"Sublatis vestimentis ostendunt id, quod reconditum vult natura"*: "By taking off their clothes, they expose that which nature intends to be hidden." This is not a direct quotation of Kant; the reference is to anecdotes in *Physical Geography* which relate how the female physical shape is said to deter the attacks of lions. See *Gesammelte Schriften,* ed. Royal Prussian Academy of Sciences, 28 vols. (Berlin: Walter de Gruyter & Co., 1910-1972, IX, 336).]

For Certain Dogmatists

They now need special characteristics in order to recognize the
    Savior,
For shallowness long ago effaced his essential nature.

"What Is Proper to Christianity"

Nowadays, every Tom, Dick, and Harry sees one thing as essen-
    tial to the Savior;
But still, that which belongs exclusively excludes one from the
    other.

209   ### See How Far Things Have Gone

Ever since the Savior was forced by these gentlemen to abdicate
    his throne,
He has been living quietly as a man of private means.

The Connection between Judaism and Christianity[43]

Something of the Jewish Spirit still clings to the Christians:
    They are somewhat stubborn, particularist, and narrow.
But if they do not continue to confine God to the Holy Land,
    Do they believe that God will manifest himself somewhere
    else?
If they believe that their God should be the God of the heathen
    and Turks,
    Is he not as narrow as the God of the Jews?

Polytheism and Monotheism

The belief that many things are divine engenders a beautiful life,
    But only the dried-up "one and only one" is acceptable to a
    Jewish nature.

Christian and Pagan Dress

The pagans kept their heads bare; among the Christians, night
    caps obstruct

The influx of the fresh air of nature. The pagan practice was
more healthy.

An Idiosyncrasy

As the tones of the lyre once caused only the evacuation
  Of the mourner's urine, but not the raising of his Spirit,
So the sweet music of philosophy works
  Only on the mystic's bladder.

The Ultimate Sin

Sinning is a common phenomenon, but the sin thinking and sin
    speaking
  Of our pietists are sins against the Holy Spirit.

The Modern Narcissus

Greek! You perished while viewing your own beauty.
  Modern Narcissus! You perish while being enchanted by the
  filth of your sins.

Forget not only the Sins of Others,
but also Your Own

Whatever you make into an object takes on existence; so forget
    your sins
  And do not fixate on them. Then you have no more sins.

The Most Effective Baptism

210

Whatever life brings it also blots out;
  Thus life offers us both guilt and reconciliation.

The Effects of Grace and Nature

The pagan had defects, but he was not yet tortured by sins;
  Nature produces defects, grace produces sins.

Nature and the Doctor

What was a defect for the heathen became a sin for the Christian;
   Nature heals the heathen, while the artificial methods of a
   doctor heal the Christian.

The Universal Cure

Zeus was a great sinner, but the God of Christianity merely suffered;
   If you recognize that there are sins in God, you will be free of
   them.

"No, That Is Too Wicked!"
but, Unfortunately, True

If you wish to be delivered from sin, pious one, just become a
   pagan;
   Sin came into the world with Christianity.

What I Am

You ask what I am? A resurrected pagan
   Who returned to life through the death of the Savior.

Home Remedy

What delivers us from sin? Guilt: this infernal fire
   That is kindled by sin also consumes it.

Dietetic Recipes

Preserve the good in your mind, but not sins or faults;
   Do not allow Spirit to know what the poor self has done.

You commit a double sin, if you reflect in Spirit on sins,
   For you defile the Spirit, which knows nothing of sins.

It is the worst sin of all to make something out of sins;
   Whoever makes something out of nothing makes nothing out
   of something.

The Basis of Pietism 211

The pious one bases faith on human weakness.
   How weak must be something that is supported by weakness!

The Necessary Result

Whatever is built on sin and weakness is truly
   Far more pathetic than sin itself.

An Experience

In fact, mystics built more on human weakness
   Than on the power of the Savior, which is based on weakness
   alone.

The Absolute Beginning

Good is based on good; it originates from itself alone
   And not from sins or fallen Adam, the principles of the faith
   of the mystic.

The True Principle of Religion

True religion is based on eternal truth
   In human nature, not on the morass of sin.

The Preparations Necessary for Deliverance

In order to experience the extent of the benefit of Christian
   faith,
The pietist makes himself sick, fasts almost to starvation,

And imprisons himself in the stifling jail of the consciousness
   of sin,
   Far from the healthy air and light of nature.
It is truly no wonder that, lacking the most precious goods
   That nature grants, deliverance then tastes so good.
A different person, who always lives in the free air, does not
   need deliverance;
   He eats natural foods and at the proper time, and drinks
   within reason.

I Implore You!

Dear friend, do not take offense at the mystical scatterbrain
   Even if he constantly proclaims that we are sinners and weak,
For his entire system rests on sin alone,
   As many a stone house is built only with debts.

212   **The Elder Mystics and the Contemporary Mystics**

Mystics of old, who out of the depths of your own Spirit
   Gave new life to the Word hidden deep in your souls,
You brought forth works not merely of faith and feeling,
   Not propped and supported on the written Word,
But of reason and the idea,
   Works of the inmost possession of Spirit, of the infinite full-
   ness of life,
Works, therefore, that are a witness to autonomous Spirit itself.
   May I express to you my profound admiration, for I love you
   from the depths of my being.
But the leather bundle that presently calls itself mystical,
   Who, for lack of Spirit, stripped of inner confirmation,
Supported solely by criticism and grammar, anxiously throw
   together
   From biblical passages that which should be the most interior
   meaning
But which is pumped from external sources into their empty
   hearts

Where no living spring bursts forth from the ground,
Who act only with biblical justification but do nothing,
   Not even the most noble deed, if it does not wear the biblical
      aureole,[44]
Who consult only the Scriptures to discover whether something,
   what, and how much is to be believed,
   Who beseech Peter and Paul to find out whether their pulses
      are still beating,
Whether they still possess power and understanding or whether
   their own capacities
Cannot of themselves do good without the push of grace—
This common rabble, with its grammatically correct belief,
   Supported only by paper, no longer by living Spirit,
Who, throughout their entire boring lives, have done nothing
   But pitiably cry for a subsistence allowance before the gates
      of the apostles,
I hate, I despise, I scorn.
May even my last breath be deadly poison for them.

The Necessity of the Present

What you suffer here will never be made up in heaven;
   Only the good of today heals present pain.

The Banquet out of Season

If you have lost the spur of hunger, even the most delicious
   meal
   Is worth as much as nothing to you.

And the Superfluous Truffle Pâté

I would rather have a piece of stale bread here on earth—
   It stills the hunger that gnaws at me—
Than the most delicious truffle pâté ever prepared   213
   In the splendid hereafter, where hunger has long departed.

A Trial Cosmetic

The hereafter is beautiful only in hope, not in itself;
  It looks good to us only from a distance.

An Entirely Specific Instance

Thus the hope for the hereafter has more value than the here-
    after itself,
  For it has to do with living pain.

Consolation

Therefore, mystical scatterbrain, I take the hereafter away from
    you
  But I will never challenge your hope for it.

Idealism

Never take the hope for everlasting being from humanity,
  For this hope may be its only true possession.

O Sancta Simplicitas!

The mystic wants to pour the deep ocean of reason
  Into the brittle chamber pot of belief! What a delicate
    process!

The Torture of Belief

Why does belief take so much strain and effort?
  Because it tears the noblest capacities out of our souls.

The Same Subject

It is easy to sacrifice something cheap, but difficult to sacrifice
    something precious.
  This is why the pietist goes through so much torture until he
    captures belief.

The Content Is Decisive

It is good to give up the bad, but bad to give up the good.
So you are bad, mystic; you give up only the good.

A Hint for the Weak-minded

The mystic does not give up the self—this is the core
Of his system—in his sickness, he only gives up the Spirit.

Something for Your Entertainment   214

What are mystics? Only little wooden puppets, marionettes
Moved by a foreigner, never by indwelling Spirit.

A Historical Reflection

Once belief was not coerced, but came out of the human inte-
    rior;
    It was the Spirit of the world, therefore, truth and reason.
In those times belief was the future, still locked in the seed;
    But then the future matured into blossom and fruit.
Even time and place are not far from truth,
    For God himself freely obeys their laws:
Only at the proper time and place
    In the course of history is something rational and true.
Therefore the belief of the present is nothing but coercion and
    oppression of Spirit,
    Is an irrational, false, burdensome, miserable pressure,
Because belief fulfilled its exalted destiny long ago
    So that the human Spirit does not need it any more.

The Only Rational Memento Mori

Be not aristocratic; rather, lower yourself to the status of a
    stone
    And feel yourself at one with that which has no feeling;
Share your life with that which lives eternal death,
    And death will certainly be as easy for you as love.

Do Not Consider It Robbery to
Assume the Form of a Servant

What is death? It is not primarily being dead, but it is only the
  action
  Whereby you put down the crown and the scepter that you
  carried in life.

The Living Death and the Dead Death

In life, Spirit consumes you; in death, nature consumes you;
  Spirit consumes your core; nature consumes your outer shell.

A Critical-Exegetical-Dogmatical-Philosophical
Doubt

Adam lays the blame for the Fall on you; but is it not possible
That the fruit fell from the tree by itself?

215   ### Confirmation of the Doubt

At least it can be said that the fruit was almost overripe, and, as
  is well known,
  Ripe fruit falls from a tree by itself.

A Qualification

Meanwhile, even if the fruit did not fall from the tree of itself—
  Which is very dubious, as I have just noted—
Then it was high time that Adam had knowledge of the vulner-
  ability of simple innocence
  And gathered a more noble fruit.

I Am Totally Certain, I Can Assure You

If faith* could make me free of consumption, then I,

---

*When the author speaks of faith and Christianity, he understands by these—as the perceptive
reader will see on his own—not faith and Christianity *as such,* but the definite form of contemporary faith, the particular Christianity of the present. So, too, when he speaks of grace, providence,
and the like, he is indicating only the previous theological representations of these, not the realities
to which they refer. Finally, when he speaks of himself as a naturalist, a pagan, and the like, he uses
these expressions, not in their proper sense, but only allegorically and ironically.

Merely a naturalist at this point, really would become a believing Christian, too.

The Distinction between a Naturalist and a Christian

By pursuing nature alone, by learning the inner constitution of
  things
By their own scent, the naturalist discovers
What is wholesome, and correctly puts food into his stomach
  Through his mouth out of instinct, not out of inspiration.
But the Christian, who finds his mouth only by the light of
  grace,
  Needs the Holy Spirit to teach him not to shove
Food into his backside, needs instruction in the Scriptures to
  learn
  To distinguish water from wine and healthy fluids from
  poison.

A Modest Wish

Should we be Christians? It would be better to be healthy;
  Only medicine and chemistry can still give us health.

The Alliance between Medicine and Theology   216

Truly our doctors and ministers are a helpful team:
  The cleric makes reparation for the blunders of medicine.

Thinking This Over Again

If medicine were able to prevent untimely death
  And to allow the human to die at the time that nature has
  appointed,
Then humanity would no longer demand life after life,
  And the ground on which the cleric now stands would disappear.

Lord! Lord!

Therefore, only the mistakes that doctors have made from time
    immemorial
Are the supports—how sad!—of our spiritual leaders.

To the Superfluous People

Hear this, you of the care of souls: we need only people who
    care for our bodies.
Spirit helps itself; only the body needs doctors.

The Proper Time and the Wrong Time

Death is acceptable if it arrives at the proper time,
    But if it arrives too early, it is a burdensome guest.
It's no wonder: even the most cherished visitor is a pain
    If he arrives before dinner is ready.

The Only Redeemer

As often as I have been up to my ears in trouble,
    The only redeemer I found was manly courage.

Grinding Remorse

The dry self has no taste; only when pulverized by remorse
Does the dry seed become delicious syrup for you.

The Light of Grace

What is the light of grace? The lantern that shines only by night
    So that you do not break your leg when you have to walk in
    the street.

217

The Distinction between the Light of Grace
and the Light of Nature

The natural light awakens blossoms out of the cold, hard
    ground

And evokes merry songs of joy even out of the breasts of ani-
mals;
It raises the human out of the prison of the self
To the pure feeling of infinite beauty and love,
And it lays before him the magnificent treasures of the bound-
less universe
So that he forgets himself.
But the light of Christian grace is only a night lamp
For keeping a little light in the bunk of the poor weakling
So that he can rest more securely, and so that, if he has an acci-
dent,
He can find his way to the door of health, as it were.
Thus even the weakling lights his night lamp only at bedtime;
But by day he, and all of us, need only the light of nature.

The Mediator

God and nature are total extremes; God first united himself
With nature in humanity; therefore the mediator is humanity.

The Mystery That Is As Clear As Daylight

You call it a mystery that God became human, you fool?
It would be a miracle if he had never become a human.

The Best Exegetes of the Bible

The only consistently faithful interpreters of the Bible from
time immemorial
Were senseless visionaries.

Ergo

If you wish to expound the Scripture accurately, faithfully, and
honestly,
With facts and not hot air, then you must become a visionary.

A Play on a Famous Anecdote

The two who once explained the Bible by hitting it
Truly gave a fine interpretation.

Christian Humility

The condemned race of the heathen always ascribed
    Its good and evil acts only to itself.
But the Christian of humble mind ascribes good acts to the
        Savior
    And evil acts to the devil alone.

It Is Self-evident

218

The pagan ascribed heroic deeds to himself. My dear mystic,
    It is natural for you to ascribe no deeds to yourself, because
    you accomplish none.

If Only I Knew This!

Tell me, pious one, what is so special about you?
    What do you have that wasn't given to you?

To You

I admit it: the Christianity that you proclaim is pure;
    But for this very reason it is colorless, odorless, and tasteless.

A Philosophy of Nature

Where many kinds of power and quality are united
    The elements become clouded; but they also obtain more
        Spirit.

The Necessary Ingredients

Every head of lettuce needs vinegar and oil, salt, pepper, even
        onions and chives;
    Otherwise, even the freshest tastes flat.

The Noble Intention of a Purist

"Poor lettuce, from now on I want to enjoy you
    As purely as you came naked out of the womb.

How terribly has human seasoning disfigured you,
    How horribly have human wit and intelligence soiled and
        desecrated you;
Reason has inflicted all sorts of things on you, vinegar and oil,
    salt, pepper,
    Even onions and chives, even taste itself.
But now I wish to lead you back to your former simplicity
    When you were pure lettuce without taste.''

The Salad Transfigured in the Concept

The Catholicism of old was the lettuce that
    Vinegar and oil, pepper, onion, and chives had disfigured.
But, fortunately, Protestantism finally purified the lettuce
    Of its burdensome pomp in the water of the Bible.

On the Pure and the Sullied Christianity

219

Whatever you take in, you mix with your own juices;
    Otherwise it lies in your stomach as indigestible as a heavy
        stone.
When Christianity was still sullied and infected by human
    juices,
    It was also an interior good.

The mystical souls of the present are very ordinary windows
    Through which you can read everything as it stands in the
        Scriptures.
The former mysticism was painting in glass; it burned into its
    material
    The Christian story, clouding the light with color.

Light becomes color on earth. As Christianity became the Spirit
    of the world,
    It was natural that the light became clouded into colors.

Food Gone Bad

Your biblical Christianity blends very well with the Bible,
    But it lies like a heavy stone in our bellies.

The History of a Flea: A Fragment from My Life

It is strange to tell, and yet it is the pure truth
    That it only took a flea to make me into a pagan.
One day, while I was raising my folded hands to heaven—
    At that time, I was still a pietist—and was praying with great
      devotion,
It bit me! Think of it! Right at the point of my most devout out-
      pouring,
    Right in the middle of the stream of prayer a flea took a
      healthy bite of my arm,
Causing me to pull apart my folded hands as fast as I could,
    To lose the thread of my devout prayer,
And to pursue the infamous destroyer of my devotions
    Until I had captured it and smashed it in a rage.
Now the flea was dead, yet the painful wound that the blas-
    phemer
    Had inflicted on me still burned in my heart.
"Destroyer of devotion!" Thus I spoke to the flea in my anger,
    "Who engendered you? What is your purpose in the world?
You parasite, you bloodthirsty monstrosity,
    Did a wise Sovereign, a loving Father who arranges
All in his mansion for an intelligent purpose,
    Create you only to give others burdensome torments?
If indeed he did create you, then I committed murder most foul
    When I dispatched you, flea, for you are a creature of God
220   Which he once cherished in his understanding; when he found
      you worthy
    Of being our guest here on earth, he sent you into the world
      out of love."
But then I said to myself, "I had to murder that flea
    Unless I wanted to sacrifice my life to it."
And this objection catapulted me down
    To the dark abyss of titanic naturalism.
Now, for the first time in my life, I really saw nature,
    Saw how it produces from itself out of its own power,
How it is its own ground and source of eternally struggling life,
    How it knows no laws besides those of its own being.

So there! It was through a flea that I fell from faith;
  I would still be a believing Christian if there were no fleas in
  the world.

The Incomprehensible Tail of the Devil

Our present-day theology is acquainted with the devil's tail
  Only up to a few inches short of its end. Thus, how an inde-
  pendent tail
For which a body has never been discovered
  Came into creation remains a mystery to it.

Conjectures Concerning the Devil's Tail

Rationalists are of the opinion that it is the clitoris
  Of a bestial woman, which arouses sensual drives;
Mystics think that it is the rattle of a dangerous snake
  That lures its prey into its deadly throat,
Or else that it is from a species of carnivorous beasts,
  Which, like the horrible lion, gulps down even humans.
But I am of the opinion that it is best of all
  Not to waste a word on the dismal thing.

A Recommendation to Study the Sources

Grab the devil by the head, not by the tail;
  Then you will know for certain that he fits well in the world.

A Directional Signal

If you grasp the devil only while he is among humans, you will
  get only his tail;
  You must go higher if you want to battle him head to head.

Practical Applications of the Devil's Tail
in Theology

For rationalists, it serves as a military moustache
    In order to maintain respect for moral upbringing,
And to show that evil is the discharge of fluid
    That breaks forth in the body at puberty,
And that it would certainly be more beautiful if one's face
      stayed smooth
    But that the essence is not disfigured by a beard,
And that therefore it is very easy to shave it off the devil
    But that his face quickly becomes full of bristles even in one
      night.
In contrast, this tail is an inherent part of the mystic,
    Which stays on him from birth—he never gets rid of it.
A primitive heirloom from Adam on,
    This burdensome tail hangs completely attached to him.
Nevertheless, it is not, let us say, an elongation of the coccyx,
    So that, as with animals, it grows from an inner root,
But it is similar to a tuft of feathers on a military dress hat,
    Which is attached by being jammed into a hidden hole
That the mystic discloses to groups of children in order that he
      will
    Receive the entail that father after father bequeaths to him.
However, the appendix does grow attached to him to the extent
    That he can even do clever tricks with it,
For he hangs on this inherited tail as securely as a monkey,
    Even using it to climb up the tree of deliverance.

On Death and Eternity

The human lives eternally. Therefore humans die,
    For the eternal is nothing but the death of all that is temporal.

True, you will turn to dust someday; but whatever noble
      thoughts you had,
    Whatever you have deeply loved never passes.

The only object that the human loves is the human essence;
    If the human never loves an object he is as empty as straw.

Practical Applications of the Devil's Tail in Theology

or rationalists, it serves as a military moustache
    In order to maintain respect for moral upbringing,
nd to show that evil is the discharge of fluid
    That breaks forth in the body at puberty,
nd that it would certainly be more beautiful if one's face
        stayed smooth
    But that the essence is not disfigured by a beard,
And that therefore it is very easy to shave it off the devil
    But that his face quickly becomes full of bristles even in one
        night.
n contrast, this tail is an inherent part of the mystic,
    Which stays on him from birth—he never gets rid of it.
A primitive heirloom from Adam on,
    This burdensome tail hangs completely attached to him.
Nevertheless, it is not, let us say, an elongation of the coccyx,
    So that, as with animals, it grows from an inner root,
But it is similar to a tuft of feathers on a military dress hat,
    Which is attached by being jammed into a hidden hole
That the mystic discloses to groups of children in order that he
        will
    Receive the entail that father after father bequeaths to him.
However, the appendix does grow attached to him to the extent
    That he can even do clever tricks with it,
For he hangs on this inherited tail as securely as a monkey,
    Even using it to climb up the tree of deliverance.

On Death and Eternity

The human lives eternally. Therefore humans die,
    For the eternal is nothing but the death of all that is temporal.

True, you will turn to dust someday; but whatever noble
        thoughts you had,
    Whatever you have deeply loved never passes.

The only object that the human loves is the human essence;
    If the human never loves an object he is as empty as straw.

How terribly has human seasoning disfigured you,
    How horribly have human wit and intelligence soiled and
        desecrated you;
Reason has inflicted all sorts of things on you, vinegar and oil,
    salt, pepper,
    Even onions and chives, even taste itself.
But now I wish to lead you back to your former simplicity
    When you were pure lettuce without taste.''

The Salad Transfigured in the Concept

The Catholicism of old was the lettuce that
    Vinegar and oil, pepper, onion, and chives had disfigured.
But, fortunately, Protestantism finally purified the lettuce
    Of its burdensome pomp in the water of the Bible.

On the Pure and the Sullied Christianity

219

Whatever you take in, you mix with your own juices;
    Otherwise it lies in your stomach as indigestible as a heavy
        stone.
When Christianity was still sullied and infected by human
    juices,
    It was also an interior good.

The mystical souls of the present are very ordinary windows
    Through which you can read everything as it stands in the
        Scriptures.
The former mysticism was painting in glass; it burned into its
    material
    The Christian story, clouding the light with color.

Light becomes color on earth. As Christianity became the Spirit
        of the world,
    It was natural that the light became clouded into colors.

Food Gone Bad

Your biblical Christianity blends very well with the Bible,
    But it lies like a heavy stone in our bellies.

The History of a Flea: A Fragment from My Life

It is strange to tell, and yet it is the pure truth
  That it only took a flea to make me into a pagan.
One day, while I was raising my folded hands to heaven—
  At that time, I was still a pietist—and was praying with great
    devotion,
It bit me! Think of it! Right at the point of my most devout out-
    pouring,
  Right in the middle of the stream of prayer a flea took a
    healthy bite of my arm,
Causing me to pull apart my folded hands as fast as I could,
  To lose the thread of my devout prayer,
And to pursue the infamous destroyer of my devotions
  Until I had captured it and smashed it in a rage.
Now the flea was dead, yet the painful wound that the blas-
    phemer
  Had inflicted on me still burned in my heart.
"Destroyer of devotion!" Thus I spoke to the flea in my anger,
  "Who engendered you? What is your purpose in the world?
You parasite, you bloodthirsty monstrosity,
  Did a wise Sovereign, a loving Father who arranges
All in his mansion for an intelligent purpose,
  Create you only to give others burdensome torments?
If indeed he did create you, then I committed murder most foul
  When I dispatched you, flea, for you are a creature of God
Which he once cherished in his understanding; when he found
    you worthy
  Of being our guest here on earth, he sent you into the world
    out of love."
But then I said to myself, "I had to murder that flea
  Unless I wanted to sacrifice my life to it."
And this objection catapulted me down
  To the dark abyss of titanic naturalism.
Now, for the first time in my life, I really saw nature,
  Saw how it produces from itself out of its own power,
How it is its own ground and source of eternally struggling life,
  How it knows no laws besides those of its own being.

So there! It was through a flea that I fell fro
  I would still be a believing Christian if there
    the world.

The Incomprehensible Tail of the I

Our present-day theology is acquainted with tl
  Only up to a few inches short of its end. Thu
    pendent tail
For which a body has never been discovered
  Came into creation remains a mystery to it.

Conjectures Concerning the Devil's T

Rationalists are of the opinion that it is the clitc
  Of a bestial woman, which arouses sensual dri
Mystics think that it is the rattle of a dangerous
  That lures its prey into its deadly throat,
Or else that it is from a species of carnivorous be
  Which, like the horrible lion, gulps down even
But I am of the opinion that it is best of all
  Not to waste a word on the dismal thing.

A Recommendation to Study the Source

Grab the devil by the head, not by the tail;
  Then you will know for certain that he fits well ir

A Directional Signal

If you grasp the devil only while he is among human
  get only his tail;
  You must go higher if you want to battle him hea

Neither your personhood nor your flesh lives for eternity;
  Only in love do you live after death.

Exegesis

This mark is decisive. But, oh dear, it will never be known
  Whether it is a fly dropping or from God's dictation.

The Same as in the Case of Buridan's Ass[45]

222

Indeed the Holy Scripture is the lock on the portals of salvation,
  But paganism is, sadly, the only key that fits it.

Inspiration

"The Scripture is inspired." Certainly! But the ground on
    which
  Spirit poured itself out was dry; hardly a single flower grows
    there.

Pardon Me! Every Seat Is Taken

Naturally. Here sits Lady History at the spinning wheel
  Dampening the dry yarn with driblets of prosaic moisture.
This chair belongs to Mademoiselle Morality, and on that one
  Mrs. Praxis teaches wisdom very appropriate for housekeep-
    ing.
Here sits James the Greater, there Peter, here Luke and Paul:
  The places are all taken. Please leave, Holy Spirit!

I:

"Did the Holy Spirit take away the individuality
  Of the different evangelists over whom he poured?"

The Learned Pietist from Berlin:[46]

"Not on your life! That would be barbaric;
  He urges up the flowers only with light drops of heavenly
    dew, as it were."

The Same Gentleman Again, Deeply Sighing
in the Glow of His Radiant, Interesting
Human Characteristics:

"Inspiration is mild; it merely brightens the blossoms of
　　humanity
So that one can better see the contrasting colors in the
　　heavenly glow."

His Dear Friend Supports Him:[47]

"The evangelists were only instruments, though they remained
　　free."
(Free? Maybe they played some little tricks of their own.)

The Ironically Happy Rationalist:

"What a small terrain modernity has left the Holy Spirit to live
　　on!
Soon even this tiny plot will be sold off."

I:

223

"It's no wonder then if today's gentlemen of divinity
　　Only grow potatoes on their small acreage."

The Philistine:

"What good to us are stock, sunflowers, or roses?
Let us grow potatoes! Only these keep us alive."

The Pietist from Berlin:

"Flowers belong to heaven, and if we do not look at them
Even though they bloom here on earth, our sight will be
　　spared for the hereafter."

Practical Christianity:

"On earth, we need only potatoes to be able to live;
  Therefore, whoever does not grow potatoes alone is not a believing Christian."

A Noble Maxim

Traveling journeymen are sparing during the week; they drink
  only water
So that on Sunday they can drink beer till they're plastered.

The Unveiled Portrait

While on earth the pietist drinks only water and hoards his
  money so that in heaven
He can get drunk and squander his savings.

The Layman Sighs:

"Alas! The Holy Spirit could only write in Hebrew and Greek!
Woe to us laity, who only understand German!"

The Philosopher:

"A Bible that is written in a particular language
  Cannot be the divine Word."

The Same Philosopher:

"Only a particular spirit, not the universal, divine Spirit,
  Uses a particular language as its instrument."

The Historian: 224

"The period of the Babylonian confusion
  Is not yet closed, and the Holy Scripture belongs to this
    time."

The Public Confession of an Honorable Exegete, Who Passed Away under the Burden of Theological Scholarship:

"Alas! By the time the Holy Spirit reaches us,
   He is already exhausted to the point of death by the strenuous
   journey."

The Rationalist:

"The Holy Spirit, in order to emigrate from Asia to Europe,
   Takes a route through America."

"Moreover, he is so complex that he writes folio volumes
   As introductions to the tiniest pamphlets."

"He wants to quench our thirst, not with the spring of reason,
   But only by letting tiny drops seep through goose feathers."

The Cunning Pietist Retorts:

"That the process of inspiration is a slow dripping
   Is precisely a proof of the divine wisdom."

"Do you not know that the smallest dose makes the greatest
      effect,
   And that even coffee makes you drunk when you drink it by
      the spoonful?"

"And do you not know that the Holy Spirit himself chooses
      only goose feathers as his instrument?
   Do you know an instrument more suited to him?"

"You demonstrate mental incompetence to call him complex;
   He rouses the appetite by teasing us with a little piece of bread
      before he gives it to us."

I:

"Behold the divine care! Instead of loosening the knot
  It makes the skein of nature ten times more tangled that it
  already is."

The Christian Labyrinth

225

A Theseus could easily find his way through the labyrinth of
  nature
But not through the labyrinth of divine providence.

The Spider Web of Theological Sophistry

Whoever gets lost and entangles himself in the web of divine
  providence
Doesn't get out; he is stuck there for all eternity.

Malheur

Nature is blind and divine Providence is lame;
  Tell me how far this pair of cripples can lead us?

A Portrait

Look! There is the pious one, carefully counting how many sins
  he has
In the knapsack of his memory.
Observe how, after he has made the proper reckoning,
  He drags the heavy sack up a hill!
"What does this man have in mind?" He goes shopping in
  heaven
  To purchase supplies for the sins that he has so assiduously
  saved up.

A Conversation between Two Merchants

"So there is a lot of profit in the sin trade these days?"
   "Why, yes, I'm making a living on this one article alone."

"Are sins ready-made or manufactured?"
   "The factory turns out just as many as nature."

"Where can I pick up the manufactured sins?
   Can you show me the factory?" "Over there in theology."

"What kind is better?" "Without a doubt, the manufactured
      ones;
   The natural sins are never as durable and thick:
They tend to lose their colors in the light. But manufactured sins
   Resist the brightest light."

226   **Mercantilistic Speculations, together with**
Complaints about the Bad Times of the
Present and the Poor Products of
the Christian Lands

Ever since belief became the mode, all business has stagnated,
   Even ideas in the head, even blood in the veins.

What a solid foundation we had when bourgeois virtue
   And a sure sense for what is right built the cities!

In those days, when the public was not yet prohibited from
      access to virtue,
   There were a lot fewer bankruptcies than today!

These are really bad times; the most oppressive misery in the
      land
   And yet the Christians won't let us import any foreign
      product.

For our spiritual customs officers prohibit the entrance
   Even of good products if they don't have a crucifix on them.

Meanwhile, the Christian lands grow only corn and potatoes
But their soil yields nothing for the enjoyment of life.

Certainly agricultural livestock, excellent cattle and sheep,
But the broad expanse of nature does not thrive in the Christian lands.

We have plenty of horses, too, but they are better suited for plowing,
Than for riding, for they are almost as sluggish as asses.

For those who carry a parasol for defense on the charger of faith,
A Christian nag is, at best, fit for the glue factory.

An Excursion

But our one defender, with fire still coursing in his veins,
Bravely mounts an Arabian and travels throughout the world.

Something for the Everyday Horse Philistine

Perhaps he will break his neck. Well and good!
A noble death is better than the life you spend riding plugs.

Duration Doesn't Matter

227

Year after year you trot along on the Christian nag,
And yet, you coward, you have not yet learned how to ride.

A Worthwhile Ride

A half hour's ride on an Arabian charger has more value
Than ten hours of trotting on a Christian nag.

The Boring Slow Trot into the Hereafter

I admit it, you do not fall off of an old plug; you can amble
along at your drowsy pace
Even to heaven. But I do not envy you.

An Important Remark on Language

Just think of this important fact! In our language, belief is
masculine
But dear reason is only the little woman.

Prelude

Your attention please! I will reach a conclusion in your best
interests:
Eve was reason, Adam was faith.

The Curtain Rises on
the Lost Paradise of Faith

In the beginning faith was alone and in a condition of inno-
cence,
But, sadly, this innocence was of short duration.
Adam had a normal growth as long as he was alone;
Thus he developed a strong yearning for a female companion.
God pitied his plight, took a rib out of the body of faith,
And created for him Eve, that is, reason.
"You are bone of my bone, flesh of my flesh,"
He said to reason (truly his best speech!).
At first they were naked but not ashamed in front of one
another;
For Adam had not yet known Eve.
But, alas, Eve! Unhappy Eve!
But, alas, Eve! Lustful reason!
But, alas, Eve! She seduced upright faith
Into plucking the fruit from the tree of knowledge.
And an angry God now drove the pathetic pair

Out of Paradise, the land of simple innocence.
Now a cherub watches at the gates of Eden
  With a fiery sword and never lets the little pair in.
So the lovely Eden of belief is lost forever!
  God himself threw you out; you can never go back.
Perhaps you could still pin the fruit that was picked from the
    tree
  Back onto it, but it will not grow any more.
You must now work, bring forth in pain; you must no longer
    merely believe,
  But must earn on your own what you need for life and salva-
    tion.

Intermission and Change of Scene: Pastoral Medicine Is Revealed in Its Total Nakedness

Hear this, you totally ordinary cleric, you pietistic dandy:
  Had you ever suffered what I have inwardly suffered,
You certainly would not be trotting around in heaven
  On the gray horse of faith, which went to seed long ago.
If you had experienced as deeply as my heart
  What sin is, how terrible its pain,
You certainly could not be standing like a servant
  In the garden of the Lord, waiting for plants that withered
    long ago,
And you would not want to press juice from fully trampled
    grapes
  And suck on faith to obtain your cure.

Believe me, I have gone through much
  And constantly strove for the truth with a sense of nobility,
Yet I have found that only nature
  Can prepare the remedy for real suffering.

Certainly the doctor can cure the sniffles and catarrh,
  But only one's own Spirit cures consumption and other seri-
    ous diseases.

Medicines are only ways of stimulating nature
    To help itself; the cure comes from inside.

The true diseases, my dear cleric, are incurable:
    Only death heals them. This verse is no fable.

The diseases that medicine cures are butterflies
    That harmlessly suck nectar only at the tip of the flower,
While that which consumes the plant comes from deep under it;
    The seriously ill plant becomes healthy only when it exists no
        longer.
Can you, my clerical friend, cure the lettuce
    When the worm has already gobbled up its roots?
Thus, I believe that the diseases that you clerics cure—
    But please do not take offense at me, you fashionably dressed
        dandies—
Are freckles that, on hot summer days,
    Break out only on your sensitive skins.
But in your apothecaries you have only cosmetics
    And you can only remove spots from smocks.
The beauty cure requires much expenditure and much belief,
    But nature heals serious disease in silence.

229

With Your Permission, One More Postscript

What is it that I call nature, my dear clerics?
    Anything that you cannot feel or see.
The nature of God is as clear as soft, pure light;
    Only nature is a mystery.
Nature is a strange genius in everything
    So philistines and clerics never understand it.

The Theater is Closed

Out with you, you feeble philistines, you boring men!
    But to you, fair sex, I dedicate Spirit with love.

To a Pietist Maiden

Young maiden, when you sacrificed nature for belief, you committed
Your only sin; otherwise, you still would be pure.

The Evident Mystery

You philistine, you call the unity of Spirit and nature a mystery.
Yet behold the woman; the unity lies before your very eyes.

Something for Gynecologists

The male can endure much; his nature is robust.
He can even endure pietism in a pinch.
But a woman who bubbles with piety loses her inmost essence;
Her beautiful nature loses its reconciling Spirit.

The Different Offices of Man and Woman   230

Men preserve the essence, women the existence of humanity;
Thus the man strives for the hereafter, but the woman attains
nothing but reality.

The Superiority of the Woman

The man must sweat to attain what he should be,
But the woman already is by nature what she should be.

Natura se potissimum prodit in minimis[48]

Most men don't go out without walking canes,
But I have never yet seen a woman with one.

The Pietists, for Example

Often men use the knot of a dead tree
For stability even when they have other means of support.

The Secure, Happy Woman

Your nature alone, which is one with your destiny, supports
you, dear woman;
    It requires and strives after only that which duty impels you
to do.
What the man unites only by action is one in you by nature.
    Happy woman! You therefore have no need of faith.

A Confused Custom

It's all right if the student carries a shillelagh;
    He has to go through much misery for which only a cane will
help.
But that the maidens of today must carry the shillelagh of
Faith! God knows, this is a bit too much.

Examples of the Most Glorious and Noble
Deeds of Women:
(1) The Fall

"Eve led Adam astray." I certainly am not upset by the fact
    That she finally pulled the night cap off the head of the pious
fool.

231   A motion for a new feast day

We should celebrate gratefully the day when
    Eve misled Adam, for she only did it out of her love for us.

(2) World creation and philosophy of nature

Māyā once drove away the melancholy of the ancient Brahmā[49]
    So that a depressed person was changed into a creator of the
world.

(3) Trojan War and poetry

Helen pulled the Greeks out of their mystical nooks and
    crannies
So that, on her account, they bravely smashed heads.

An Appeal to the Fair Sex

Dear maidens and women! Take the noble ancients as your
    example
And once again drive away theology.

Notes to the Introduction

1. Originally titled *Thoughts on Death and Immortality from the Papers of a Thinker, along with an Appendix of Theological-Satirical Epigrams, Edited by One of His Friends,* this work was edited and published in Nuremberg by Johann Adam Stein in 1830, its author vainly hoping to remain anonymous. By the time Feuerbach came to review it for the edition of his collected works, he had departed so far from his early speculative and metaphysical bent that he thoroughly rearranged the prose, leaving out almost half of it in the process, and he included only one-third of the epigrams. Under the title *Thoughts on Death and Immortality,* this revised version appeared in 1847 in Vol. III of his ten-volume *Sämtliche Werke* (Leipzig: O. Wigand, 1846-1866). It was this second version that Wilhelm Bolin and Friedrich Jodl published in the first volume of their edition of Feuerbach's collected works (1903-1911); in turn, they left out still more of the epigrams and the entirety of the rhyming verse of the original edition, while changing some of the technical philosophical terms in order to reach a wider audience. (They said nothing about the existence or nature of the version of 1830). Because of the unavailability of the original edition, a facsimile reprint was included in the first of three supplementary volumes (Vols. XI-XIII) to the reprint of the Bolin and Jodl edition (Ludwig Feuerbach, *Sämtliche Werke,* ed. Wilhelm Bolin and Friedrich Jodl, 2nd ed. unrev., 13 vols. in 12 [Stuttgart-Cannstatt: Friedrich Frommann Verlag, 1959-1960], Vols. XI-XIII ed. Hans-Martin Sass); this reprint was the source for the present translation. References to *Thoughts on Death* (the abbreviated title that I will use hereafter) are located throughout the Introduction and will refer to the pagination of the original German edition, which is located in the outside margins of the translation. Vols. XII-XIII (a double volume) contain Feuerbach's correspondence; these will be referred to as Sass. (Still another version of the edition of 1830 is scheduled to appear in Vol. I of *Gesammelte Werke* under the general editorship of Werner Schuffenhauer, published in the German Democratic Republic by Akademie-Verlag of Berlin.)

2. See Ludwig Feuerbach, "An Carl Riedel: Zur Berichtigung seiner Skizze," *Kleinere Schriften II (1839-1846),* ed. Werner Schuffenhauer and Wolfgang Harich, in Ludwig Feuerbach, *Gesammelte Werke,* ed. Werner Schuffenhauer, 16 vols. (Berlin: Akademie-Verlag, 1967-), IX, 12 (hereafter cited as *GW*), where Feuerbach, although restricting his criticism to the abstractness of speculative philosophy, discusses the method of overcoming this division.

3. This is a conclusion of Marx W. Wartofsky in a book that, for understanding Feuerbach and assessing his achievement, has by far surpassed over

one hundred years of scholarship: *Feuerbach* (New York: Cambridge University Press, 1977), p. 48. Although the absence of an interpretation of *Thoughts on Death* leaves a serious gap, Wartofsky's otherwise unrelenting pursuit of Feuerbach's developing thought sheds new and startling light on the meaning of most of his mature works.

4. I have attempted to explain some of the connections between these two works in "Feuerbach and Religious Individualism," *Journal of Religion* 56, 4 (October, 1976): 366-381.

5. An excellent introduction to the history of modern Germany is Hajo Holborn, *A History of Modern Germany,* 3 vols. (New York: Alfred A. Knopf, 1959-1969); the second and third volumes treat the prerevolutionary period.

6. Ludwig Feuerbach to Wilhemine Feuerbach, October 22, 1820, Sass, XII, 215.

7. Ludwig Feuerbach to Paul Johann Anselm Feuerbach, 1823, ibid., p. 223.

8. The quotation is from an autobiographical sketch written in 1846, as cited in Karl Grün, ed., *Ludwig Feuerbach in seinem Briefwechsel und Nachlass sowie in seiner philosophischen Charakterentwicklung,* 2 vols. (Leipzig and Heidelberg: C. F. Winter'sche Verlagshandlung, 1874), I, 16.

9. Ludwig Feuerbach to Karl Daub, August, 1824, in Uwe Schott, *Die Jugendentwicklung Ludwig Feuerbachs bis zum Facultätswechsel 1825,* Studien zur Theologie und Geistesgeschichte des Neunzehnten Jahrhunderts (Göttingen: Vanderhoeck & Ruprecht, 1973), 10:120. This treatment of Feuerbach's life up to his decision to devote himself to philosophy does a good job of sorting out and assessing the sketchy material from his early years.

10. The writings that resulted from this confrontation were *A History of Modern Philosophy from Bacon von Verulam to Benedict Spinoza* (1833), *A History of Modern Philosophy: Presentation, Development, and Critique of the Philosophy of Leibniz* (1837), and *Pierre Bayle, Presented and Evaluated according to His Most Important Moments for the History of Philosophy and Humanity* (1838).

11. A chronological list of Feuerbach's works may be found in Sass, XI, 341-346.

12. Ludwig Feuerbach, *Briefwechsel,* ed. Werner Schuffenhauer (Leipzig: Philipp Reclam, 1963), pp. 53-60.

13. Grün, *Nachlass,* I, 29.

14. Feuerbach, "An Carl Riedel," *GW,* IX, 10-12.

15. Ludwig Feuerbach, "Vorwort," *Kleinere Schriften III (1846-1850),* ed. Wolfgang Harich, in *GW,* X, 183.

16. Grün, *Nachlass,* I, 29.

17. Ludwig Feuerbach to Paul Johann Anselm Feuerbach, 1823, Sass, XII, 223.

18. For example, John S. Dunne, *A Search for God in Time and Memory* (New York: Macmillan Co., 1967), p. 21. See also Dunne's treatment of the light and dark sides of God and humanity, pp. 169-205.

19. This theme, though, is implied in the poetry, pp. 154-157.

20. See, for example, John S. Dunne, *Time and Myth: A Meditation on Storytelling as an Exploration of Life and Death* (Notre Dame, Ind.: University of Notre Dame Press, 1975), pp. 59-69.

21. Some of my reflections in this discussion were suggested by Ernest Becker, *The Denial of Death* (New York: Free Press, 1973). See especially pp. 198-207.

22. See my Introduction.

23. Part of the reason for this drastic cutting of the *Epigrams* may have been the fact that all of them were not his: in his Foreword (p. vii of the German edition), editor-publisher Stein admits to having added a few of his own! For the entire publishing history, see n. 1 above.

24. I have taken seriously the advice of editor-publisher Stein concerning an error of the compositor (p. viii of the German edition) and have placed the concluding prose (pp. 232-247 of the German edition) immediately after the rhyming verse, instead of after the *Epigrams,* where it appeared in the original edition.

Notes to Thoughts on Death and Immortality

1. *Camera obscura:* a primitive camera, in which a reversed and upside-down image appears on the transparent back wall of a dark chamber, the front of which contains a convex lens.

2. Feuerbach is referring to Jakob Böhme (1575-1624), the theosophist, mystic, and visionary whose works had a profound influence on nineteenth-century German romanticism and idealist philosophy. The quotation that follows is from *Christosophia, oder der weg zu Christo* (1624), in *Sämtliche Schriften,* ed. August Faust and Will-Erich Peuckert, 11 vols. (1730; facsimile reprint ed., Stuttgart: Friedrich Frommann Verlag, 1955-1961), IV, 151-152.

3. Feuerbach omits the following phrase from this sentence: "as you can see in the humanity of our dear Lord Christ, whom love led to the most exalted throne, into the power of the godhead" (ibid., p. 151).

4. *Die natura... einen horrorem vacui hat:* "Nature... abhors a vacuum."

5. *Habitus:* "condition."

6. *Crimen laesae majestatis:* "crime of treason."

7. *Sit venia verbo:* "if you will excuse the expression."

8. *Pinsel,* the word used here for "brush," can also mean "simpleton."

9. The reference is to the *Orbis pictus* (1658) of Johan Amos Comenius (1592-1670), whose pietism and educational theories contributed to reforms after the Thirty Years' War. The work, extremely popular throughout the eighteenth century, was an encyclopedic textbook, a guide to the reality of the world in pictures, informed by the theory that empirical reality was the best guide to the understanding of both language and concepts.

10. *Himmelschein:* Feuerbach often uses the ambiguity of *Schein,* which can mean physical light, the appearance of a reality, and the semblance or illusion of reality. Thus *Himmelschein* could mean "the heavenly glory" or "the illusion of heaven."

11. In Greek mythology Niobe, the queen of Thebes, was the daughter of Tantalus and the wife of King Amphion; in punishment for her desire for equality with the gods, she was forced to witness the killing of her twelve children by Apollo and Artemis, who were the children of her rival, the Titan Leto. The "weeping stone" into which Zeus transformed her was said to be located on Mount Sipylus.

12. *Rübezahl:* the mountain spirit, ogre, or gnome of the *Riesengebirge,* the range extending along the Silesian-Bohemian border.

13. In Greek mythology the music of Orpheus was capable of enchanting even inanimate objects. The word *Klotz,* here translated "log," as well as

indicating a lump of wood, can mean "lout" or "clod." Feuerbach uses *Klotz* in this second sense twice in the following lines.

14. See n. 13.

15. See n. 13.

16. Besides being a church father whose name conveniently rhymes with *onanism (Athanasie, Onanie),* Athanasius (293?-373) opposed the Arian belief that Christ was not fully divine by stating that the essence of God completely penetrated the human nature, or personhood, of Christ, and he formulated a doctrine of the Trinity in which the three personae had as much weight as the divine essence. Thus, if Feuerbach intended the historical reference, he is implying that the pietist also wrongly attributes too much to personhood.

17. The pagination to the original edition changes at this point in the translation because this prose section was mistakenly printed after the *Epigrams,* while these immediately followed the poetry of *Thoughts on Death.* In the original edition, the prose bears the title "Conclusion Belonging to Page 171," the last page of the poetry.

Notes to the Epigrams

1. For the pagination of the original edition, see n. 17 to *Thoughts on Death.*

2. For the probable author of epigrams that are too mild, see my Introduction.

3. For the relationship of Orpheus to stones and the double meaning of the word *Klotz* ("clods"), see n. 13 to *Thoughts on Death.*

4. Feuerbach here invokes Pallas Athena in her role of granting and protecting Greek culture; in Attic Greece she also was the source of olive trees.

5. Parnassus is the mountain in southern Greece which was the sacred dwelling of Apollo and the Muses of Greek poetry. The *Palmesel,* here translated "Palm Sunday donkeys," were life-sized, carved wooden statues of Christ sitting on a female donkey, which from medieval times were carried or pulled in procession on Palm Sunday.

6. Ernst Moritz Arndt (1769-1860) first became well known for the writings that urged the German people to overthrow French control during the years of the Napoleonic Empire. The poetry that he wrote during the French occupation shows the influences of both pietism and romanticism; one of its major themes is a longing for paradise which combines nationalism and religion with metaphors derived from classical antiquity. A small cottage in a garden is a common symbol for his desire to return to German freedom and innocence. Examples of his style are "Paradisal Wine Song" (1807) and "Life-Vision of the Future, Painted at Reichenbach in Summer, 1813," in *Arndts Werke,* ed. August Leffson and William Steffens, 12 pts. in 4 vols. (Berlin: Bong & Co., n.d.), I, 36-37, 150-154. The spring of Castalia, which was located on Parnassus, was one of the Greek oracles and symbolic of poetic enthusiasm.

7. *Ad vocem:* "a remark concerning."

8. Feuerbach uses *Essenz* here instead of the more common *Wesen* to denote "essence"; the context suggests that he also had in mind "concentrate of Spirit."

9. I have translated *Grabmahl* as "tomb," although the proper spelling for this word is *Grabmal;* Feuerbach inserts the *h* to make the word mean, literally, "meal of the grave."

10. In this line and the following, Feuerbach uses *Satz* to mean both "sediment" and "proposition."

11. See n. 10.

12. See n. 10.

13. The years after the Congress of Vienna saw the first great burgeoning of popular periodical literature in Germany, much of it inspired by the pietistic

and mystical religious revival. Feuerbach could be referring to any number of journals in the following four epigrams; the only hint he gives, in "Interesting Variety," is that two of them are from Prussia, one from Bavaria. The most famous of these, all of them apologetic in tone, were: in Prussia, the *Evangelische Kirchenzeitung* (1827-1869), edited by the pietist and strict confessionalist theologian of the University of Berlin, Ernst Wilhelm Hengstenberg (1802-1869), who belonged to the powerful and reactionary circle of the crown prince (who reigned as Friedrich Wilhelm IV from 1840 to 1861), and the *Literarische Anzeiger für christliche theologie und wissenschaft* (1830-1849), edited by one of the leaders of the German Awakening, the eclectic pietist exegete and theologian of the University of Halle, Friedrich August Gottreu Tholuck (1799-1877); in Bavaria, *Eos* (1828-1832), edited by the Catholic reformer Joseph von Görres (1776-1848), who had been called by King Ludwig I of Bavaria to the University of Munich.

14. *Schein* is translated as "halo" but can also mean "illusion."

15. The metropolitan of the Archdiocese of Munich-Freising was Lothar Anselm Freiherr von Gebsattel (1761-1846), who out of concern about bringing his clergy into line with the decrees of the Council of Trent began a series of visitations to the rural parishes in 1822. Feuerbach is referring either to one of the pastoral letters that resulted from these visitations or to the announcements of the new seminaries that Gebsattel created (a major seminary in 1826, a minor seminary in 1828).

16. *Afflabit Deus, et dissipabuntur:* "God shall blow on them, and they shall be put to flight."

17. *Corpus juris:* "body of law."

18. The phrase *grows horns* can mean "to cuckold."

19. *Canes Domini:* "the dogs of the Lord."

20. The object of the following five epigrams is a work edited by the romanticist and pietist historian of Christianity of the University of Berlin, Johann August Wilhelm Neander (1789-1850): *Denkwürdigkeiten aus der Geschichte des Christenthums and des christlichen lebens*; 2d rev. ed., 3 vols. (Berlin: Ferdinand Dümmler, 1825-1827). A major purpose of this work, which was originally published from 1822 to 1824, was to contrast the beliefs and moral life of early Christianity with those of its Greek and Roman environment. The first essay, by Tholuck ("Das Wesen und die sittlichen einflüsse des Heidenthums besonders unter Griechen und Römern, von dem standpunkte des Christenthums aus betrachtet," ibid., I, 1-233), revels in demonstrating the immorality of pagan religious practices, and "For Th." is clearly addressed to him (although not Socrates but the cynic philosophers are found guilty of relieving nature in public [ibid., p. 112]). For Tholuck, see n. 13; for Feuerbach's opinion of Neander, see the Introduction.

21. The entire quotation is *"Parturiunt montes, nascetur ridiculus mus,"* meaning, literally, "The mountains are in labor and give birth to a ridiculous mouse," from the *Ars Poetica* of Horace.

22. *"Pectus facit theologum"*: this is the motto of the first volume (1826)

of Neander's *Allgemeine Geschichte der christlichen religion und kirche,* which reached five volumes by 1845. The full motto is *"Pectus est, quod theologum facit,"* meaning, "It is the heart that creates the theologian." For Neander, see n. 20.

23. *Tempora mutantur, et nos mutamur cum illis:* "The times change, and we with them."

24. *Lirumlarum:* a nonsense word primarily used in children's verses.

25. Johann Friedrich Blumenbach (1752-1840) was one of Germany's first great natural scientists; the work that Feuerbach cites is the *Handbuch der Naturgeschichte,* which was first printed in 1779 and reached thirteen editions by 1830.

26. The vinegar eel, or vinegar worm, is a minute nematode worm often found in vinegar, sour paste, and other acid fermenting vegetable substances.

27. The mount of the Hindu god Vishnu was Garuda, often represented as a small hawk.

28. Lucian was a Greek rhetorician, pamphleteer, and satirist of the second century A.D. (120?-180?). Feuerbach's statement that Greek inspiration descends to mockery in Lucian may be ironical, for Lucian was famous for his dialogues mocking the vanity and folly of the religious beliefs and intellectual life of his own day; his *Dialogues of the Gods* and *Dialogues of the Dead* were written in the late 150s.

29. *Pars pro toto:* "the part for the whole."

30. *Ingenia tarda:* "slow minds."

31. Many of the following epigrams are directed at Philipp Konrad Marheineke (1780-1846), professor of theology at Berlin and the leader of those followers of Hegel who believed that it was possible to reconcile Hegel's philosophy with the doctrines of Christianity. The work that Feuerbach attacks is *Grundlehren der Dogmatik als wissenschaft* (1827), first published in 1819 as *Grundlehren der christlichen Dogmatik,* which argues that it is possible to state the content of faith in philosophical terms by removing from doctrine its representational character, or, in other words, that the form in which faith is expressed is not essential to its content. Feuerbach counters this argument in "Can You Parry *This* Thrust, Sophist?"

32. *Haec fabula monet:* "this tale admonishes."

33. M—— is Marheineke (see n. 31); the dash surely stands for Hegel.

34. M—— is Marheineke.

35. See n. 31.

36. *Auf ihn kannst du Haüser bauen* (literally, "You can build houses on him") is an expression meaning "You can pin your faith on him."

37. The following six epigrams are again directed at Marheineke and his *Dogmatics* (see n. 31). The attack on "dry bones" comes from the "skeletal framework" organizing this work, while the nickname "The Theological Jupiter" was probably a result of Marheineke's rather grandiose style of preaching; he was also called "the cardinal."

38. Bruno is Giordano Bruno (1548-1600), the philosopher, astronomer, and mathematician, who countered Aristotelian philosophy with a monist conception of the world. For Jacob Böhme, see n. 2 to *Thoughts on Death*.

39. Feuerbach refers here to the Berliner Dom, standing opposite to the Royal Palace on Museum Island in the River Spree, which was originally built in 1747-1750 and was reconstructed between 1816 and 1821 in neoclassical style by the great architect, Karl Friedrich Schinkel (1781-1841).

40. Wilhelm Traugott Krug (1770-1842) was professor of philosophy at the University of Leipzig, becoming its rector in 1830. Feuerbach here attacks his apparent compulsion to write on practically every contemporary event or object of discussion, the most striking example of which was *System der kriegswissenschaft* [System of the science of war], published in 1815, for which he had no background besides a few years' duty in the War of Liberation.

41. *Brachybiotik:* "the brevity of life."

42. "Gives off a light": the verb is *scheinen,* which can mean both "shine" and "appear."

43. In this and the following epigram, Feuerbach repeats commonplaces of the dangerous German anti-Semitism of his day.

44. "Aureole": *Schein* means both "light" and "semblance."

45. See the footnote relating to p. 174 of the German text.

46. This is probably a reference to Neander (see n. 20), because of the reference in the following epigram to the pietist's "radiant, interesting human characteristics." Neander cut an extraordinary figure in Berlin intellectual circles because of his unconventional dress and inspirational manner of lecturing.

47. Neander remained close to the pietist circle around Hengstenberg (see n. 13) until, in 1830, he objected to Hengstenberg's call for the censorship of more liberal theological opinions; moreover, Tholuck (see n. 13) taught at Berlin until 1826. But most probably the reference is to his old friend, the emotional pietist theologian, Gerhard Friedrich Abraham Strauss (1786-1863), who from 1822 served as court and cathedral preacher and at the University of Berlin as professor of practical theology.

48. *Natura se potissimum prodit in minimis:* "Nature produces itself principally in the smallest realities."

49. In Hindu mythology Mahā Māyā was the virgin Mother of Gautama Buddha, and she is worshipped in Mahayana Buddhism as the personification of supreme wisdom and the Mother of all Buddhas. Brahmā is one of the major gods of the late Vedic period; he came to assume the identity of the creator god Prājapati. I am not aware of the particular legend to which Feuerbach refers.